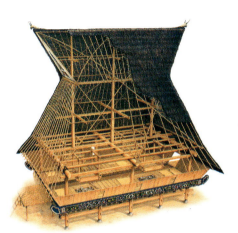

Architecture

BOARD

(..air)
Dr. S. Somadikarta
Dr. Aprilani Soegiarto
Dr. Taufik Abdullah
Paul Sochaczewski
Dr. John Miksic

...NG TEAM

Studio Managers
Tan Tat Ghee
Tan Seok Lui

Designers
Nelani Jinadasa
Lee Woon Hong
Joseph G. Reganit
Norreha Bt. Sayuti
Wong Yit Har

Series Illustrator
Anuar Bin Abdul Rahim

Production Manager
Edmund Lam

Project Coordinators, Jakarta
Seti-Arti Kailola
William Woodruff

Editorial Coordinator, Jakarta
Judi Achjadi

Administrative Coordinators, Jakarta
Nunun Daradjatun
Tjetjep Suparman

Editorial Assistant, Jakarta
Rafli Lindaryadi

Dr. ...

Editors
Dr. Julian Davison
Goh Geok Yian
Amita Sarwal
Irene Toh Lay Kuan

SPONSORS

This encyclopedia project was initiated and guided by the **Yayasan Dana Bakti**

with the support of the **Shangri-la Hotel**, *Jakarta.*

It was also made possible thanks to the generous and enlightened support of the following companies:

PT. Makindo
Sinar Mas Group
Bakrie Group
Bank Artha Graha
Satelindo
Telekomindo
Telekomunikasi Indonesia
Indobuildco
Indosat
Inti
Pasifik Satelit Nusantara

Plaza Indonesia Realty
Siemens Indonesia
WES Intratama Consortium
Wahana Tigamas Buana/AT&T
Konsorsium Pramindo Ikat
Artha Telekomindo
Amalgam Indocorpora
Elektrindo Nusantara
PT. Ratelindo
Komselindo

© Editions Didier Millet, 1998
Reprinted 1999, 2001
Published by Archipelago Press,
an imprint of Editions Didier Millet Pte Ltd,
121, Telok Ayer Street, #03-01
Singapore 068590
Tel: 65-324 9260   Fax: 65-324 9261
E-mail: edmbooks.com.sg

www.edmbooks.com

www.indonesianheritage.com

ISBN 981-3018-30-5
ISBN 981-3018-58-5 (multi-volume set)
All Rights Reserved. No part of this book may be reproduced, stored in a retrieval system, or transmitted in any form or by any means without permission from the publisher.

Jakarta Office:
Buku Antar Bangsa
Menara Batavia 11th Floor Kav. 126
Jl. K. H. Mas Mansyur
Jakarta 10220 Indonesia
E-mail: bab@dnet.net.id
Tel: 62-21-574 9147   Fax: 62-21-574 9148

Printed by Tien Wah Press (Pte) Limited

INDONESIAN HERITAGE

Architecture

VOLUME EDITOR

Gunawan Tjahjono *Department of Architecture, University of Indonesia*

CONSULTANT EDITOR

John Miksic

VOLUME EDITORIAL TEAM

Editors
Julian Davison
Goh Geok Yian

Designer
Lee Woon Hong

Picture Researcher
Helen West

AUTHORS

Agoes Arismunandar - *Department of Archaeology, University of Indonesia*
Bea Brommer - *Amsteldijk, Amsterdam*
Julian Davison - *Centre for South-East Asian Studies, University of Hull*
Gaudenz Domineg - *Institute of Cultural and Social Sciences, Leiden University*
Jacques Dumarçay - *Ecole Française d'Extrême-Orient, Paris*
Gregory Forth - *Department of Anthropology, University of Alberta*
James Fox - *Department of Anthropology, The Australian National University*
Sandrine Germain - *Independent writer, Paris*
Ronald Gill - *Progressive Design, Curaçao*
Beatrice van der Goes - *Department of Anthropology, Leiden University*
John Miksic - *Southeast Asian Studies Programme, National University of Singapore*
Soetrisno Murtiyoso - *Lembaga Sejarah Arsitektur Indonesia, Bandung*
Hugh O'Neil - *Faculty of Architecture Building and Planning, University of Melbourne*
Cor Passchier - *Passchier and Visser Architects, Hertogenbosch*
Josef Prijotomo - *Department of Architecture, Institut Teknologi Surabaya*
Thomas Reuter - *Department of HPS, The University of Melbourne*
Yuswadi Saliya - *Department of Architecture - ITB, Ujung Pandang*
Suryadi Jo Santoso - *PT. Bumi Serpong Damai, Jakarta*
Reimar Schefold - *Faculteit der Sociale Wetenschappen, Rijksuniveriteit Leiden*
Edi Sedyawati - *Department of Education and Culture, Jakarta*
Sandi Siregar - *Department of Architecture, Parahyangan Catholic University*
R.P. Soejono - *Department of Archaeology, University of Indonesia*
R. Soekmono - *(almarhum) Department of Archaeology, University of Indonesia*
Budi A. Sukada - *Department of Architecture, University of Indonesia*
Robi Sularto - *PT. Atelier Enam Architects, Jakarta*
Djauhari Sumintardja - *PT. Bina Karya, Jakarta*
Roxana Waterson - *Department of Sociology, National University of Singapore*
Johannes Widodo - *Fujimori Laboratory, University of Tokyo*
Bagoes Wiramartono - *Department of Architecture, Bandung Institute of Technology*

ARCHIPELAGO PRESS

Contents

INTRODUCTION
Gunawan Tjahjono & Julian Davison

TRADITIONAL ARCHITECTURE
Julian Davison

Austronesian-Indonesian Connections........... 10
R.P. Soejono

Common Features:
Raised Pile Foundations............................... 12
Roxana Waterson

Common Features:
Extended Roof Ridges................................. 14
Roxana Waterson

Construction Techniques..............................16
Gaudenz Domineg

The House as a Ritually Ordered Space......... 18
Julian Davison

Construction Rites...................................... 20
Roxana Waterson

The Toraja Tongkonan............................... 22
Roxana Waterson

Batak Architecture of Sumatra...................... 24
Sandrine Germain & Beatrice van der Goes

Rumah Gadang:
the Minangkabau Great House......................26
Roxana Waterson

Mentawai Longhouses..................................28
Reimar Schefold

Houses and Megaliths of the Nias Island........ 30
Bagoes Wiramartono

Longhouses of Kalimantan:
the Kenyah Umah Dadoq..............................32
Gunawan Tjahjono

The Javanese House.....................................34
Gunawan Tjahjono

The Balinese House..................................... 36
Robi Sularto

Houses and Compounds
in the Mountains of Bali................................ 38
Thomas Reuter

Houses and Rice Barns
of the Sasak in Lombok................................40
Roxana Waterson

Uma Mbatangu of Sumba............................42
Gregory Forth

Timorese Houses... 44
James Fox

The Dani Compound:
an Irian Settlement Pattern............................ 46
Djauhari Sumintardja

Houses for the Dead..................................... 48
Roxana Waterson

INDONESIA'S CLASSICAL HERITAGE
Josef Prijotomo

Abode of the Gods:
Architecture and Cosmology.......................... 52
John Miksic

Sources of Early Indonesian
Stone Architecture.......................................54
John Miksic

Indonesian Methods of
Buildings with Stone.....................................56
Jacques Dumarçay

Perspective Effects in Javanese
Temple Architecture......................................58
Jacques Dumarçay

Ornamentation of Classic
Javanese Stonework.....................................60
John Miksic

Hindu Architecture of Central Java................. 62
Jacques Dumarçay

Candi Borobudur..64
Soekmono

Buddhist Architecture of Central Java............. 66
Jacques Dumarçay

Stone Architecture of East Java......................68
Jacques Dumarçay

Brick Architecture of Majapahit 70
John Miksic

A traditional Minangkabau house with its characteristic horned roof. West Sumatra.

Architecture in Ancient
Javanese Inscriptions.....................................72
Edi Sedyawati

Terraced Temple Sites................................. 74
John Miksic

Brick Temples of Sumatra............................76
John Miksic

Artificial Caves and Rock-cut Temples............78
Agoes Arismunandar

Conservation and Reconstruction................. 80
John Miksic & Soekmono

CITIES, MOSQUES AND PALACES
Gunawan Tjajhono

The Genesis of an Urban Tradition.................84
Gunawan Tjajhono & John Miksic

Architecture of the Early Islamic Period..........86
John Miksic

Early Muslim Places of Worship.....................88
Budi A. Sukada

Palace and City.. 90
Gunawan Tjajhono

The Mosque as a Sacred Space.................... 94
Hugh O'Neil

Regional Indonesian Mosques:
Tradition and Eclecticism.............................. 96
Hugh O'Neil

Taman: an Earthly Paradise..........................98
Soetrisno Murtiyoso & John Miksic

Muslim Tombs and Cemeteries....................100
Hugh O'Neil

Cities of the Pesisir................................. 102
Jo Santoso

ARCHITECTURE OF THE
17TH TO 19TH CENTURIES
Yulianto Somalyo

Town Formation in 19th-Century Java..........106
Ronald Gill

Batavia: the Realisation of an Ideal City....... 108
Bea Brommer

Country Houses in the 18th Century.............110
Ronald Gill

Dutch Townhouses..................................... 112
Ronald Gill

Shop Houses and Temples:
the Chinese Connection............................. 114
J. Widodo

The Introduction of New Building Types........116
Ronald Gill

MODERN ARCHITECTURE
AND IDENTITY
Yuswadi Saliya & Sandi Siregar

The Emergence of a New Indies Style.......... 120
Budi A Sukada

Attempted Synthesis:
Dutch Architects in the Indies..................... 122
Yulianto Somalyo

Garden Cities and Suburban Bungalows...... 124
Cor Passchier

Modernism and the International Style..........126
Yuswadi Saliya

The Architecture of Early Independence....... 128
Budi A Sukada

The Architecture of
Modern Indonesian Cities........................... 130
Sandi Siregar

Regionalism and Identity
in Contemporary Architecture...................... 132
Budi A Sukada

Towards a Maturity of
Indonesian Architecture.............................. 134
Gunawan Tjajhono

Glossary.. 136

Bibliography.. 138

Index... 140

Photo Credits....................................... 142

INDONESIA:
Architecture of Indonesia

The architecture of Indonesia represents a kaleidoscope of different forms and technological traditions which reflect both the cultural diversity of the region and a rich historical legacy. In trying to draw together the multiple elements that constitute the Indonesian architectural record, it is useful to consider the separate geographical origins of the different traditions that have contributed to Indonesia's architectural heritage. These diverse influences can all be arranged in a rough chronology.

An Ancient Vernacular Tradition

The vernacular architecture of Indonesia — the traditional Indonesian house in all its many regional forms — belongs to an ancient building tradition which can be found throughout most of island Southeast Asia and parts of the mainland too. Characteristic features include post foundations, an elevated living floor and a pitched roof with an extended roof ridge and outward leaning gable ends. Variants on these general themes occur throughout the Archipelago testifying to the gradual dispersal of this ancient architectural tradition, over several millennia, from a common point of origin which may have been the island of Taiwan. Being more or less constructed from wood and other perishable organic materials, the oldest vernacular buildings in Indonesia are no more than about 150 years old. However stone carvings on the walls of 9th-century Hindu and Buddhist temples in central Java reveal close correspondences between the domestic architecture of that time and contemporary vernacular forms which are still being built today.

The Karo Batak house of north Sumatra, with its post foundations, raised floor, high roof profile and extended roof ridge with outward leaning gables, exhibits many of the characteristic features of Indonesian vernacular architecture.

Classical Heritage

Although the architecture of Indonesia's Hindu-Buddhist past (9th-15th centuries) drew its initial inspiration from Indian forms, the latter were from the outset subjected to strong local influences which in time led to the emergence of an entirely separate architectural tradition with its own distinctive temple typology, construction techniques and decorative features. The great monuments of Indonesia's Classic Era, such as Borobudur and Candi Lara Jonggrang testify to a style of architecture which is wholly Indonesian in its conception and execution.

The quintessential feature of Indonesian Classical architecture is the *candi*—a tower-like structure, built of stone, which is raised on a basement and surmounted by a stepped pyramidal roof, ornamented with antefixes and finials. In

(Below) The Gedung Saté building in Bandung, now the headquarters of the West Javanese provincial government, reflects a conscious attempt to create a new Indonesian architectural identity during the 1920s.

symbolic terms, the building was conceived as a representation of the legendary Mount Meru, which in Hindu-Buddhist mythology is identified as the abode of the gods. The gods reside in caves set in the sides of this mythical mountain and these are replicated in architectural terms as chambers and niches containing statues of the deities to whom the sanctuary is dedicated. Buddhist structures such as the famous 9th-century Candi Borobudur in Central Java similarly invoked this idea of a cosmic mountain.

Islamic Architecture

The gradual spread of Islam through the region from the 12th century onwards introduced another important set of architectural influences. In this instance, however, the changes were more ideological than technological, the advent of Islam did not lead to the introduction of an entirely new building tradition, but rather saw the appropriation of existing architectural forms, which were reinvented or reinterpreted to suit Muslim requirements. The Kudus drumtower, on the north coast of Java, is a case in point. Resembling a candi built of the 14th-century Majapahit era, the tower was adapted for use as the drumtower for a more recently built Islamic mosque following the collapse of the Majapahit kingdom and the coming of Islam. Similarly, the earliest Indonesian mosques draw their inspiration from existing building traditions in Java, and elsewhere in the Archipelago, in which four central posts support a soaring pyramidal roof. In both vernacular and Islamic structures, the four columns are attributed a special symbolic significance.

The Dutch and the New Indies Style

The 16th century saw the arrival of the first European merchant-adventurers seeking to seize control of the immensely lucrative trade in spices. The Portuguese and Spanish, and later the Dutch, introduced their own architectural agenda to the region and many elements of European architecture subsequently found their way into the local architectural traditions. However this appropriation of ideas was not simply a one-way process: the Dutch readily adopted indigenous architectural elements to create a unique form of colonial architecture known as the Indies Style. More recently in the early decades of this century, Dutch Modernists also consciously turned to the local vernacular as a source of inspiration for a new tropical architecture which combined traditional forms with modern building materials and construction techniques.

Towards an Indonesian School of Modern Architecture

The years that followed Independence saw the adoption of a largely Modernist agenda on the part of Indonesian architects. This continued into the 1970s and 1980s when the rapid growth of the Indonesian economy led to massive building programmes at every level of development from low-cost housing schemes to factories, airports, shopping malls and skyscrapers. Many of the most prestigious projects were designed by foreign architects who seldom applied themselves to designing for a specifically Indonesian context. More recently, as the world's major city centres, especially those in Asia, have come increasingly to resemble one another, irrespective of local histories, climate and cultural orientations, there has been a growing demand for instilling a sense of place in the built landscape — one that reflects local identities and sensibilities. Postmodernism has encouraged this quest for a 'new architecture' so that today one finds contemporary Indonesian architects again exploring their rich architectural heritage with a view to developing a viable alternative to the hegemony of Modernism.

(Top) The Sivaite sanctuary, Candi Badut, near Malang, East Java, was probably built around AD 760 and represents one of the earliest surviving structures of the Hindu-Buddhist era.

(Above) A gateway in the Kasepuhan palace of Cirebon, West Java. The gateway features both pre-Islamic and Chinese elements, taking the form of paduraksa portal from the Hindu-Buddhist era which has been augmented with Chinese 'cloud and stone' decorative motifs.

(Left) The soaring skyline of downtown Jakarta in the late 1990s, represents the modern face of Indonesian architecture, with its International Style skyscrapers and glittering façades of glass and steel.

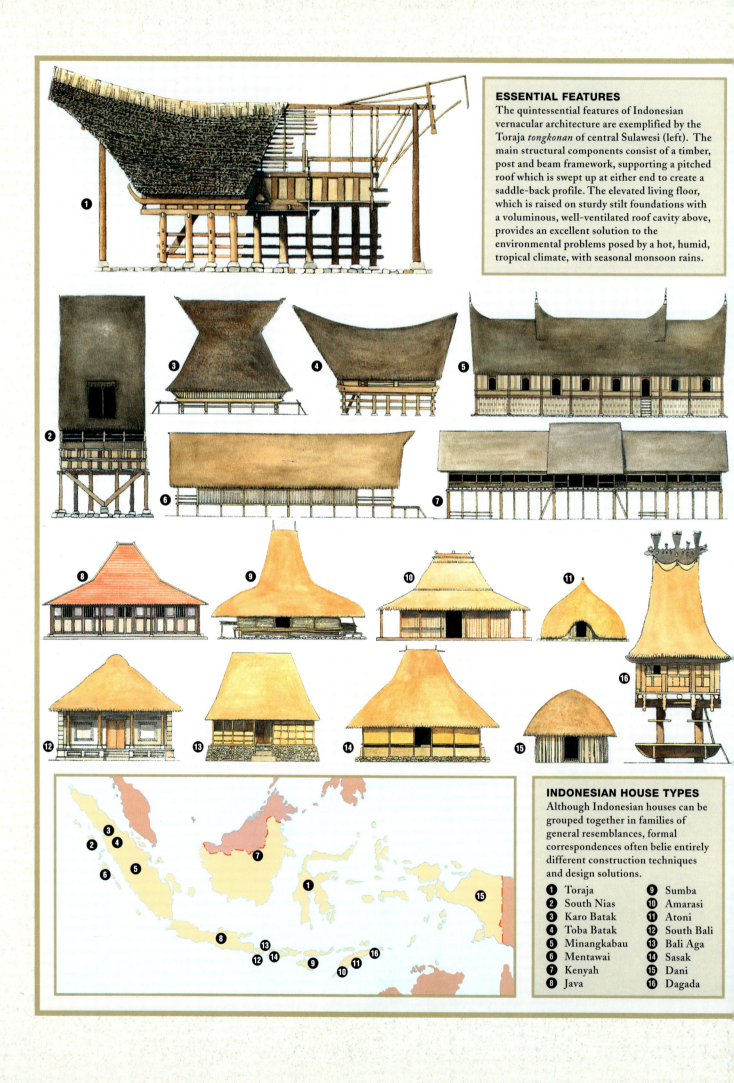

TRADITIONAL ARCHITECTURE

HOUSE POSTS AND TIE BEAMS

The archetypal Austronesian house consists of a rectangular structure, raised on wooden posts, with a pitched roof which is extended at either end to create outward-leaning gables. Until recently these structures were constructed entirely from natural building materials — timber, bamboo, thatch and fibre — and were put together without the use of nails. The basic construction techniques are the same everywhere: vertical house posts and horizontal tie beams provide a load bearing structure to which the floors, walls and roof are subsequently attached. The main framework is assembled using sophisticated jointing techniques, while the walls, roofing and other non-structural elements are typically secured in place by wooden pegs and plant fibre lashings. Given the perishable nature of these building materials, it is hardly surprising that there are very few surviving examples of vernacular architecture which are more than 150 years old. In this respect, temple reliefs from the Hindu-Buddhist era, which often include representations of dwellings and other forms of secular architecture, provide us with a unique record of ancient building types. Judging from the pictorial record at Candi Borobudur, the vernacular architecture of Java during the 9th century closely resembled present-day traditions in the Lake Toba area of north Sumatra.

Temple relief from Candi Borobudur, depicting a 9th-century Javanese house (above). Detail from a Badui house in west Java, showing the articulation of the top of a foundation post with the superstructure of the building (below).

Although the vernacular architecture of Indonesia encompasses a wide variety of styles and technologies, a number of common themes and principles can be discerned. These correspondences, which include the widespread construction of pile dwellings with pitched roofs and extended roof ridges, are the legacy of a shared Austronesian ancestry. The term Austronesian refers to a group of related languages which are spoken throughout most of island Southeast Asia, parts of the mainland, Taiwan, the Pacific and Madagascar. Although the many peoples who make up this widely dispersed language group are believed to have originated in Taiwan some 6,000 years ago, their common cultural background can still be clearly discerned. Not all Indonesians are Austronesian-speakers: the peoples of Irian Jaya, parts of Halmahera and the eastern end of Timor belong to different linguistic and cultural traditions and these differences are reflected architecturally. For the most part, however, the traditional architecture of Indonesia unequivocally declares its ancient Austronesian heritage, both structurally and in terms of symbolic significance which surrounds the house.

Today we can still identify a substratum of common cultural characteristics which occur throughout the Austronesian world. These include the idea of the house as a symbolically ordered structure through which key ideas and cultural orientations are expressed. First, the house defines a social group and here, the size and formal properties of a dwelling can serve to indicate the rank and social status of its owners. Often, the house is also identified as the physical embodiment of the ancestors and provides a depository for sacred heirlooms, handed down from generation to generation.

The symbolic organisation of space within the house is another important Austronesian characteristic. Pairs of antithetical spatial coordinates — 'inside' and 'out', 'front' and 'back', 'up' and 'down', 'left' and 'right', 'east' and 'west' — are mapped onto social categories relating to relationships between the sexes, kin and affines, junior and senior generations, even between the living and the dead, to create a symbolic topography which both organises and represents these social relations. These associations between domestic space and the social order are often linked to local cosmologies in which the house is construed as a microcosm of the macrocosm. A house may also be imbued with a spiritual identity — in this respect, the house provides not only shelter from the elements, but also protection from less tangible forces.

Austronesian-Indonesian Connections

The vast majority of Indonesians are Austronesian speakers and in this respect they share a common cultural heritage. The Austronesian language group, which numbers some 700 to 800 languages, embraces most of island Southeast Asia, as well as parts of south Vietnam, Taiwan, Micronesia, Polynesia and Madagascar. In addition to linguistic affinities, one also can discern a core of distinctive cultural attributes, including architectural features, which are found throughout the Austronesian region.

Austronesian Expansion

It seems likely that a considerable number of Austronesian-speaking peoples were living in coastal and riverine areas of southern China and north Vietnam by the middle of the 4th millennium BC. The expansion of these peoples from this ancestral homeland commenced some 6,000 years ago, and culminated in the eventual dispersal of Austronesian speakers half-way around the world by about AD 500. This movement can be reconstructed chronologically from archaeological and linguistic sources. They suggest that Taiwan was settled around 4000 BC, the Philippines by about 3000 BC, and Borneo, Sulawesi and eastern Indonesia a thousand years later. Micronesia and Polynesia were first reached by 1500 BC and western Indonesia by about 1000 BC. The relatively recent date for the arrival of Austronesian speakers in western Indonesia might indicate that densely populated islands such as Java could have been occupied by smaller and more gracile Australoid hunter-gatherers right up until the first millennium BC. Alternatively, the situation may reflect a later expansion of Malayic and Javanese languages in the region which replaced Austronesian languages of greater antiquity.

Early Austronesian sailing vessels may well have resembled this outrigger canoe from the Tucker Isles. Although such craft were mainly intended for inshore navigation, they were capable of carrying ancient Austronesian seafarers across the Pacific and Indian Oceans, to destinations as remote as Easter Island and Madagascar.

Life and Material Culture

Based on a reconstructed vocabulary of words used in the earliest Austronesian languages, it seems that the first Austronesian settlers in island Southeast Asia were cultivating taro, yam, banana, breadfruit, coconut, rice and millet by about 2500 BC; they also raised buffaloes, pigs, dogs and chickens. Important cultural features shared by many Austronesian societies include headhunting and the erection of megaliths, either in commemoration of the dead or else to mark the occasion of a great sacrificial feast. Other common elements in terms of material culture included outrigger sailing craft, pottery, weaving and a stone age tool kit consisting of polished adzes, bark-cloth beaters and a distinctive type of reaping implement for harvesting rice (modern iron counterparts still adhere to the same basic pattern).

Austronesian Houses

The Austronesian house typically consists of a rectangular structure, elevated on posts, with a thatched roof. It is entered by means of a notched tree-trunk ladder and features a hearth with a rack above for firewood and storage. This basic form has been subject to elaborate refinements in many parts of the Austronesian region. Structures of remarkable form and size are found among the Dayak peoples of Kalimantan, the Minangkabau and Batak of Sumatra and the Toraja of Sulawesi. Cognates of the Indonesian terms for a dwelling (*rumah*), meeting hall (*balai*) and granary (*lumbung*), occur repeatedly through the Archipelago and the Austronesian region as a whole. Significantly, for many Austronesian peoples, the house is much more than simply a dwelling place, rather it is a symbolically ordered structure in which a number of key ideas and cultural concerns may be represented. Thus, the Austronesian house may variously be seen as a sacred representation of the ancestors, a physical embodiment of group identities, a cosmological model of the universe and an expression of rank and social status.

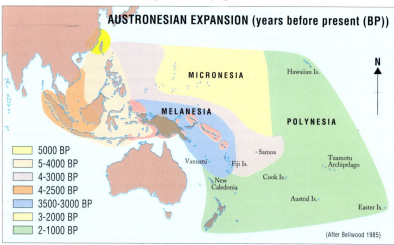

STONE AGE TOOL KIT

The principal components of the Austronesian tool kit consisted of highly polished adzes with a quadrangular cross-section ❶ and pick-adzes with a pentangular or triangular cross-section and a longitudinal ridge along the upper surface ❷ - ❹. The simple, polished stone adze with a quadrangular profile is mainly found among the islands of the western and central parts of the Archipelago; the highly-specialized pick-adze occurs only in south Sumatra, Java and Bali.

AUSTRONESIAN WORD LIST

Many words in present-day Austronesian languages seem to share a common root. Attempts to reconstruct archaic Austronesian languages have identified several ancient linguistic strata, including (in order of appearance) Proto-Austronesian (PAN), Proto-Malayo-Polynesian (PMP) and Proto-Hesperonesian-Formosan (PHF) which is compatible with Western-Malayo-Polynesian which includes the modern Indonesian languages. The fact that many contemporary architectural terms seem to have their origins in this remote linguistic past supports the hypothesis that the Austronesian house form is of considerable antiquity.

English	PAN/PMP	Minangkabau	Javanese	Toraja	Roti
House	*Rumaq (PAN)	rumah	omah	banua	uma
Post/pole	*ha-d₂iRi (PMP)	tongga	čaga	a'riri	di
Ridge pole	*bubung (PMP)	-	karpus	bubungan	to a-k
Roof/thatch	*qatep (PMP)	ato	payɔn	papa	uma lala-k
Stone	*batu (PAN)	batu	watu	batu	batu
Door	*qe+Neb (PHF)	kaporo	lawang	ba'ba	le-lesu
Room	*bilik (PAN)	biliə	gutak-an	bilik	[kama]
Hearth/kitchen	*d₂apúR (PMP)	dapuᵉ	pawon	dapo'	[dapu]

Megaliths and Stone Terraces

Megalithic monuments, though absent in most areas of mainland Southeast Asia, are a common feature of Austronesian societies in both Indonesia and Oceania, where the erection of menhirs, dolmens and stone terraces seems to have predated the more complex stone graves of the Metal Age. In the case of the Indonesian Archipelago, prehistoric megaliths have been found in Sumatra, Java, Bali, Kalimantan, Sulawesi, Sumbawa, Timor and several smaller islands. A megalithic tradition still flourishes in some parts of Indonesia, most notably the island of Nias off the west coast of Sumatra, and Sumba, in the Nusa Tenggara chain. The evidence provided by these surviving megalithic traditions would seem to indicate that the erection of megaliths was associated with mortuary practices, ancestor worship and the marking of social status and deeds of merit.

Ceremonial stone terraces, constructed for ritual purposes, have also been found in many parts of Indonesia and Oceania. The Indonesian version (*punden berundak* in Bahasa Indonesia) consists of a series of stepped terraces with stone retaining walls and menhirs erected on the upper levels. Gunung Padang, in west Java, is the best-known example of such a site, and represents the local counterpart of Polynesian *marae* (the terraced edifice as a whole) and *ahu* (the platform with menhirs), found in Oceania.

A contemporary megalithic tomb (detail) from east Sumba. The female figure represents a papanggu, *or mourning slave, who attends to the deceased in the Afterlife, while the turtle is a symbol of royalty.*

AUSTRONESIAN ARCHITECTURE

The Toba Batak house of north Sumatra exhibits many key Austronesian features in its design. Robust timber house posts ❶, standing on stone foundations ❷, support an elevated living floor, while mortised cross beams ❸ lend rigidity to the structure. The building is dominated by the roof, whose extended ridge piece ❹ creates a characteristic saddle-back profile. Ornamented gable ends ❺, which slope outwards, complete the ensemble, and are a typical Austronesian feature which occurs widely throughout the Indonesian region.

(After Gaudenz Domenig)

Common Features: Raised Pile Foundations

Building on piles is an almost universal, and undoubtedly ancient, feature of Indonesian vernacular architecture. Its history in mainland Southeast Asia can be traced back to Neolithic times, and its wide distribution in island Southeast Asia and the Pacific suggests that the technique was used by the early Austronesian settlers of the Archipelago. As well as being well-adapted climatically, symbolic significance has become attached both to house-posts and to the space they create beneath the house floor.

A 9th-century relief from Borobudur, depicting a house, or granary, raised on foundation posts, which are topped by wooden discs, intended to deter rats from climbing up and entering the building. Similar anti-rodent devices can be found to this day, throughout the Archipelago.

A Dayak settlement in west Kalimantan, mid-19th century. Inter-tribal warfare was endemic in Borneo and the employment of such exceptionally tall piles was probably for reasons of defence as the surrounding stockade would suggest.

An Austronesian Legacy

Buildings with pile or stilt foundations are a pervasive feature not only in mainland and island Southeast Asia, but also in parts of Micronesia and Melanesia, giving way in Polynesia to stone platforms. The occurrence of this type of structure, along with other characteristically Austronesian features, in parts of Madagascar and in the ancient Japanese shrines at Ise and Izumo, bears witness to the far-flung influence of Austronesian seafarers.

Historical linguistics, as much as archaeology, provides crucial evidence in the search for the origins of Austronesians and their architecture, and tentative reconstructions of Proto-Malayo-Polynesian include terms for house post and notched ladder which points to the ancient origins of this construction technique. In Indonesia, rare exceptions to the practice of pile building in Indonesia are found in the mountains of Timor and highland Irian Jaya. In Java and Bali, where the Indian cultural influences of the Hindu-Buddhist era have had an enduring impact, houses and other buildings are constructed on a raised stone stereobate or plinth, but Javanese temple reliefs testify to the previous existence of pile-built structures in the distant past. Images from Borobudur show people engaged in daily activities, sitting in the shaded space beneath the floor, just as they do in many parts of Indonesia to this day, while in the case of Bali, traditional rice barns are still constructed in a typically Austronesian manner.

SEISMIC ACTIVITY: A NIASAN SOLUTION
The massive foundation posts of the chief's house in Bawömataluo village, south Nias, are braced by equally massive diagonal struts. The latter are a distinctive feature of Niasan architecture and are probably an adaptive response to earthquake stresses in this region of constant seismic activity.

Climatic and Geographical Appropriateness

Pile foundations have several advantages in a tropical climate. They raise the living floor above the mud and flood waters which occur during seasonal monsoon rains, while providing excellent underfloor ventilation in hot weather — warm air within the house rises and escapes through openings in the roof, drawing a current of cooler air from beneath the house, through gaps in the floor. Furthermore, a small fire, lit under the house, drives away mosquitoes, while the smoke, as it escapes through the thatch, effectively fumigates it. Housework is also quick and easy when dust and rubbish can be swept through these same gaps in the floor.

The underfloor space is often used as a pen for stabling domestic animals, and as a place for storing utensils. It can also provide a shaded daytime work space for tasks such as weaving and basketry.

In many areas, house posts simply rest on top of foundation stones, rather than being driven into the ground. This ensures that the building has enough flexibility to survive earthquakes in this seismically active region. At the same time, should one wish to move house, the entire structure can literally be picked up and carried to a new site.

Piles built of hardwoods like teak, *cengal* (*Balanocarpus heimii*) or ironwood (*Eusideroxylon zwageri*), may endure for over a hundred years, while some palm trunks, especially *nibung* (*Oncosperma tigillarium*), also make excellent, long-lasting piles. Easily available and replaceable, bamboo is widely used for ordinary houses or temporary structures.

TRADITIONAL ARCHITECTURE

CROSSED-LOG FOUNDATIONS

A different method of stabilising the lower part of a building is to anchor the posts in a crossed-log foundation. This was quite common in central Sulawesi and is still used in north Sumatra for houses and granaries of the Karo and Simalungun Batak (photo). In the case of a Karo Batak granary, the foundation typically consists of six horizontal logs and a pair of broad planks. These elements are piled up so as to form a rectangular framework in which the members are separated by intervals, except at the corners where they meet and cross. The posts of the granary superstructure, which end at the bottom in long tenons, pierce this substructure at the corners, thus locking the components firmly together. In this way the posts stabilise the crossed-log foundation, which in turn holds them in an upright position. Granaries built with piled up logs are depicted on bronze age drums from Yunnan (2nd-1st centuries BC), but these differ significantly from the crossed-log structures which are found in Indonesia.

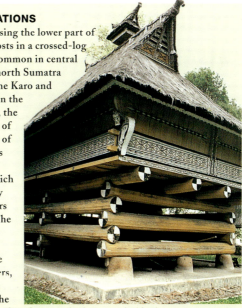

STRUCTURES WITHOUT NAILS

Indigenous Indonesian buildings are held together entirely without nails, relying instead on a variety of jointing techniques, which are sometimes reinforced by pegging, wedging or binding. Not surprisingly, similar construction methods are employed in local boat building traditions — no doubt they share the same origins in a common Austronesian seafaring past. In the case of foundation posts, these may either be buried in the ground or else placed on top of flat stones. In the latter instance, the rigidity of the structure is typically reinforced by cross beams mortised through the posts as in the case of Toba Batak or Toraja houses. The space under the house may then be used as a stall for buffalo or pigs, though this is not as common today as it once was.

Most Indonesian built forms represent variations of a post and beam construction technique, where walls (if they exist at all) are seldom load-bearing, and proportionally, the roof dominates. Sometimes house posts run through the entire structure to support the roof, but in other instances, for example, Karo Batak granaries in north Sumatra, the foundation structure is topped off by two (or more) parallel tie-beams and the superstructure sits on top of this, rather like a box. In the case of traditional houses built by the Manggarai of West Flores, the floor is supported by an entirely separate system of foundation posts to those which hold up the roof. The illustrations here demonstrate indigenous construction techniques from north central Sulawesi. In these examples, robust foundation posts support the floor and provide a framework for the walls, while the roof consists of a lightweight frame which rests on top. (Gaudenz Domenig)

13

Common Features: Extended Roof Ridges

The most distinctive feature of Southeast Asian vernacular architectural forms is the extended line of the roof, often with outward-sloping gables. This style is not only ancient, but is often carried over into modernised forms, being made to stand as a visual symbol of local ethnic identities. The extended ridge, sometimes developing elegant curves, cannot be explained in functional terms, nor is it integral to a particular mode of construction. Its appeal is aesthetic, and it is achieved by a variety of different building techniques.

Detail from a Dong Son drum (above), showing a typical Austronesian-style habitation with a saddle-back roof similar to that of Toraja houses in south Sulawesi (below).

↗ *The palace of Rajas of Simalungun in Pematang Purba on the northern shore of Lake Toba. Roof profile of Toraja rice barn (lower photograph) echoes that of the house.*

(Below) Elevation of a Toraja origin-house.

Evolution of a Style

The wide distribution of extended or curved roof ridges throughout the Indonesian Archipelago suggests that the form is a very ancient one. This kind of roof style is also found in Micronesia, and in pockets along the coasts of New Guinea, where it acquires the most fantastic elaboration in the men's houses of the Sepik river. Generally, the evidence indicates that it is almost certainly much older than the earliest surviving pictorial representations of such roof forms which first appear on Dong Son bronze drums of north Vietnam (c. 500 BC - AD 100). Although these drums were traded widely throughout island Southeast Asia, Dong Son influence never extended eastward beyond Indonesia, which suggests that this type of roof might have dated back to a much earlier Austronesian period. There is interesting archaeological material from Japan where it has been demonstrated how pile-built structures, with extended gables, could have evolved from prehistoric pit dwellings. Bronze artefacts from the 1st-4th centuries AD depict various structures of this type and Neolithic southern China has been suggested as a common point of origin for the architecture of both Indonesia and Japan.

Variations on a Theme

The extended roof ridge has been elaborated in a number of different ways throughout the Archipelago. Karo Batak houses of northern Sumatra are sometimes topped by a cluster of smaller roofs with gable

ends (see p. 25), while among the Minangkabau of west Sumatra, the roof is swept up at either end to finish in elegant points like the horns of a buffalo. Among the Toraja of Sulawesi, the roof ridges of noble houses were extended so far and high beyond the gable ends that they required an extra free-standing post (*tulak somba*) to support them.

Construction Methods

Although many Indonesian roofs have a similar form, construction techniques differ. In Toba Batak houses, the extended ridge line is achieved by a graduated angling of the rafters, to produce a fan shape, which is reinforced by diagonal ties. The Minangkabau however use a truss and cross-beam structure, with many small rafters and battens to build up the roof peaks. Then again, the Toraja roof has a straight ridge beam to which additional members are added at each end, angling upward and outward to produce a cantilevered framework for the eaves which require the additional support of free-standing *tulak somba*. But whatever form it takes, the roof is without

TRADITIONAL ARCHITECTURE

HORNED HOUSES
Crossed gable finials, which are often elaborately carved, are a very characteristic feature of Southeast Asian roofs, derived, no doubt, from the solution to a technical problem of how to hold the rafters together at the ridge. Often there is a symbolic association of the house with the body of a buffalo in which case the gable finials are identified as the horns of the beast. This idea is quite explicit in southeast central Sulawesi (right) where the silhouette of buffalo horns can be clearly distinguished in the elaborate carvings that ornament the gable finials. Among the Karo Batak of north Sumatra, buffalo heads, fashioned from *ijuk* palm fibre complete with real horns, are placed at either end of the roof ridge as a protective measure (see p. 25), while in the case of the Minangkabau house (above), the roof as a whole is identified with the horns of the animal (see pp. 26-27).

RICE BARNS AND RAFTERS
The roof profile of a Toba Batak rice barn (*sopo*) (top), closely resembles that of a 9th-century structure depicted in relief at Borobudur (above). The roof of the *sopo* is mainly supported by the rafters, and this is also the case elsewhere in Indonesia, though larger structures may be reinforced by additional load-bearing elements.

doubt the dominant architectural element in Indonesian houses, with walls being either very low or even absent altogether — in Roti, Savu and Manggarai (west Flores), the house consists simply of a platform under an expansive roof.

Traditional Roofs in a Modern World
Indigenous roof forms have a continued appeal today as images of a local identity. One sees them everywhere, grafted onto hotels, airports, municipal buildings and even reproduced in miniature for tourists. As traditional images are lost or change their meaning in a modern context, archaic roof forms continue to persist as a convenient symbol of ethnic identity.

SACRED PEAKS
Not all Indonesian houses have extended roof ridges: in many areas of eastern Indonesia, the ridge piece is reduced in length, though the height of the roof may still be impressive. The most dramatic expression of this style may be seen in the Sumbanese clan house, with its tall peak known as *toko*, which resembles, both structurally and morphologically, the *joglo*-style roof found in Java (p. 35). In both instances, the space beneath the raised roof ridge is considered the most sacred part of the building, while the four columns supporting this central section are endowed with a special symbolic significance. In the case of the Sumba clan house, the attic is where seed rice, sacred heirlooms and other house treasures are stored. Some of these buildings become so sacred and taboo-ridden that their owners fear to live in them, preferring to reside in ordinary, profane houses elsewhere. In such instances, the clan house acquires the character more of a temple than a dwelling.

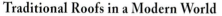

15

Construction Techniques

The vernacular architecture of Indonesia is characterised by its use of natural building materials and post and beam construction methods. The wooden framework is assembled without nails, using sophisticated jointing techniques. The rafters of the roof are typically supported by wall-plates, with additional support often provided by a ridge piece and purlins — elements that variously transmit the load to other structural members. Walls and floors do not constitute a part of the main load-bearing elements but may brace the structure as a whole.

Dayak carpenters prepare massive posts for a Kalimantan longhouse.

A typical post and beam structure from central Sumatra (above) and different types of bamboo joinery (below) from the same location.

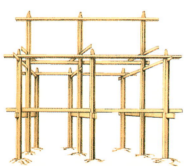

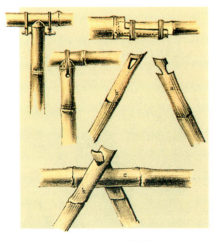

The Timber Framework

The vernacular architecture of Indonesia typically employs a post and beam method of construction. Putting this together is largely a matter of shaping and jointing wooden members with a range of specialised tools which include axes, adzes and chisels. Rounded logs are squared by splitting or by means of a pit-saw worked by two men.

Pile structures, with posts buried in the ground, have been mostly superseded by stilt structures where the house posts rest on top of foundation stones, and stability is achieved by horizontal rails running through apertures cut into the posts. Often, the post and beam framework is loosely assembled on the ground before being placed on the foundation stones. The joints are then secured by wedging or pegging, with full stability only being achieved when the floors and the walls are added.

An alternative strategy for stabilising the lower part of a post and beam building is to anchor the posts in a crossed-log foundation. This was common in central Sulawesi and is still employed by the Karo Batak of north Sumatra (see p. 13). A third method, also rare in Indonesia, is to add diagonal struts or braces. The best known example of this is in Nias where thick logs are employed for this purpose. In the southern part of the island, these come in pairs, which are arranged in the form of the letter 'V' (see pp.12-13).

Box-frames

Sometimes a box-frame is employed for the upper portion of a building. This consists of vertical studs that are slotted into horizontal sills and held together at the top by wall-plates. This sits like a bird cage on top of the main posts. A variety of jointing techniques may be used, including mortise and tenon joints, lapped joints and notched joints. Often the frame is first put together on the ground and then taken apart, to be re-assembled again in place on top of the posts.

Walls

Box-frames are often further stabilised by wooden panels that are fitted to the main framework using tongue and groove, or mortise and tenon joints. This method is commonly found, for example, among the Sa'dan Toraja of south Sulawesi and also in southern Nias. Here, the ensemble operates like a load-bearing wall, but usually the walls of vernacular structures serve only to provide protection from the elements and secure privacy. As such, they may consist of matting, *atap* thatch (palm leaves folded round a lath and stitched together with a strip of rattan), flattened or plaited bamboo panels, as well as wooden boards and panels, depending on the use and status of the building. These non-structural walls are sometimes fixed in an outward sloping position — a familiar feature of traditional Batak architecture.

TRADITIONAL ARCHITECTURE

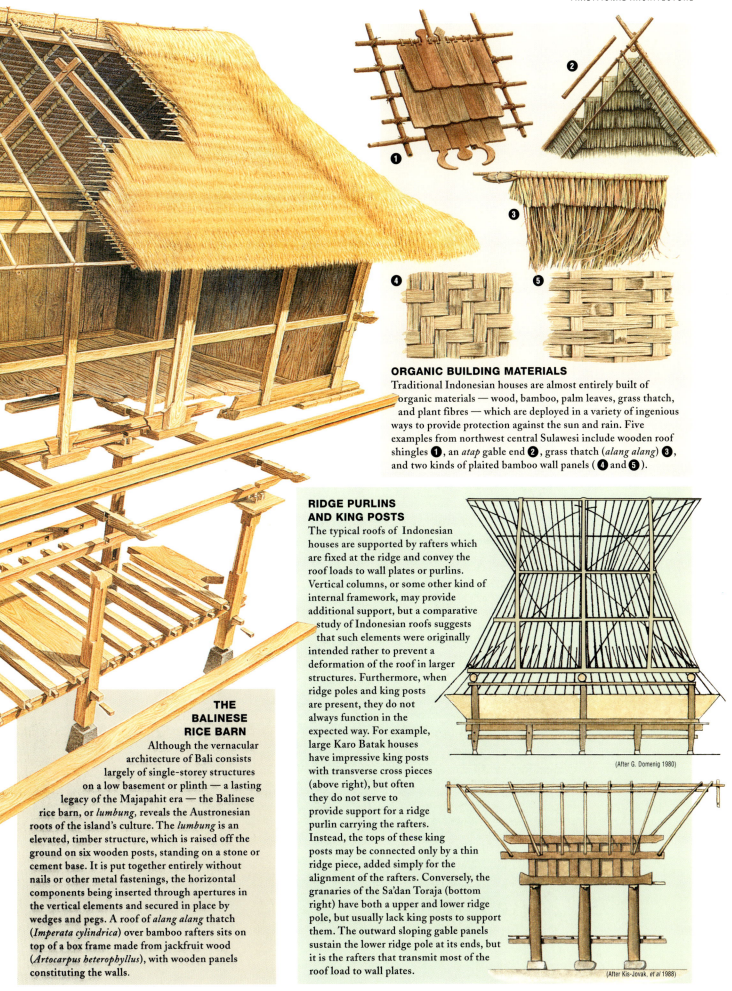

ORGANIC BUILDING MATERIALS
Traditional Indonesian houses are almost entirely built of organic materials — wood, bamboo, palm leaves, grass thatch, and plant fibres — which are deployed in a variety of ingenious ways to provide protection against the sun and rain. Five examples from northwest central Sulawesi include wooden roof shingles ❶, an *atap* gable end ❷, grass thatch (*alang alang*) ❸, and two kinds of plaited bamboo wall panels (❹ and ❺).

THE BALINESE RICE BARN
Although the vernacular architecture of Bali consists largely of single-storey structures on a low basement or plinth — a lasting legacy of the Majapahit era — the Balinese rice barn, or *lumbung*, reveals the Austronesian roots of the island's culture. The *lumbung* is an elevated, timber structure, which is raised off the ground on six wooden posts, standing on a stone or cement base. It is put together entirely without nails or other metal fastenings, the horizontal components being inserted through apertures in the vertical elements and secured in place by wedges and pegs. A roof of *alang alang* thatch (*Imperata cylindrica*) over bamboo rafters sits on top of a box frame made from jackfruit wood (*Artocarpus heterophyllus*), with wooden panels constituting the walls.

RIDGE PURLINS AND KING POSTS
The typical roofs of Indonesian houses are supported by rafters which are fixed at the ridge and convey the roof loads to wall plates or purlins. Vertical columns, or some other kind of internal framework, may provide additional support, but a comparative study of Indonesian roofs suggests that such elements were originally intended rather to prevent a deformation of the roof in larger structures. Furthermore, when ridge poles and king posts are present, they do not always function in the expected way. For example, large Karo Batak houses have impressive king posts with transverse cross pieces (above right), but often they do not serve to provide support for a ridge purlin carrying the rafters. Instead, the tops of these king posts may be connected only by a thin ridge piece, added simply for the alignment of the rafters. Conversely, the granaries of the Sa'dan Toraja (bottom right) have both a upper and lower ridge pole, but usually lack king posts to support them. The outward sloping gable panels sustain the lower ridge pole at its ends, but it is the rafters that transmit most of the roof load to wall plates.

(After G. Domenig 1980)

(After Kis-Jovak, *et al* 1988)

The House as a Ritually Ordered Space

The Indonesian house is much more than simply a place of residence affording somewhere to sleep, eat and take shelter from the elements. Rather, it is a symbolically ordered structure which provides a series of spatial metaphors for the expression of key cultural concerns and social values.

(Above) A hearth in a Rotinese house.

↗ *Interior of a Mentawai* uma. *The distribution of space within the* uma *reflects the order of social relationships within a single longhouse.*

Houses and Ancestors

First and foremost, the house in Indonesia defines a social group — the people who live in it. Typically this social group is identified with the original founders of the house. Ancestral origins constitute an important cultural orientation in many Indonesian societies, both conferring and confirming group membership, inheritance rights, social status, gender relations, and succession to office. In this respect, the membership of a particular household defines an individual's place in society.

These ideas are commonly portrayed in terms of a botanical metaphor — the imagery of organic growth readily lends itself for the representation of more abstract concepts such as precedence, continuity and social unity or cohesiveness. This in turn is embodied in the way that houses are constructed: house posts are 'planted' and other timbers are arranged according to their direction of growth. In this light, the house in Indonesia can thus be seen as the 'living' embodiment of the social group it represents, and indeed, in many instances, houses are said to possess a 'soul', or animating principle, which is brought into being by the original founders during construction ceremonies or rites of consecration. House parts are oftenly named after body parts in elaborate ways, for example, in Savu, the house is said to have a head, a tail, a neck and cheeks etc.

The House as a Microcosm of the Macrocosm

A number of different frames of reference may be simultaneously invoked. These commonly include an alignment with the path of the sun or an orientation in relation to geographical features such as the sea or a mountain. Together, these cosmological elements create a ritual order that organises activities taking place within the house. For example, the east is often identified with life-giving properties while the west is linked to death and one frequently finds that women give birth in the eastern 'half' of the house, while the dead are laid out in the west.

In the vertical plane, the house is typically divided into a tripartite scheme of things, where the roof space is identified with the realm of the gods and ancestors, the floor level represents the mundane world of everyday experience, and the void beneath the house is linked to an underworld populated by malevolent spirits, the souls of the dead and other supernatural agencies. In symbolic terms, movement from one part of the house to another represents a cosmological journey between these different realms whose mystical geography is delineated in myth and ritual: in the rarefied atmosphere of a shamanic séance, the familiar interior of the house is transformed into another reality in which the gods may descend from the heavens and the dead can be summoned from the grave.

ATONI HOUSE

The symbolic organisation of space within the Atoni house (West Timor) involves a complex interweaving of planes and axes. Some general correspondences can be drawn between pairs of spatial coordinates, such as 'high' and 'low', 'inner' and 'outer', 'right' and 'left', and various social categories — 'male' and 'female', 'kin' and 'affines', 'senior' and 'junior', 'high status' and 'low status'. Thus, in the horizontal plane, Atoni men are associated with the outer part of the house and the right hand side, while women are identified with the inner part of the house and the left. These spatial associations, however, are both relative and contingent. For example, Atoni society is subdivided into a number of patrilineal clans and women who go to live with their husbands after marriage are denied access to the innermost section of their new home until they have been initiated into their husband's patriclan. Similarly, women are not allowed to sleep on the 'great platform' situated on the right side, but on special occasions, their fathers and brothers may be honoured by being seated here.

Vertically, the attic is the most sacred part of the house — this is where the family heirlooms are stored, together with the altar stone used in agricultural rites and other ritual paraphernalia. Rice and maize are also kept here and only agnates who are related to the householder through the male line may enter this sacred space; non-agnates will cause the soul of rice and maize to flee, adversely affecting harvests.

① *mone*: 'outside'/'male' – yard
② *si'u*: 'elbow' – outer section
③ *harak*: 'platform' – high status guests are seated here
④ *eno*: 'door'
⑤ *nanan*: 'inside'/'centre'
⑥ *ni ainaf* (*nakan*): '(head) mother post' and entrance to attic
⑦ *harak ko'u*: 'great platform'
⑧ *harak tupa'*: 'sleeping platform'
⑨ *harak maba'at*: 'agreement platform' — where food is served to guests and women give birth
⑩ *tunaf*: 'hearth'

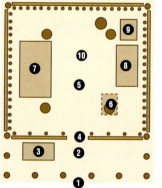

THE TORAJA HOUSE AND COSMOS

The Toraja house (*banua*) is a microcosm of the macrocosm. In the vertical plane, the roof space is identified with the heavens (*langi'*) ❶, the interior, with the realm of the living (*padang*) ❷, and the space beneath the house, with the underworld ❸. The latter is supported on the head of the deity Pong Tulak Padang ❹, while the 'Old Lord', Puang Matua, resides in the highest level of the heavens (*ulunna langi'*) and is identified with the sun at its zenith ❺. In houses of aristocratic families, there is a central house post which though it does not serve any structural function is identified as the *a'riri posi'*, or 'navel post' ❻, and constitutes a kind of *axis mundi*, or cosmic centre of the universe (a central pole (*petuo*) ❼ continues this vertical axis in the living space above). The space beneath the house is conceived as a place of danger, where malevolent spirits prowl seeking to eat the livers of those who sleep.

The north is associated with life and the source of life-giving waters that irrigate the terraced rice fields ❽. The headwaters of Sa'dan river ❾ are also in the north and the river which flows on a roughly north-south axis provides one of the two principal axes in the Toraja universe, the second being an east-west axis charted by the daily passage of the sun. To the south lies the sea and beyond, the island of Pongko ❿, homeland of the ancestors before time. The land of dead souls ⓫ is also located to the south, near the legendary Mount Bamba Puang ⓬ — the souls of aristocrats or wealthy commoners who have had the highest order of mortuary rites performed on their behalf, ascend this mountain, or an associated palm tree ⓭, to become deified ancestors in the heavens.

Toraja houses are laid out on a north-south axis. The most sacred part of the house is the upper part of the northern gable ⓮ which is called *lindo puang*, 'face of the lords', and which is said to be the place where the gods make their entry into the house. The southern end, on the other hand, is identified with the dead who are also associated with the west and the setting sun: corpses ⓯ are laid out on the west side of the house with their heads pointing towards the land of dead souls in the south. This is only carried out at a very late stage in final funeral rites; until then, the corpses lie east-west like the living and are treated as if they are not really dead. The initial rites for the dead are performed here and the body is removed from the house via a door situated in the west wall ⓰. The south and west are also identified with the ancestors from before time and family heirlooms are often stored in the southwest corner of the southern room ⓱. The eastern side of the house is associated with life-enhancing activities — this is where the hearth ⓲ is located and fertility rites are performed, while the umbilical cord of newborn infants is buried outside the house but on the east side. Similarly other architectural components of the house such as the ridge poles, roof beams, entrance ladders and other house parts are endowed with a cosmological significance to create a symbolic mirror image of the world.

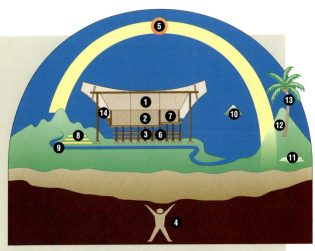

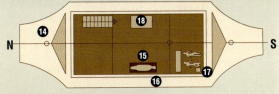

(Left) The northern gable of a contemporary Toraja tongkonan *is typically ornamented with mythological and cosmological symbols reflecting its symbolic significance as the most sacred part of the house.*

The Representation of Gender and Status

The cosmological orientations of the house dovetail with other symbolic orderings of space — for example, inside and out, upper and lower, front and back — to provide a set of spatial coordinates for the representation of social categories such as senior and junior, affine and agnate, close kin and distant. These divisions are frequently linked to gender-based concepts and ideas of appropriate male and female behaviour. Thus one finds that women are often associated with the inner or rear portion of the house while men are identified with the front of the building.

Changing statuses in the course of an individual's life time — from child to adult, unmarried to married — are reflected in how a person is physically situated within the house. Among the Minangkabau of western Sumatra, for example, the organisation of domestic space within the house, in terms of sleeping, seating and eating arrangements, charts the social trajectory of women from childhood, through marriage and motherhood, to old age.

Although one finds a common repertoire of symbolic elements in traditional Indonesian architecture, the significance or meaning of these elements differs between societies and even within the same society according to context.

SIGNIFICANT POSTS

The idea of having four principal posts is a common feature which occurs throughout most parts of the Indonesian Archipelago, in Java, Sumatra and Sumba to name a few. In Sumba, the right front house post is the most sacred just as the *soko guru tatal* of the Javanese mosques is supposed to be imbued with special symbolic meaning.

Construction Rites

Indigenous belief systems in Indonesia place humankind within an animated cosmos, permeated by a vitality which pervades all things. Even man-made objects are regarded as having their own lives and personalities which interact with those of the people who use them. This attitude informs the entire house-building process: the different stages of construction, with their attendant rituals, bring the vitality of the house into being, and any subsequent misfortune that may befall its occupants can be blamed on procedural errors which have created a disharmony between the building and the people who reside in it.

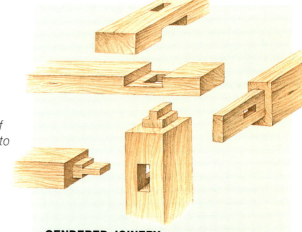

Roofing a house is often a communal effort, as seen here in Sumba (above), and its completion is cause for celebration. In Java (below), a red flag and an offering of fruit is tied to the roof ridge to encourage local spirits to favour future inhabitants of the house.

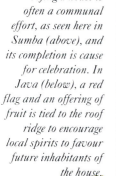

Selecting a House Site

Almost every stage in the house-building process is circumscribed by ritual observations including the selection of a new house site. This usually involves obtaining permission from the spirits of the earth or the gods who own the land. Among the Sa'dan Toraja of south Sulawesi, for example, a small bamboo, filled with water, is placed at the proposed house site and if, after three days, it is found to be still full to the brim, this is taken as a sign of spirit acquiescence. A chicken is then offered in propitiation and a piece of iron and a bead, representing longevity and nobility respectively, is buried on the spot.

'Planting' the House Posts

Trees, especially large, mature ones sought for house timbers, are often conceived as possessing a powerful 'life force' which must be dealt with respectfully in order that this 'wild' vitality can be safely contained when converted into 'domesticated' house parts. Most Indonesian societies observe some sort of ritual procedures when felling large trees and there are often special conditions relating to the transportation of timbers and their storage, prior to construction. The Nuaulu of Seram, for example, take care to prevent them from touching the ground and, in particular, from being 'inverted' — i.e. turned upside-down in relation to the direction in which they were growing. The last point is crucial: everywhere in Indonesia, house posts are 'planted' with the root end down, while even the 'trunks' and 'tips' of horizontal members must be ordered correctly, often according to a rule of 'moving to the right' (see box). In the eastern Indonesian island of Kedang, inversion of a house post is referred to by the same term used for 'incest', which literally means 'to turn upside-down', while in Sumba it is said that should a house post be placed the wrong way up, then the building will rot and illness will strike down its inhabitants. The imagery of 'trunk' and 'tip' and other related botanical metaphors are often used to describe many other kinds of relationships, especially kinship ties and the relation between founding and 'branch' houses.

GENDERED JOINERY

Javanese mortise and tenon joinery is explicitly identified with human sexual relations, the male component being the tenon pin and the female component the socket into which it is inserted. The complementarity of male and female establishes a harmonious arrangement of structural elements and their secure fit, while the actual bringing together of components mirrors the act of procreation and finds an ancient resonance in the *lingga-yoni* rituals of the Hindu-Buddhist era (see glossary).

House Posts Personified

House posts are almost everywhere the recipients of ritual attention — iron or candlenut, signifying strength and durability, may be placed in the post hole and often a propitiatory sacrifice is necessary before they are raised (in the past, a human head was sometimes required for important buildings).

House posts are also frequently personified as 'male' or 'female'. In Aceh, for example, the two principal house posts are identified as 'prince' and 'princess' (*raja* and *putròë*) and during wedding ceremonies they symbolise the bride and groom who are seated at their foot. The central, 'navel', post of aristocratic Toraja origin houses may similarly be identified as 'male' or 'female' and should be suitably 'dressed' before being erected — in this instance the male-female symbolism refers to a 'paired'

TRADITIONAL ARCHITECTURE

INAUGURATING THE NEW HOUSE
The completion of a noble origin house (*tongkonan*) in the Toraja highlands of south Sulawesi requires that the building, which up until this time has been under the control of the head carpenter, be formally handed over to the owners. Accordingly, the carpenter and the senior house owner sit themselves down on a mat with a basket of rice between them and the carpenter's tools laid out beside him. The house owner calls down blessings on the carpenter and expresses the hope that he will long continue to excel at his craft, while the carpenter responds by asking for health, wealth and a long life for both of them. Later, as a priest (*to minaa*) prepares to spend the night in the still unoccupied house, the owner comes knocking at the door. The priest calls out 'Who is it? What have you brought?', and the house owner presents him with a basket filled with pieces of wood and stones, which he declares to be rice, buffalo, pigs, gold and other items valued by the Toraja. The basket is taken up into the house and the priest and house owner then spend the night there.

The following day is marked by a dramatic ritual called *ma'bubung*. A chunk of pig fat is set alight on the roof ridge of the newly completed house (*bubung* means 'roof ridge'), and as it melts, the fat is allowed to run over an offering of rice. At the same time, water is sprayed from a bamboo tube over the people gathered below — the latter is said to be 'cooling' and symbolises a state of good health and spiritual well-being for the future occupants of the house. In the past, these rites were performed by a slave with a flaming brand who would run up and down the roof ridge three times, dancing and shouting as he went. Coming to a halt at the northern end — i.e. over the front façade of the house — the slave, or his modern substitute, hurls his torch to the ground, aiming to strike a wooden bowl containing water in which various ritual items are immersed. These include a piece of iron signifiying longevity, a gold bead representing health, a ceramic bead symbolising nobility, and a selection of leaves with 'cooling' properties. A big feast then follows, attended by relatives of the house's new occupants.

relationship between two related origin houses. On the island of Roti, the principal house post was traditionally clothed like a king and identified as the guardian of the house's power: in the case of newly built houses this was considered to be so potent that it could kill people, and participants at the inaugural rites had to wear new clothes, gold and beads, which were supposed to protect them from harm.

Living Houses
The idea that houses have a 'life' or 'personality' of their own is closely linked to the Indonesian belief in two different planes of existence, represented, on the one hand, by the mundane world of everyday experiences, and on the other, by an unseen yet parallel universe, which is encountered only in dreams and other exceptional circumstances. Everything we observe in the mundane world, including houses and other man-made objects, has a non-material presence, or 'spiritual' counterpart (*semangat* in Indonesian, in the latter realm. Furthermore, there is a direct correlation between the health and well-being of everything that occurs in the everyday world and that of their mystical counterpart in the invisible realm. In the case of human habitations, this 'spiritual' dimension is often bound up with the past lives of the ancestors and may influence the health and fortunes of those who live there, hence the care taken with construction rituals and subsequent house-maintenance rites.

*The 'navel' post (*a'riri posi'*) of a Toraja origin house. The post does not fulfill a structural role and is only found in the origin houses of noble families, which in the past were the seat of local political power.*

MOVEMENT TO THE RIGHT
In many Indonesian societies, the order in which the various structural elements of a house are assembled is significant. In the district of Rindi, in eastern Sumba (photo and diagram), the four principal house posts supporting the central portion of the roof are endowed with a ritual significance (see p.43), and the order in which they are erected is crucial to the future well-being of the building's inhabitants. The first post to be raised is the front right ❶, followed by right-hand rear ❷, left-hand rear ❸ and finally the front left-hand post ❹. They must, of course, be placed in the ground according to their direction of growth, with the root end down and the growing tip uppermost — were they not 'planted' in this way, then the posts would rot in the ground and the health of the occupants would be adversely affected. Horizontal timbers must also be arranged in a systematic manner with the 'root' end (*pingi*) ⓟ of one element meeting the 'tip' end (*kapuka*) ⓚ of another. This generates a circular 'motion' proceeding from root to tip (⟶), which in conjunction with the order of erecting the house posts creates a systematic directional movement to the right within the Rindi house.

21

The Toraja Tongkonan

With the daring upward sweep of their gravity-defying roofs, and the rich harmonies of their carved and painted decorations, the origin-houses of the Toraja make a dramatic and unforgettable impression. While the pile structure and extended roof ridge indicate a common ancestry with other Austronesian dwellings, the ingenuity with which this structure has been pushed to extremes in Tana Toraja represents a special architectural achievement. At the same time, the Toraja house exemplifies many of the themes that make houses so central to social organisation throughout the Archipelago.

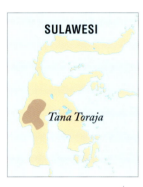

A contemporary tongkonan *with massively extended roof (below). The buffalo horns attached to the post supporting the roof ridge reflect the wealth and status of the householders, being the legacy of numerous funerary sacrifices.*

Rice barn under construction (bottom).

Houses as History

In an oral society, architecture can embody the past in a particularly significant way. Traditionally, only the nobility had the right to build elaborate, carved origin-houses (*tongkonan*), and only they had an interest in remembering long genealogies to go with them. Most ordinary folk live in undecorated common houses called *banua*. When people tell their genealogies, they always name first the founding couple of an origin-house, both husband and wife, and then the names of children and later descendants who spread out over the countryside, with the names of the new houses they founded, and sometimes also the heirlooms that they took with them when they moved. The result is a sort of geographical and historical map of settlement.

The most important noble houses were the seats of political power of local rulers who controlled small groups of villages. Such houses often have myths and legends associated with them which tell of ancestors who performed amazing feats, and magical heirlooms still stored in the house, or perhaps long since lost. The founding couples of some houses are said to have been *to manurun* or 'ones who descended': a man who came down from the sky and wed a woman who rose out of a river pool. In the past, these stories helped to legitimate the power of the nobility, but people still continue to argue over the details today in the interest of maintaining the prestige of a particular *tongkonan* — perhaps because they wish to see it included on the tourist circuit.

House styles have changed somewhat over time. The oldest surviving structures tend to be small, with only a slight curve to the roof. As the house came to embody aristocratic ambitions, it was gradually built higher and the curve of the extended eaves has become more and more exaggerated, actually reducing the usable interior space even as the exterior conveyed an increasingly impressive message about power and prestige.

Body, House and Cosmos

Like most vernacular architectures of Indonesia, the layout of the Toraja house is imbued with symbolic significance. The orientations of the Toraja house have cosmological meaning, and the design and arrangement of carved motifs on the façade convey a variety of other messages about social structure and relations with the spiritual world. Houses must always face north — the direction associated with a creator deity, Puang Matua. The south end, by contrast, is the 'posterior' of the house (*pollo' banua*), and is associated with the ancestors and the afterworld, Puya. The west and east sides correspond to the left and right hands of the body. The east is also associated with the deities (*deata*), while the west is identified with the ancestors in their deified form.

The spatial organisation of Toraja villages in the hilly areas is different from that found on the plains. The orientation of these houses depends largely upon the geography of the area.

(Left) A modern day tongkonan *raised on slender polygonal piles with an elegant soaring roof line supported by a free standing column (*tulak somba*).*

HOUSE DECORATION

Many house carving designs are derived from plant and animal motifs. The names of some of these designs have quite humble, everyday referents — for example, trailing water weeds, tadpoles or pumpkin vines. The significance of these seems to lie in their ability to multiply or spread rapidly; they represent a hope that the house descendants will likewise be numerous. Other designs represent buffaloes, heavy ears of rice, or heirloom ornaments — all symbols of desired wealth and plenty. The load bearing wall studs are always decorated with stylised buffalo heads (above left), and some say these stand for the aristocracy, who 'holds up' the rest of society. Near the top of the façade, one typically sees designs of betel leaf motifs and banyan trees — both have ritual associations — and in the topmost gable triangles, two sunbursts, surmounted by cocks (above right). The latter images are variously said to be emblems of high rank, bravery or greatness, or to stand for Tana Toraja itself, sometimes poetically referred to as *tondok lepongan bulan, tana matarik allo*, 'village of the circle of the moon, land of the circle of the sun.' The cock is an important mediating figure in myth, who is able to revive the dead and fulfill wishes by crowing, and who eventually flew up into the heavens and was transformed into a constellation.

Batak Architecture of Sumatra

Batak architecture is distinguished by dramatic roof profiles and elaborately ornamented surfaces. The type of roof employed differs between regional sub-groups, the best known examples being from the Toba, Karo and Simalungun areas. Traditionally, the Batak house was home to a number of related families, but the adoption of Christianity in the 19th century resulted in the abandonment of rituals designed to foster harmonious relations between the occupants of these communal houses and led to the building of smaller, single-family dwellings in their place.

A Toba Batak house with its traditional saddle-back roof.

The Toba Batak ruma gorga *is decorated with motifs (*gorga*) painted in traditional colours of black, white and red which reflect the social status of the householder.*

A traditional Simalungun house, standing on crossed-log foundations.

The Batak Homeland

The Batak of Sumatra are one of Indonesia's largest ethnic minorities. Their homeland lies to the north, where the central mountain range spreads out around Lake Toba to form the Batak tablelands at an altitude of more than 1,500 metres. They can be sub-divided into six or seven regional groupings or clans: Toba, Karo, Simalungun, Pakpak, Angkola (Sipirok), Mandailing and Pardembanan (now assimilated into the Malay communities of Asahan). The architecture of the Toba, Karo and Simalungun regions, is the best known since these remain the most traditional areas in terms of building houses.

General Principles

Although each Batak group is distinguished by its own distinctive architectural tradition, a number of general principles may be discerned. A variety of different building types exist, which include, depending on the region, dwellings, meeting houses, granaries, communal rice-pounding sheds and charnel houses. All of these structures are rectangular in plan and consist of an elevated floor supported on posts with a large pitched roof overhead. The latter is thatched with *ijuk* palm and the gable ends lean outwards. Traditional Batak houses are constructed entirely of wood and other natural materials, without using nails: individual components are held together by mortise and tenon joints or fastened with *ijuk* fibre bindings. In general, house posts rest on stone foundations and the space beneath the floor is closed in to create a buffalo pen. In the past, the Batak house was home to several families, whose physical distribution inside the building reflected their social relationship to the principal householder. Family units were grouped around a hearth and the living space was subdivided at night by hanging mats or textiles which afforded a measure of privacy. Apart from that there were no interior divisions.

Toba Batak

Although several different Toba Batak house styles exist, they all have the same generic form — a saddle-back roof and outward leaning gables. Larger dwellings can accommodate several families, each with their own hearth, though contemporary Toba houses tend to be much smaller than in the past. The front façade is often articulated by a series of tiered balconies, which may be used by musicians as a kind of minstrel's gallery during outdoor ceremonies. The lower balcony extends inside the house and may again be used by musicians during the performance of rituals inside the building.

The most refined type of Toba Batak dwelling is the *ruma gorga*. These are entered from below, through a trap door in the living floor, and are richly decorated with wood carvings. The latter include representations of the Batak deity Tapak Raja Suleiman and the mythical creature known as *singa-singa*, which combines the body of a man with the head of a horse.

Ruma siampore, at the other end of the social spectrum, are much simpler structures. They are entered through a door in the front façade and lack the minstrel's gallery and elaborately sculpted façade of *ruma gorga*. Their less affluent owners, however, will often decorate the front and sides of their houses with paintings depicting scenes of everyday life.

Toba granaries (*sopo*) (see p. 15) are situated directly opposite the house: the open-sided platform beneath the storage space provides a cool and shaded area for daily activities and socialising.

TRADITIONAL ARCHITECTURE

KARO BATAK

The Karo Batak have the greatest variety of house styles. These are classified according to the kind of construction techniques employed for the foundations or the type of roof structure which sits on top. The latter reflects the prestige and social status of the house founder — a particularly fine, though rare, example is the *rumah anjung-anjung* of a local Karo ruler, or *sibayak*, where the main roof is surmounted by an upper storey with a cruciform plan and gable elevations on all four sides (right). The huge size of Karo roofs, generally, requires a complex roof structure to carry the proportionally greater loads in comparison to Toba Batak houses. Nevertheless, the construction principles are recognizably the same which allows them to be considered as part of the same architectural tradition.

Karo Batak houses can accommodate between 8 and 12 families, which are arrayed on either side of a central passageway, connecting the two doors at either end of the building. The spatial distribution of individual families within the house is prescribed by customary law (*adat*) and is always the same irrespective of the house type, each hearth being shared by two families. Entry to the Karo house is gained via a bamboo platform (*ture-ture*), and women gather here to talk and gossip, and carry out their daily chores. Karo houses are rarely decorated with wood carvings like Toba Batak dwellings, but are often richly painted in traditional Karo colours — red, black, blue, green and yellow — which represent the five original clans (*marga*) from which today's lineages are descended.

Rumah Gadang: the Minangkabau Great House

The Minangkabau people of West Sumatra have developed one of the most distinctive and refined variations of the Austronesian saddle-back roof to be found in all of Indonesia. The traditional house, called rumah gadang, *or 'great house', is still a striking feature of the Minangkabau highlands, though they are not as common now as in the past. Some of the older houses were really enormous, providing accommodation for several matrilineally related families under one roof.*

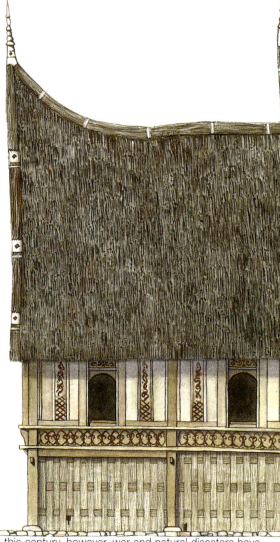

*Minangkabau society is sub-divided into matrilineal clans, which fall into two categories: the aristocratic (*koto piliang*), and the democratic (*bodi caniago*). This distinction has an architectural register: the living floor of aristocratic houses steps up towards the ends (below) while that of bodi caniago houses remains level throughout. Another distinction is the existence of the 'anjuang' (raised area) which can only be found in* koto piliang *houses.*

The Minangkabau

The roof of the Minangkabau house soars up to delicate points at the gable ends. Often the ridge line is broken into tiers, creating as many as six or more such pinnacles on the largest and finest buildings. The Minang compare these graceful spires to the horns of the legendary 'victorious buffalo' (menang kerbau) which prevailed in a tournament organised by Javanese rivals, and from which, according to popular etymology, they take their name. In 1990, the Minang numbered close to 4 million in their home province, but at least 1 million more live outside their homeland, having migrated (merantau) to other parts of Indonesia and beyond to work and trade. The migrant spirit is deeply embedded in Minangkabau culture and has been responsible for an exposure to many exotic influences. The practice of matriliny, in which descent is traced through women who inherit the house and all ancestral lands, is an important feature of the Minangkabau. The matrilineal system has survived several centuries of Islam — the religion has been thoroughly integrated into Minang culture since the 16th century — as well as the many changes of the colonial and modern eras.

Great Houses

In the past, Minangkabau 'great houses' lived up to their name: a Dutch colonial officer in 1871 found over 100 people living in a single house in Alahan Panjang, and between 60 and 80 resident in another. The largest structure still standing measures 120 x 15 metres with 20 biliak, or family apartments. During this century, however, war and natural disasters have caused the destruction of many older houses. Some were toppled by a severe earthquake which hit Padang Panjang in 1926; thousands more were destroyed in the war for Indonesian Independence (1945-49), and during the unsuccessful PRRI Rebellion in the 1950s. Afterwards, it proved too expensive to rebuild these great houses and finance the rituals which must accompany their construction. Deforestation has also made it increasingly difficult to find trees large enough to furnish the central pillars of *rumah gadang*. Today, many people think it more prestigious to build modern homes in concrete. Nevertheless, the old houses still remain important as places of origin and as the proper sites for ceremonies.

Construction Techniques

The Minangkabau house is put together without nails, the mortised post and beam framework being pegged or wedged in place. The central house post is set vertically, while in older houses the outer posts slope slightly outwards, to accentuate the roof line. The latter is built upward and outwards by means of internal crossbeams and trusses, the peaks being extended by an assembly of struts and battens. Thatching was traditionally made from tough, black sugar-palm fibre, capable of lasting a hundred years, though corrugated zinc became a popular alternative as early as 1907. Other building types, such as rice barns, prayer halls, and meeting-houses, echo the basic form of the house.

TRADITIONAL ARCHITECTURE

Rumah gadang *are raised one or two metres off the ground on stilts. The space beneath the living floor is often closed in with plaited bamboo panels to create a buffalo pen. The roof is thatched with* ijuk *palm and the pinnacles are tipped with metal finials. The longitudinal elevation is unusual for Indonesia in that the walls are quite high in proportion to the roof. These surfaces are often elaborately carved and painted. Minang wood carvings, like their textiles, make extensive use of plant motifs which are rich in symbolic significance.*

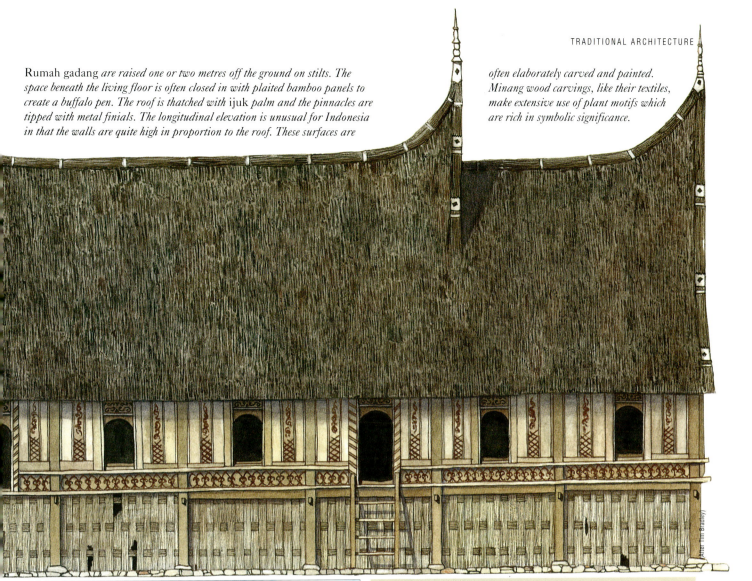

(Above) *A recently constructed Minangkabau house built in the traditional style. Unlike the* rumah gadang, *many houses hold only single families. Traditional houses are decorated by carving which are derived from plant and animal motifs.*

HOUSE PLANS AND SPATIAL ARRANGEMENTS

Minangkabau houses are rectangular in plan, with the entrance in one of the longitudinal sides. This opens into a capacious hall (*ruang*), where meals are taken and social activites take place. At one end of the hall, there is a raised area called the *anjuang*. In matrilineal Minang society, husbands live in their wives' houses, and traditionally, the *anjuang* is where the most recently married daughter of the house and her husband reside. Other married women and their spouses occupy apartments, or *biliak*, at the back of the house. As each girl gets married she moves into the *anjuang* while the other married women shift down one room towards the kitchen. Ideally, the oldest woman in the house should sleep in the *biliak* next to the kitchen. If there are no vacant *biliak* to accommodate her, she will move into the space called *pangkalan* (central post) reflecting her status as the senior matriarch. Nowadays, newly wedded women often prefer to move out and build a new dwelling in the house compound if they can afford it.

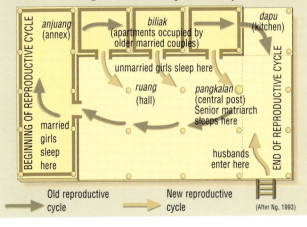

Mentawai Longhouses

Many aspects of the traditional culture of the Mentawai Islands, off the west coast of Sumatra, bear witness to an ancient, Neolithic, Austronesian past. The economy is based on simple gardening and animal husbandry, with a division of labour determined by gender. Formerly, stone tools were used, though today these have been replaced by metal imports obtained from Sumatra. Nevertheless, despite this simple technology, the Mentawaians are the creators of impressive longhouses called uma.

Siberut sapou (above right) are typically situated along one of the many rivers which intersect the vast stretches of hilly jungle covering most of the interior of the island.

Longhouse Society

In most parts of the Mentawai Archipelago, modern influences have led to drastic changes in the traditional culture, but longhouses can still be found in some regions of Siberut, which is the largest island in the group. A single *uma* may be home to up to a dozen families and together they constitute a discrete social unit — also called an *uma* — which is the basic building block of Mentawaian society. Relations, however, between neighbouring *uma* can be equivocal. Every *uma* belongs to one of the many patriclans which are distributed through the islands and wives should always be sought in another clan — preferably from an *uma* in the vicinity. Friendly alliances are the usual consequences of this, but good relations between neighbouring *uma* are constantly countered by rivalry and mutual distrust which threaten the peace and often lead to open hostility.

Residence Patterns

Each family owns a private dwelling (*sapou*), near their plantations, and this is where they live on a day to day basis, coming together at the *uma* for ritual and festive occasions. At such times, family life is subordinated to the concerns of the group as a whole. In the *uma*, family members do not even sleep together, with men and older boys fixing up their mosquito nets on the verandah, while women and children occupy the rear of the house.

Omens and Auguries

Mentawai house building is supervised by a *rimata*, or master of ceremonies. He is usually an elderly man who is an expert at interpreting omens and religious traditions. For him, especially, the *uma* is his actual home and it is he who makes the most substantial contributions to its construction. However, all the other members will also provide both materials and labour, while neighbouring groups are invited to help with the building. The latter are regaled with generous meals and participate as guests in the various ceremonies that accompany the different stages of construction.

Although the Mentawai longhouse is not oriented according to the cardinal points, an *uma* will only prosper in a place which is agreeable to both the ancestors and local spirits. Before construction starts, a small spot is cleared and in the process special attention is paid to augural signs. The calls of specific birds, the appearance of certain animals, climatological peculiarities and so forth, are all regarded as

The roof ridge of present-day Mentawai longhouses is straight, but the huge uma *of pre-colonial times had saddle-back roofs with a beak-like 'peak' and projecting gables at either end. These features are widespread in Indonesia, reflecting a common Austronesian inheritance.*

THE MENTAWAI *UMA*

The Mentawai *uma* stands on piles and is constructed without nails, making the most of mortise and tenon construction techniques and lap joints. As in many Indonesian houses, the arrangement of vertical and horizontal timbers must follow the direction of growth of the plant materials employed.

The ritual centre of the house is marked by the *siegge legeu* post, which stands to the right of the entrance to the innermost room ❶. It is believed that the spirit of a protective culture hero dwells beneath this sacred post and when a house is consecrated, upon its completion, this is where the *bakkat katsaila* is attached. The latter is the principal household fetish, and consists of a bunch of sacred leaves which have a benign, 'cooling' influence on the house and the lives of its inmates.

In terms of layout, there is a covered front verandah ❷ for daily activities and relaxing; an outer room ❸ for the preparation of communal meals, and for feasting and dancing; and an inner room (which may sometimes be sub-divided into smaller units) ❹, which is where women carry out most of their household chores and where they sleep at night, together with their children.

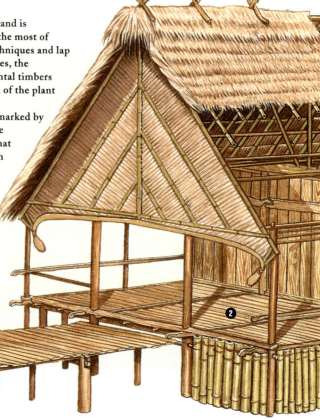

messages from the spirits, and if the signs are unfavourable, another site must be sought. Similar procedures are observed when seeking house posts and other structural elements: a bad omen indicates that the material in question should be discarded.

An important moment is the setting up of the main house post. This post, which is the last to be raised, is called *siegge legeu*, 'the one who is waiting in a cloudless period'. If rain falls in the night after its erection, if someone dies in the vicinity, or if there is an earth tremor, then all the work will have been in vain: the whole building is dismantled and the material set aside until a new site has been chosen. All being well, however, the floor is fixed in place, with special attention paid to the dance floor in the outer room, which is constructed from boards. In this instance, a thunderstorm is regarded as a good omen: everyone is delighted to hear the claps of thunder, since thunderous stamping is part of the dancing.

Inaugural Rites

Inaugural rites last several weeks and begin with a sacrifice to propitiate the ancestors and local spirits. There are regular banquets and for every pig slaughtered a decorated bamboo stake several metres high is set up by the riverbank. These announce to the spirits how many animals have been sacrificed on their behalf. There is also a ceremonial hunt for a male monkey, whose skull is subsequently attached to an intricately carved and painted wooden board (*jaraik*) which is then hung above the entrance to the innermost room as a guardian against evil influences. As time goes by, daily activities are gradually resumed in a ritual way to ensure a propitious new beginning in the lives of *uma* members. Finally, the whole group moves away for several days to stay with neighbours, but in pre-colonial times, this concluding stage was marked by a headhunting expedition.

❶ Interior view of the gable end of a Mentawai *uma*, showing the principal house posts and transverse beams under construction.
❷ A plaited basket containing sacred leaves and other ritual items, suspended from the rafters.
❸ Pig skulls hanging from the eaves are testimony to past sacrifices.
❹ Man sitting in the front room of an *uma*; the mosquito nets behind indicate sleeping places on either side of the central gangway.

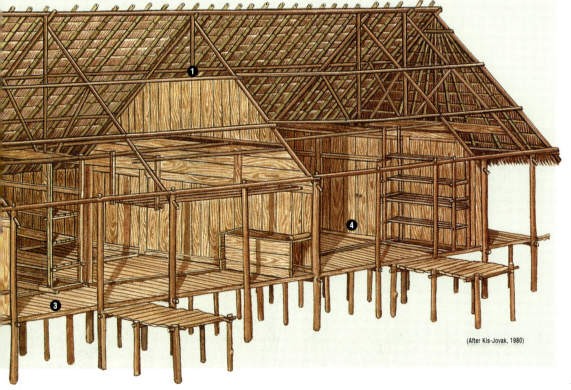

(After Kis-Jovak, 1980)

Painted wooden house carving, commemorating a successful headhunting expedition.

Houses and Megaliths of the Nias Island

The island of Nias, off the west coast of Sumatra, is justly famous for its magnificent houses, paved streets and megalithic culture. Massive pile structures with soaring roofs and opening skylights are the distinctive features of a unique architectural tradition which has no parallel in other parts of the Indonesian Archipelago.

The main street in a southern Nias village is bisected along its linear axis by a pavement. The paved area on either side is a semi-public space and is identified with the house which fronts it.

(Below) Northern Nias houses are distinguished by their unique oval ground plan. The roof is a much lighter structure with an unobstructed roof space which allows for an upper storey over the main living floor.

Nias Society and Culture

The people of Nias refer to their island as *'tano niha'*, meaning 'land of mankind'. Headhunting, ancestor worship, feasts of merit, and a stratified society composed of chiefs, noblemen, commoners and slaves, were once the definitive characteristics of Nias society. Today, differences of social organisation and village formation divide the island into three distinct regions: north, central and south. Southern Nias villages have been described as mini 'republics' whose leaders are appointed by a village assembly (*orahua*). Villages in the centre of the island also form politically autonomous entities, only in this instance they are organised around a patriarchal system of hereditary chiefs. Those of the north, however, are quite different, being more like hamlets which in times of war were organised into loose confederations.

Salient Architectural Features

The houses of Nias are notable for their foundations which consist of a complex arrangement of vertical and oblique posts. This structure is designed to withstand earthquakes and the assembly as a whole retains a high degree of elasticity because the posts themselves are not settled in the ground, but rest instead on top of stone foundations. Other notable features include steeply pitched roofs with opening skylights that allow daylight to enter the interior of the building and encourage the circulation of air. The skylight is peculiar to the island of Nias and is not found elsewhere in the Archipelago.

Southern Nias Villages

Southern Nias villages are situated on hilly sites and take their name from their location. They are often approached by a grand staircase built of stone and can consist of several hundred dwellings arranged on either side of a paved street which may be hundreds of metres in length. Neighbouring houses are interconnected, forming long terraces with entrances shared by pairs of adjacent households. The basic linear street pattern may, over time, take on an 'L' or 'T'-shaped configuration as new houses are added to the settlement. Sometimes the main street (*ewali*) will be bisected at right angles by a second axis, creating crossroads at the centre of the village.

Megaliths are situated immediately in front of the culvert in the semi-public domain. Referred to as the 'wall of stones' (*öli batu*) they indicate the rank of the householders, being the physical reminder of past feasts of merit and a lasting memorial to those who hosted them. In this respect they represent a kind of petrified model of the social hierarchy within the village community — the erection of a menhir (*fa'ulu*) by a chief or nobleman is in effect a public proclamation of his status within the community. It also marks the completion of a privately sponsored 'feast of merit'. In the past, the bones of the dead were placed in jars and buried beneath these sacred stones. Eligibility to erect a megalith is decided upon by the village assembly, whose members base their consideration on wealth (*mokho*), leadership (*molakhomi*), seniority (*fa'asia*) and intelligence (*onekhe*). The stones are classified by gender, and come in a variety of forms which include menhirs, benches and circular seats.

The chief's house (*omo sebua*), which naturally has the biggest and best megaliths, is always the largest structure in the village and is located at the centre of the community, overlooking the main square (*gorahua newali*). The public meeting house (*bale*) is also situated nearby. In the past, when warfare and headhunting raids were endemic, the village was fortified by an outer palisade of sharpened bamboo stakes with a deep ditch behind. An inner bailey, consisting of a stout masonry wall with a single entrance protected by a guardhouse, provided the main line of defence, while the house itself, with its stout posts and elevated floor level, afforded a last opportunity for resistance.

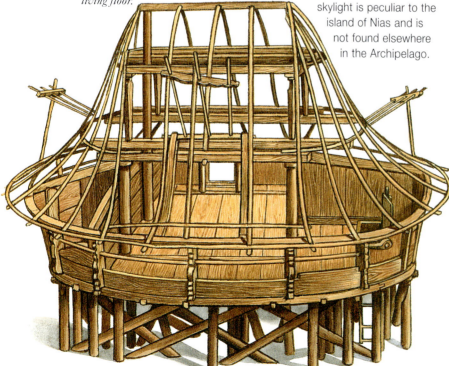

TRADITIONAL ARCHITECTURE

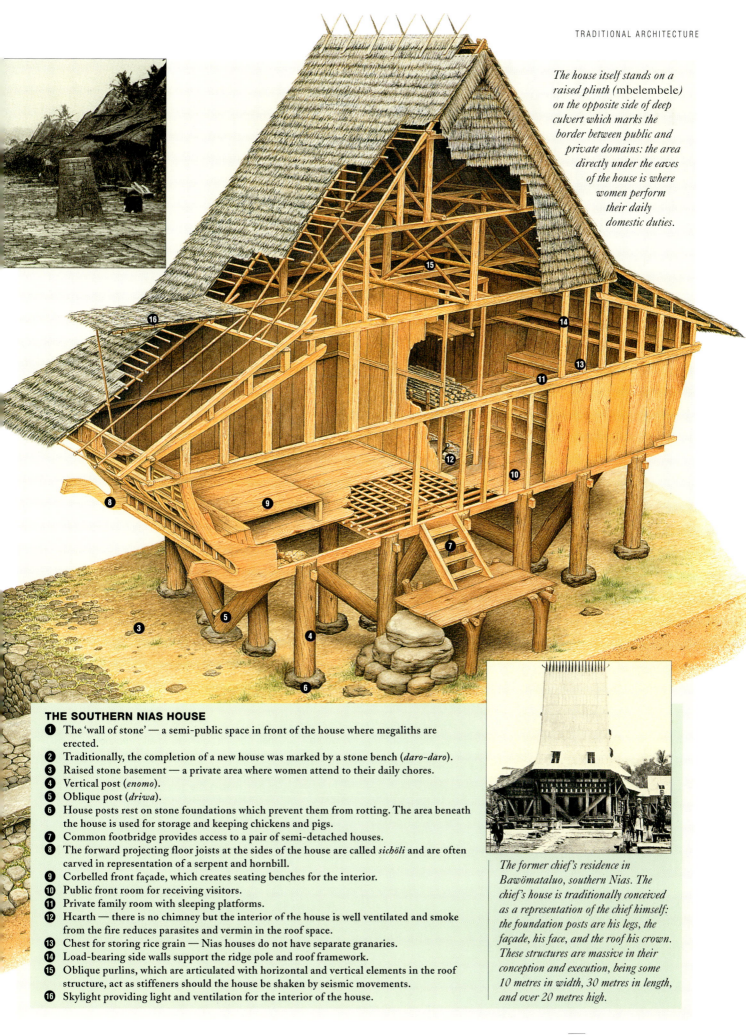

The house itself stands on a raised plinth (mbelembele) on the opposite side of deep culvert which marks the border between public and private domains: the area directly under the eaves of the house is where women perform their daily domestic duties.

THE SOUTHERN NIAS HOUSE

① The 'wall of stone' — a semi-public space in front of the house where megaliths are erected.
② Traditionally, the completion of a new house was marked by a stone bench (*daro-daro*).
③ Raised stone basement — a private area where women attend to their daily chores.
④ Vertical post (*enomo*).
⑤ Oblique post (*driwa*).
⑥ House posts rest on stone foundations which prevent them from rotting. The area beneath the house is used for storage and keeping chickens and pigs.
⑦ Common footbridge provides access to a pair of semi-detached houses.
⑧ The forward projecting floor joists at the sides of the house are called *sichöli* and are often carved in representation of a serpent and hornbill.
⑨ Corbelled front façade, which creates seating benches for the interior.
⑩ Public front room for receiving visitors.
⑪ Private family room with sleeping platforms.
⑫ Hearth — there is no chimney but the interior of the house is well ventilated and smoke from the fire reduces parasites and vermin in the roof space.
⑬ Chest for storing rice grain — Nias houses do not have separate granaries.
⑭ Load-bearing side walls support the ridge pole and roof framework.
⑮ Oblique purlins, which are articulated with horizontal and vertical elements in the roof structure, act as stiffeners should the house be shaken by seismic movements.
⑯ Skylight providing light and ventilation for the interior of the house.

The former chief's residence in Bawömataluo, southern Nias. The chief's house is traditionally conceived as a representation of the chief himself: the foundation posts are his legs, the façade, his face, and the roof his crown. These structures are massive in their conception and execution, being some 10 metres in width, 30 metres in length, and over 20 metres high.

31

Longhouses of Kalimantan: the Kenyah Uma Dadoq

The vernacular architecture of Kalimantan is typified by the Dayak longhouse, an attenuated pile dwelling with a pitched roof and verandah, which may be home to literally hundreds of people. Dayak is a generic term for the many ethnic groups that live along the major river systems of Borneo such as the Kapuas, Barito, Mahakam and Kayan. Although each group builds its own distinctive type of longhouse, these structures nevertheless share a number of common features in terms of their layout and construction methods.

A mural at Umah Rukun Damai, east Kalimantan. The upper portion of the wall is identified with the sky and is decorated with images of clouds and birds; the middle section contains representations of the human face, tigers and other animals; the bottom is filled with reptiles and other crawling creatures.

An Iban longhouse in West Kalimantan.

Kenyah Settlements

The Kenyah come from the Apo Kayan Plateau, near the headwaters of the Mahakam River in east Kalimantan. Their longhouses resemble those of their neighbours, the Kayan, and there is speculation that the Kenyah may once have been nomadic people who subsequently adopted a longhouse lifestyle in imitation of the Kayan.

The Kenyah refer to their longhouses as *uma dadoq* (*uma* means 'house' or 'farm'; *dadoq* means 'big', 'long' or 'tall'), and they are well named — some longhouses may reach over 250 metres in length and comprise more than 30 independent family apartments (*amin*). These are situated side by side, and are joined by a common verandah (*useh*), running the full length of the building. This covered verandah, or gallery, is a public area which is used for both work and recreation. It is also a place for receiving guests and where major rituals are performed.

The longhouse community is typically made up of close relatives and new apartments can be easily added at either end of the building should other families wish to join the community. Conversely, existing apartments can be readily dismantled simply by disengaging the mortise and tenon joints of the principal timbers, should a family wish to move to another community.

Longhouse Construction

The Kenyah longhouse stands on wooden piles which are sunk in the ground, the space beneath the living floor being used for storage and keeping livestock. The main load-bearing components are mortised, while lighter elements are simply lashed in place. House posts are ideally made from iron wood (*Eusideroxylon zwangerii*), with wooden shingles made from the same material for the roof. Access is gained via notched tree trunk ladders, located at either end of the building and other convenient points along its length.

Social Stratification

Kenyah society was traditionally divided into three classes: aristocrats, commoners and slaves. Aristocratic families are entitled to bigger apartments, with that of the chief being the largest of all. The latter is located at the centre of the longhouse, with close relatives situated on either side — their relative rank or position in society can be calculated in relation to the distance they are removed from the headman's apartment. The roof ridge of the headman's apartment is higher than those of other *amin*, while the portion of the covered verandah in front of his door is extended outwards to create a public space where members of the longhouse community can gather to discuss important issues. The headman's position in society is also reflected in the construction of new longhouses, which always commences with erection of the central post which supports the floor of his apartment. The seven remaining posts of the headman's *amin* follow, before the rest of the community can begin building their own apartments which progressively extend the longhouse on either side of the headman's *amin*.

The Longhouse Community

In essence, the longhouse community is a village whose members live together under a single roof. They are typically situated on the banks of rivers which have traditionally provided the main arteries of communication in the densely forested interior of Kalimantan. With the exception of the nomadic Punan, most of the major non-Malay ethnic groups in Kalimantan are longhouse dwellers. In addition to the Kenyah, they include the Kayan, Maloh, Ngaju,

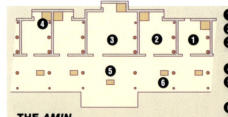

1. Commoner's *amin*.
2. Aristocrat's *amin*.
3. Chief's *amin* (at centre of longhouse).
4. Hearth.
5. Communal verandah.
6. Fireplace.

THE *AMIN*
The average size of individual apartments is roughly nine metres wide by 6-9 in depth and relations with neighbours are intimate, the party walls between adjacent *amin* reaching less than halfway to the roof ridge. There are no windows but some *amin* have an opening in the outer wall, while others have a back door leading on to a platform at the rear.

TRADITIONAL ARCHITECTURE

Iban, Kantu', Mualang and Ot Danum.

Within the Longhouse

The *amin* apartment is home to an extended family which constitutes the basic economic and social unit of Kenyah society. The interior of the apartment (*dalem amin*) is a private, family space to which only close relatives are admitted. Family members sleep on mats which are unrolled at night along the wall separating the apartment from the common verandah. Although this sleeping area is not physically divided from the rest of the apartment, a portion will be screened off during childbirth. The rear half of the *amin* apartment — i.e. the far side from the entrance — is conceived as a sacred domain (*sinong*) and should always be kept clean. This is where family heirlooms and ritual items are stored. Meals were traditionally prepared within the apartment proper, but the hazard of fire has led to the hearth being removed to a separate structure (*atang*), joined to the longhouse by a short catwalk.

In addition to the main entrance which opens off the common verandah, there is a second, smaller door, concealed in the same wall. Corpses make their final exit from the *amin* via this latter portal, the idea here being that the dead take a different route from the living.

Notched-log entry ladders (top left), interior of an amin *(top); and communal gallery (above).*

The Javanese House

Temple reliefs from the 9th century clearly indicate that the vernacular architecture of Java at that time conformed to an Austronesian archetype with pile foundations, pitched roofs and an extended roof ridge. Today, however, the traditional Javanese house is built on the ground with a raised floor and a roof form more closely resembling the houses of eastern Indonesia. In general, most Javanese houses conform to a similar ground plan but differences in the type of roof employed are indicative of the social and economic status of the house owners.

The front verandah of a house in Kudus, Central Java. The houses from this region are famous for their rich ornamentation and high standards of craftsmanship.

A Hierarchy of Roofs

Javanese domestic architecture distinguishes three main types of roof — *kampung, limasan* and *joglo*. The *kampung* roof is the simplest, structurally, and is identified with the domicile of the common man. It consists of a pitched roof erected over four central columns, braced by two layers of tie beams. The roof ridge is supported by king posts and is typically aligned on a north-south axis. The structure can be enlarged simply by extending the roof, at a lesser inclination, from the eaves of the existing roof.

The *limasan* roof is a more elaborate version of the *kampung* roof form and is used for the houses of higher status Javanese families. In this instance the basic ground plan of four house posts is extended by adding a pair of posts at either gable end; rafters running from the end of the ridge beam to these outer posts transform the pitched roof into a hipped roof with a trapezoidal longitudinal section and five roof ridges.

The *joglo* roof is traditionally associated with the residences of noble families. It exhibits a number of distinctive features. The main roof is much steeper and the roof ridge greatly reduced in length. The four main house posts support a roof which is surmounted by a unique structure consisting of layered beams referred to as the *tumpang sari*.

JAVANESE HOUSETYPES
❶ Typical *kampung*-style house, with extended front verandah, near Mojokerto, East Java.
❷ *Limasan*-style house, also with extended front verandah, Yogyakarta, Central Java.
❸ *Joglo*-style house, near Jepara, Central Java.

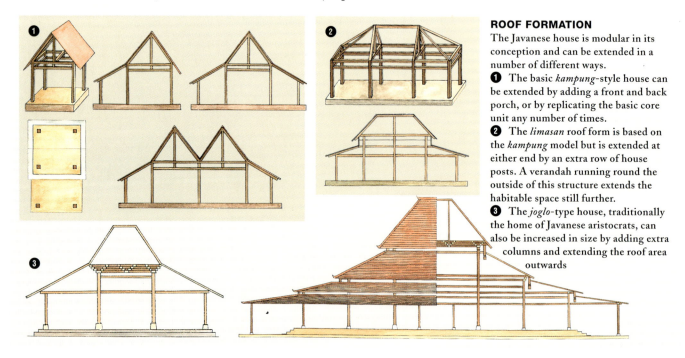

ROOF FORMATION
The Javanese house is modular in its conception and can be extended in a number of different ways.
❶ The basic *kampung*-style house can be extended by adding a front and back porch, or by replicating the basic core unit any number of times.
❷ The *limasan* roof form is based on the *kampung* model but is extended at either end by an extra row of house posts. A verandah running round the outside of this structure extends the habitable space still further.
❸ The *joglo*-type house, traditionally the home of Javanese aristocrats, can also be increased in size by adding extra columns and extending the roof area outwards

TRADITIONAL ARCHITECTURE

(Main illustration) The upper roof of the joglo-*type building is supported by four columns surmounted by the* tumpang sari. *The outermost band of beams support the rafters of both the upper and lower roofs, while the inner series create a vaulted ceiling in the form of a stepped pyramid. This composition of four central columns supporting the main roof seems to echo similar construction techniques found in eastern Indonesia and the traditional Indonesian mosques.*

(Inset) The tumpang sari *of a traditional Javanese house near Cilacap, Central Java.*

The House Compound

The ideal Javanese residence consists of three main structures — the *omah*, a *pendapa* and a *peringgitan* — enclosed by a brick wall or low fence. The latter is breached by a gateway, which both physically and symbolically connects the private, inner space of the family compound with the wider social community.

The *pendapa* is a pavilion which is situated in the front part of the compound. This constitutes the public domain of the household — a place for social gatherings and ritual performances. The *peringgitan* has either a *kampung* or *limasan* roof form, and links the *pendapa* to the *omah*. It is the place where shadow puppet plays (*wayang*) are performed during ritual and festive occasions.

The basic house unit is known as the *omah*. The plan is rectangular with a raised floor, the area under the roof being divided by wall panels into an inner and outer domain. The latter consists of an external verandah (*emperan*) which is used for public activities. It is also provided with a raised bamboo platform which is used for reclining or sleeping during the day. A wide door in the front wall connects this verandah with the inner domain (*dalem*). The *dalem* is an enclosed structure and is subdivided along a north-south axis into different domains. In the case of *kampung* and *limasan* models this is a simple distinction between the front and rear parts of the inner house, but in *joglo* houses a more complex tripartite division between front, middle and back is used.

The eastern part of the front portion of the *dalem* is where family chores are performed and where all the members of the family sleep, on a large bamboo bed, prior to the puberty of the children. The middle section of the *dalem* in *joglo* houses is defined by the four principal house posts. Today, the area has no specific usage, but traditionally, this area was where incense was burnt once a week in honour of the rice goddess Sri; it is also the place where the bride and bridegroom are seated during their marriage ceremony.

The rear portion of the house consists of three enclosed rooms called *senthong*. The western *senthong* is where rice and other agricultural produce are stored, while farming equipment is stored on the eastern side. The central *senthong* was traditionally the most lavishly decorated room being identified as the permanent abode of Sri herself. Newly married couples sleep here.

The kitchen is located outside the *omah* and is typically constituted as an independent structure, situated near the well. The well, as the provider of water, is identified as the source of life, and is always the first thing to be completed when building a new house compound. As the size and wealth of a family grows, additional structures (*gandok*) may be added.

JAVANESE HOUSE COMPOUND
1. *lawang pintu*
2. *pendapa*
3. *peringgitan*
4. *emperan*
5. *dalem*
6. *senthong*
7. *gandok*
8. *dapur* (kitchen)
9. *kamar mandi* (bathroom)

The Balinese House

Balinese culture represents a syncretic blend of Hindu and Buddhist beliefs, fused with an underlying Austronesian animism, and it is this mélange of indigenous and exotic influences which informs the layout and construction of the residential compound. Correct orientation in space, combined with ideas of ritual purity and pollution, are the key concepts here, providing a cosmological framework for maintaining a harmony between the lives of those who live within the compound walls and the rest of the universe.

Macrocosm and Microcosm

The Balinese conception of *dharma* affords a holistic model of the universe in which the ultimate aim in life is to reach *mokhsa*, the point at which an individual achieves a perfect state of being and merges with the infinite, thereby attaining release from the endless cycle of rebirth. This can only be achieved through being in harmony with all of creation, a sublime state which must be maintained at all times and in all places. Correct orientation is an important consideration; everything in nature is conceived as having an ideal location and must be correctly aligned or coordinated if the desired harmony between man and nature is to be achieved. Naturally, architecture plays a crucial role in this scheme of things.

Family shrine dedicated to the ancestral spirits.

Asta Kosala Kosali

Every aspect of Balinese architecture is governed by a detailed set of formulae relating to the proper size, location and alignment of building types. These principles are set down in a sacred architectural treatise, the *Asta Kosala Kosali*, which is inscribed in ancient Javanese on *lontar* palm leaf manuscripts.

The Balinese universe is divided in three: the underworld (*buhr*) which is the domain of evil and malevolent spirits; the human realm (*buwah*); and the heavens (*swah*), which is the place of the gods. This cosmological model can be readily mapped onto the local topography. The mountains and volcanoes and in particular Gunung Agung are conceived as the abode of the gods, while the sea is identified as the locus of malevolent spirits and evil influences. In between lie the coastal plains and foothills which represent the abode of mankind.

An orientation towards the mountains (*kaja*) is considered pure or sacred while the seaward direction (*kelod*) is designated as impure or profane. As most of Bali's population live on the south side of the island, this dichotomy corresponds to a north-south axis running between the central mountain range and Gunung Agung in particular, and the sea. Similar ideas are attached to the east-west axis, except that in this instance, it is the east (*kangin*) which is identified as sacred and the west (*kauh*) is often seen as being profane. The northeast (*kaja kangin*) is generally regarded to be the most auspicious direction whilst the southwest (*kelod kauh*) is the least favourable. Each of the eight cardinal points is also associated with a particular Hindu deity and is identified with a corresponding day in the Balinese eight-day week. Together with the centre, they play an instrumental role in organising the layout of the Balinese house compound and many other aspects of Balinese life.

Other frames of reference also operate, including the metaphorical representation of the compound and its various structures in terms of the human body. Thus, the family shrine is identified with the head; the sleeping quarters and pavilion for receiving guests, with the arms; the central courtyard with the navel; the hearth, with the sexual organs; the kitchen and granary, with legs and feet; and the refuse pit in the backyard, with the anus.

House building must be ritually sanctioned by the gods and before beginning work on construction, offerings must be made on an appropriately auspicious day determined from the calendar. Ritual observations accompany every stage of construction, the cycle being completed by a final ceremony, called *melepas*, which spiritually brings the building to life.

ANTHROPOCENTRIC MEASUREMENTS

The Balinese compound is laid out according to the owner's physical proportions. The basic unit is a combination of the distance between the tip of the middle finger of each hand when the arms are stretched out horizontally on either side of the body (*depa*), plus the distance from the elbow to the tip of the middle finger (*hasta*), plus the width of the fist with thumb extended (*musti*). These dimensions are recorded on a length of bamboo which serves as a yardstick for laying out the complex.

1. Depa
2. Depa media
3. Hasta
4. Musti
5. Sedemak
6. Tampak
7. Lengkat

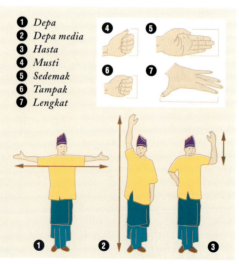

TRADITIONAL ARCHITECTURE

THE RESIDENTIAL COMPOUND

The Balinese residential compound consists of a number of pavilions (*bale*) and other structures enclosed on all sides by a wall of whitewashed mud or brick. There is a central courtyard ❶ of packed earth which is kept free of vegetation except for a few ornamental flowers or a decorative frangipani tree, while the rest of the compound is laid out according to the Balinese conception of the sacred and profane. Thus, the family shrine ❷ is situated in the northeasternmost corner of the compound, with the principal sleeping pavilion (*meten*) ❸ placed beside it, a little to the west, but still on the northern side of the central courtyard. Although the *meten* is normally occupied by the head of the family and his wife, it may be vacated for newlyweds, being the only place in the compound where privacy is available; family heirlooms are also kept here. The sleeping accommodation of other family members (*bale sikepat*) ❹ — the Balinese compound may be home to several families, the heads of which are brothers — is situated on the eastern side of the courtyard, while the pavilion for receiving guests (*bale tiang sangka*) ❺ stands on the opposite side of the courtyard, to the west. The *bale sekenam* ❻, which is where the women do their weaving is located at the southern end of the courtyard, as are the kitchen (*paon*) ❼, rice barn (*lumbung*) ❽ and pigsty ❾. The entrance to the compound ❿ should ideally be placed at the *kelod* end of the enclosure. According to the Balinese, this has a direct influence on the lives and well-being of family members: one location will promote wealth, but mean fewer children; another location will enhance popularity, but bring sickness, and so on. A small wall (*aling aling*) ⓫ is built directly behind the opening, screening off the interior and obstructing the entry of malevolent influences.

The compounds of well-to-do families, will also have a number of other buildings which provide accommodation, and may also include an ornately carved *bale gede* which is used as a place for entertaining guests.

(Above) Plan of a typical Balinese compound.

(Left) Women pounding rice inside a domestic compound (1930s).

(Below) Street scene with compound entrances.

37

Houses and Compounds in the Mountains of Bali

The geographical isolation of the mountain peoples of Bali (wong bali aga) has meant that they have been far less influenced by Hindu-Buddhist traditions than their lowland neighbours who came under the purview of the Javanese princes from the Majapahit empire from the 14th century onwards. This separate history of the Bali Aga can be seen in their vernacular architecture which clearly reveals elements of a common Austronesian tradition shared with other Indonesian peoples spread across the Archipelago.

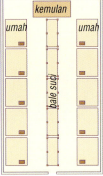

*Traditional layout of a Bali Aga compound, with the origin temple (*kemulan*) at the* kaja *end and individual houses (*umah*) arranged in parallel rows on either side of the uphill-downhill axis.*

Houses and Compounds

The Bali Aga, like their lowland neighbours, live in family compounds (*banjaran* or *pekarangan*), enclosed by an earthen wall or hedge. Furthermore, each compound contains an origin temple (*kemulan*) at the sacred, uphill (*kaja*) end, dedicated to the ancestors of the extended family who reside there. In other respects, however, the Bali Aga compound is quite different from that of the lowland Balinese. In the first place, buildings are not functionally differentiated in that each structure is a self-contained entity which is home to a married couple, their children and sometimes a dependent elderly parent. These family units are called *kuren*, this being the common term both for a hearth and the group of people who share the food cooked upon it. *Kuren* constitute the basic social and economic unit of Bali Aga society.

The layout of the Bali Aga compound also differs from other areas of Bali in that the individual houses (*umah*) are arranged either in a line, or else in two parallel rows along an uphill-downhill axis. A single row of houses, it is said, indicates a compound established by just one male ancestor, while parallel rows are evidence of more than one founder — a group of brothers or brothers-in-law. The entrances of the houses all face inwards, towards the centre line of the compound, with the layout of houses in the left and right rows reversed.

As male children marry and form their own households, new houses are added at the downhill end of the row, but when older generations die, the houses which they lived in at the uphill end become vacant and are occupied by younger couples. In this respect, residence patterns reflect the relative status of individual families within the compound. This ideal pattern of succession is not always adhered to but it is expected in several villages, that the most senior member of the extended family at least should dwell in the house at the uphill end of the row in his compound.

A Question of Space

Two sets of conceptual oppositions are fundamental to the division of space within the Bali Aga house: inside-outside (or left-right) and upward-downward (or male-female). The inside-outside distinction relates mainly to social interactions between family members and outsiders. Welcomed guests are invited to sit on the *trojogan* (from *ojog*, 'to head for' or 'to view'), which is a platform situated directly opposite the entrance. The

(Left) Bali Aga houses are arranged along an uphill-downhill axis with older, more senior, families living at the uphill, kaja, *end of the compound, while junior families reside at the* kelod *end. Trunyan.*

(Bottom left) Bale lantang, *Tenganan.*

(Below) Male members of the village council, representing individual households, are seated in order of rank in the bale lantang.

VILLAGE 'LONGHOUSES'

Bali Aga villages are notable for their community 'longhouses', or *bale lantang*. These attenuated structures are raised on a brick plinth and are oriented longitudinally on an uphill-downhill axis. They are used for village council meetings, which take place on the occasion of a new or full moon. At such times, household heads come together to discuss village affairs and to partake of a communal meal. They take their place in the *bale lantang* according to a strict order of precedence, which requires them to be seated in two parallel rows, in order of their seniority, with the most senior member at the uphill (*kaja*) end on the right. This symbolic organisation of space within the *bale lantang*, mirrors that of the family compound so that the sacred village longhouse is, in effect, like the ultimate houseyard, constituted in a single open structure wherein the entire community is represented.

TRADITIONAL ARCHITECTURE

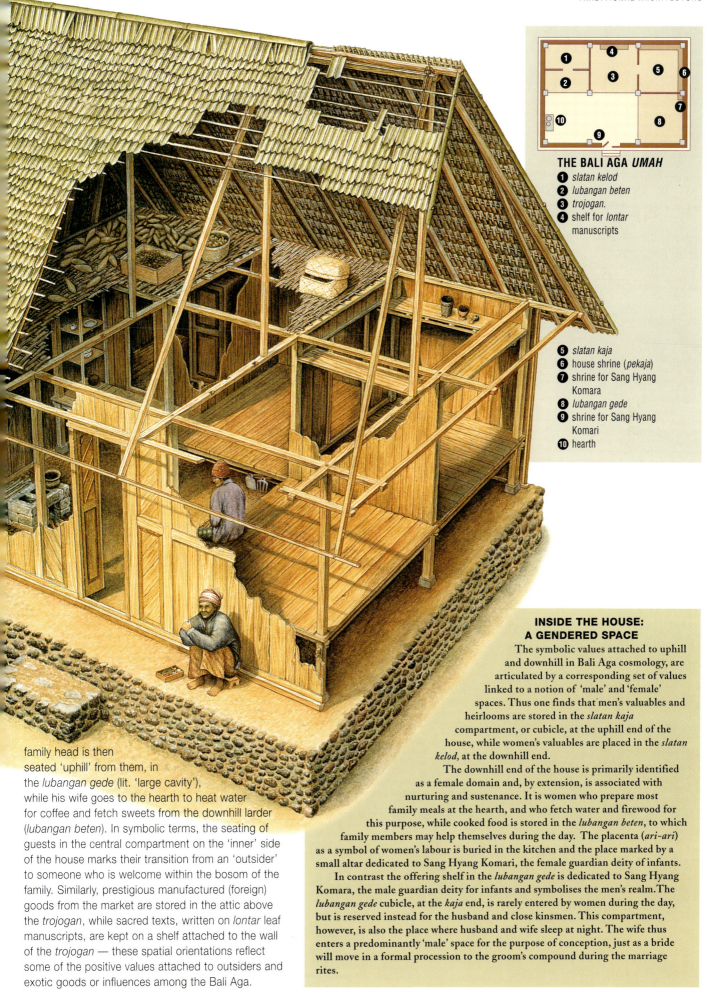

THE BALI AGA *UMAH*
1. *slatan kelod*
2. *lubangan beten*
3. *trojogan*.
4. shelf for *lontar* manuscripts
5. *slatan kaja*
6. house shrine (*pekaja*)
7. shrine for Sang Hyang Komara
8. *lubangan gede*
9. shrine for Sang Hyang Komari
10. hearth

INSIDE THE HOUSE: A GENDERED SPACE

The symbolic values attached to uphill and downhill in Bali Aga cosmology, are articulated by a corresponding set of values linked to a notion of 'male' and 'female' spaces. Thus one finds that men's valuables and heirlooms are stored in the *slatan kaja* compartment, or cubicle, at the uphill end of the house, while women's valuables are placed in the *slatan kelod*, at the downhill end.

The downhill end of the house is primarily identified as a female domain and, by extension, is associated with nurturing and sustenance. It is women who prepare most family meals at the hearth, and who fetch water and firewood for this purpose, while cooked food is stored in the *lubangan beten*, to which family members may help themselves during the day. The placenta (*ari-ari*) as a symbol of women's labour is buried in the kitchen and the place marked by a small altar dedicated to Sang Hyang Komari, the female guardian deity of infants.

In contrast the offering shelf in the *lubangan gede* is dedicated to Sang Hyang Komara, the male guardian deity for infants and symbolises the men's realm. The *lubangan gede* cubicle, at the *kaja* end, is rarely entered by women during the day, but is reserved instead for the husband and close kinsmen. This compartment, however, is also the place where husband and wife sleep at night. The wife thus enters a predominantly 'male' space for the purpose of conception, just as a bride will move in a formal procession to the groom's compound during the marriage rites.

family head is then seated 'uphill' from them, in the *lubangan gede* (lit. 'large cavity'), while his wife goes to the hearth to heat water for coffee and fetch sweets from the downhill larder (*lubangan beten*). In symbolic terms, the seating of guests in the central compartment on the 'inner' side of the house marks their transition from an 'outsider' to someone who is welcome within the bosom of the family. Similarly, prestigious manufactured (foreign) goods from the market are stored in the attic above the *trojogan*, while sacred texts, written on *lontar* leaf manuscripts, are kept on a shelf attached to the wall of the *trojogan* — these spatial orientations reflect some of the positive values attached to outsiders and exotic goods or influences among the Bali Aga.

Houses and Rice Barns of the Sasak in Lombok

Sasak houses, like those of the Bali Aga, are distinguished by not being built on piles. Instead they are set upon the ground, with the outer walls enclosing a plinth of packed mud, mixed with dung and straw; this constitutes the living floor of the dwelling. The Sasak also erect rice barns and open-sided pavilions, both of which are typical Austronesian pile structures. The latter, with their breezy, raised platforms and extended eaves, provide a cool, shady space for socialising and most daily activities other than sleeping.

(Above right) Thatching a Sasak house with alang-alang *grass.*

The Setting

Lombok is an island of considerable climatic and cultural contrasts. Topographically, Lombok is dominated in the north by a mountain range whose highest peak is Mount Rinjani (3,726 metres). The mountains draw down rainfall which makes irrigated rice cultivation possible in the fertile plain running across the centre of the island. Most of the island's population of 2.3 million (1990 census) inhabit this intensely cultivated central area. The southern landscape is one of arid limestone hills, whose unreliable rainfall makes agriculture difficult and capable of supporting only a sparse population.

A Blending of Historical Influences

For much of the past three centuries, Lombok was dominated by the Balinese. As a dependency of the Javanese kingdom of Majapahit in the 14th century, Lombok was fought over by the Balinese kingdom of Klungkung (east central Bali) and the Makassarese kingdom of Gowa (south Sulawesi), together with its vassal state of Bima (Sumbawa). After 1740, however, the Balinese kingdom of Karangasem prevailed until in 1894 the Sasak staged an uprising which, with Dutch intervention, led to the final expulsion of the Balinese *raja*.

The 18th-century temple-palace complex of Narmada and the Mayura water palace at Cakranegara are the architectural legacy of the Balinese era and some 85,000 Balinese still live in West Lombok, but the majority of the island's population are indigenous Sasak. Although the Sasak are Muslims, some Sasak villages still retain their unique traditional form of architecture, as well as local styles of dance, music and shadow-play.

RICE BARNS

The rice barn (*lumbung*) is a distinctive feature of Sasak architecture. The structure is raised on piles in typical Austronesian fashion and sports an unusual 'bonnet'-shaped roof, thatched with *alang-alang* grasses. The four foundation posts support a pair of transverse beams on top of which rests a cantilevered roof frame with bamboo rafters. The only opening is a small rectangular hatch, high up in the gable end, into which the harvested rice is placed. Large wooden discs (*jelepreng*), are set onto the top of the foundation posts to prevent rodents from getting at the rice store.

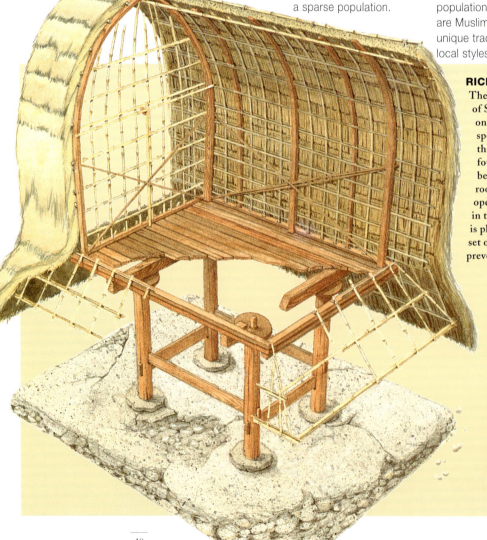

TRADITIONAL ARCHITECTURE

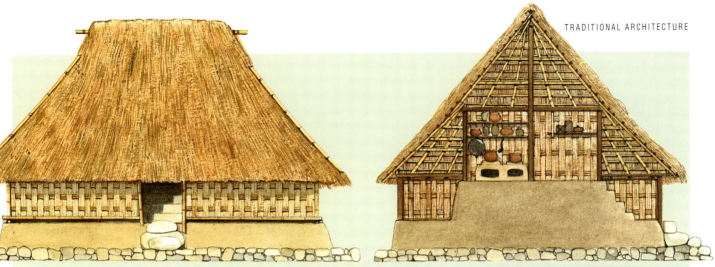

A HOUSE IN SADE
The Sasak house, roughly square in plan, is very unusual in comparison to other vernacular forms of architecture in the region in that it is not raised on piles. Instead, the steeply pitched roof, with a thatch about 15 centimetres thick, descends to low walls enclosing a raised platform about a metre and a half in height, made from a mixture of mud, buffalo dung and straw, the surface of which is smooth and polished. Three or four steps lead up to the inner house (*dalam bale*) on top of this platform, which is itself enclosed by walls of woven bamboo, often with a pair of finely carved double doors at the entrance. Boys sleep on the platform outside the *dalam bale*; girls within. The inner house contains a hearth on the right hand side with a rack for drying maize above. The left hand side is partitioned off to form a sleeping chamber, the *bale dalam*, for the householders. This contains a bed with an attic shelf for the storage of heirlooms and valuables above: this is where the children of the house are born. Firewood is stored at the rear of the house, below the platform.

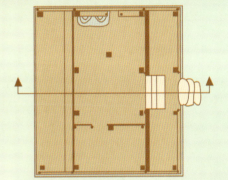

Sasak Settlements

Sasak houses differ greatly from the Balinese domestic architecture. In the plains, these tend to be large and sprawling, with populations sometimes of several thousand, and houses roughly built and crowded together. Remoter mountain villages, however, are neater and follow a definite plan. In the north, the ideal layout of mountain villages consists of two rows of houses (*bale*), with a row of rice barns (*lumbung*) to one side, and in between the houses, a row of open-walled pavilions (*beruga'*) built on six piles. Other structures in the village include large houses (*bale bele'*) belonging to religious officials, which are said to be occupied by powerful ancestral souls. The actual graves of the ancestors have small houses of of wood and bamboo constructed over them.

As in many parts of Indonesia, Sasak houses are windowless and dark, being used mainly for cooking, sleeping and the storage of heirlooms — people spend very little time in them during the day. Instead, it is the pavilion which provides a sitting platform for daily chores and social intercourse. The pavilion is also used for sleeping and for ritual functions: the dead are laid out here prior to their removal to the graveyard.

In southern villages, the platform beneath the rice barn fulfils a similar role to pavilions in the north (not all northern villages have rice barns). There are four basic types of granary and they come in different sizes. The largest usually belong to wealthy families or those of aristocratic descent. All but the smallest type of rice barn have an open platform beneath.

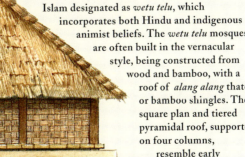

WETU TELU MOSQUES
Some 28,000 Sasak adhere to a syncretic form of Islam designated as *wetu telu*, which incorporates both Hindu and indigenous animist beliefs. The *wetu telu* mosques are often built in the vernacular style, being constructed from wood and bamboo, with a roof of *alang alang* thatch or bamboo shingles. The square plan and tiered pyramidal roof, supported on four columns, resemble early mosques from Ternate and Tidore.

*(Above) A man sitting on the lower verandah (*sesangkok*) of a Sasak house. This area is used to receive guests while male family members may sleep here at night.*

(Below) The platform or plinth beneath the rice barn is often used by Sasak women as a place to set up their backstrap looms for weaving.

Uma Mbatangu of Sumba

Belonging to the Nusa Tenggara chain of islands, Sumba comprises several cultural and linguistic groupings; yet all share a common architectural heritage. Prominent in this regard are the large, high-peaked houses found in major villages.

Houses, Ancestors and Indigenous Religion

Sumba is a dry, hilly and sparsely settled island. Proceeding from the east, relatively treeless coastal plains and inland plateaus give way in the west to an accidented yet better watered and more fertile landscape with, accordingly, a denser population and greater cultural variety. Traditional villages are typically located on elevated sites, with houses (*uma*) forming two or more rows on either side of a central plaza that contains megalithic tombs and objects of ritual significance. Most Sumbanese still adhere to the indigenous religion, which is focused on the *marapu*, the deified first ancestors of patrilineal clans. Sacred heirlooms identified with the ancestral spirits are stored inside the steeply pitched central section, the high triangular tower rising abruptly like a thatched obelisk, which distinguishes a clan's principal house. Only older men are permitted to enter this otherwise empty part of the building, and even they do so rarely. It is mostly in these houses as well that traditional priests offer food and conduct other rituals addressed to the ancestors.

(Above) Male and female ancestral figures in the loft which is the most sacred part of a Sumbanese clan house.

House Form and Construction

Houses comprise two major types. Most characteristic of an island-wide architecture is the *uma mbatangu* or 'great house' of eastern Sumba which feature a high central tower. By contrast, smaller houses lack the central

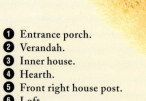

UMA MBATANGU
The Sumbanese clan house is largely a timber and bamboo construction. Tree trunks constitute the four principal house posts and other load bearing elements, while the walls are made from panels of plaited bamboo, or woven coconut leaf. Whole bamboo culms constitute the floor, and a dense thatch of *alang alang* grass, tied with coconut leaf to battens made from saplings, provides a roof.

❶ Entrance porch.
❷ Verandah.
❸ Inner house.
❹ Hearth.
❺ Front right house post.
❻ Loft.

TRADITIONAL ARCHITECTURE

tower and are known as *uma kamudungu*, 'bald houses'. They serve as common dwelling places and are also described as 'cool houses' (*uma maringu*). They are not ritually 'hot' and are thus not hedged about with religious connotations.

Varying in area from over 200 to little more than 25 square metres, Sumbanese houses can accommodate a single conjugal family or as many as five or more. The building is always rectangular in form. In the far eastern part of the island the two short sides appear at the front and back, while elsewhere the two longer sides are disposed in this way. Traditional houses are constructed of wood and thatch, with certain hardwoods being prescribed in ancestral houses (*uma marapu*). Walls are constructed of plaited palm boughs, areca sheath, or among the very rich, buffalo hide. Bamboo is more in use in western Sumba than in the east.

The framework of the house consists of series of round posts set in the ground. Also rising from the ground are a number of wooden piles, a metre or more in height, which support the raised house floor. As Sumbanese regard the earth as an abode of potentially dangerous spiritual beings, it is forbidden to build houses directly on the ground. The raised floor also allows cool air and light to enter the building through widely spaced floor planks. The space beneath the floor is also where chickens and pigs are housed and fed.

A Ritually Ordered and Symbolic Space

While symmetric in form and outward appearance, Sumbanese houses are spatially organised on the basis of symbolically important contrasts of right and left, front and back, upper and lower, and centre and periphery. Generally, the first member of each pair is considered masculine, and the second feminine. The right side of the house, called the 'big (or major) house floor' (*kaheli bokulu*), is largely reserved for ritual and other public affairs conducted by men. By contrast, the left side, named the 'cool house floor' (*kaheli maringu*), is a domestic area where daily meals are prepared and consumed and where occupants sleep in simple compartments built along the left wall. The left side is more closely associated with women, who generally spend more time at home than men. Women are even spoken of as the 'owners of houses' (*mangu umangu*), in contrast to the men, who are associated with the exterior and with external relations among houses and clans as well as communication between humans and spiritual beings. So separate are the right and left sides of the building that each is provided with two doors, one at the front and one at the back, each leading to a slightly lower verandah and thence to the exterior.

The contrast of right and left combines with the opposition of front and back to define four quadrants, each focused on one of the four main posts or pillars between which is built a central

hearth. Erected in a fixed order, defined as a 'movement to the right', each post is then named in accordance with functions associated with each quadrant. The right front pillar — always the first to be set in the ground — is called the 'augury post'. The name refers to religious services and especially divination with the organs of pigs and fowls whose flesh is offered to the ancestors, identified with the heirlooms kept in the high tower located immediately above the central hearth. It is also in this right front part of the house that Sumbanese keep bundled corpses, placed in a sitting position and facing towards the 'augury post' in the same way as a priest engaged in ritual performances. The right back pillar is then called the 'post that divides', since this is where men butcher and divide the meat of sacrificial animals. The post in the left front corner is designated the one which 'scoops the rice'. The women prepare rice here before passing it through a special aperture to a priest who formally presents the food to the ancestors in the right front part of the house. Finally, the left back post is called the 'post that feeds chickens and pigs', thereby linking this area with the care of animals sacrificed to the ancestors.

(From top right, anticlockwise) Entrance platform laid over a stone foundation.

Interior of a Sumba clan house showing the hearth.

Walls are often ornamented with buffalo horns, the reminders of past sacrifices to the gods and ancestors.

Women preparing cotton thread for dyeing on the verandah in Rindi, eastern Sumba.

(Below) A striking feature of the Sumbanese village is the intermingling of houses and tombs.

43

Timorese Houses

The island of Timor, at the eastern end of the Nusa Tenggara chain, is a place where Austronesian- and non-Austronesian-speaking populations meet and was for centuries the focus of trade in the finest quality sandalwood especially prized by the Chinese. This cultural diversity and long exposure to exotic influences is reflected in the wide variety of architectural forms found on the island.

AMARASI HOUSE
The Amarasi house is a variant of the Atoni *ume*, except that it has a more rectangular, rather than conical, roof. In 1964 the anthropologist Clark Cunningham published a seminal essay describing the complex spatial symbolism of the Amarasi house (see p. 18) which subsequently became the inspiration for countless other studies of this type in Indonesia and elsewhere. To this day, the Amarasi house occupies a special position in the ethnographic literature of the region, known to students of anthropology the world over.

The Sacred and the Profane

Although the architecture of Timor differs radically from one end of the island to the other, there are many congruences in the way houses are conceived in symbolic terms. In particular, houses tend to be laid out in accordance with specific rules of orientation which are directly linked to the performance of rituals within the building. As in other parts of Indonesia, house posts, and the order in which they are erected, play an important role in this scheme of things, with one post, or in some cases a pair of posts, singled out for special ritual attention. Similarly, the beams, planks and spars of a house are individually named and each component has specific ritual associations.

In spatial terms, the innermost part of the house is symbolically opposed to less intimate spaces, such as the verandah, and this opposition between inside and outside is typically linked to notions of gender and ritual sanctity. Invariably, the area regarded as the 'inner precinct' is defined as a 'female' space and is associated with the cooking fire and the storage of rice grain. The loft also tends to be associated with the woman of the house — often she has sole right of access to it — and is typically conceived as the most sacred part of the building.

East Meets West

Timor has two striking house forms that have become emblematic of the eastern and western halves of the island respectively. The west is represented by the bee-hive shaped houses of the Atoni Meto, while in the east there are the tall, tower-like dwellings of the Dagada, with their vaulted roofs and decorated ridges. The eastern half of the island is the most ethnically diverse region of the island and is where the greatest range of architectural variation can be found.

(Above) An Atoni house in the hill region of So'e, West Timor. The traditional bee-hive form of house structure was gradually abandoned in recent years as the local government encourages the building of rectangular forms which are generally regarded as more hygienic.

THE ATONI *LOPO*
The architecture of the Atoni Meto, in west Timor, is distinguished by circular ground plans and bee-hive shaped roofs which are used for both simple family dwellings (*ume*) and more elaborate communal meeting houses (*lopo*). In the past, the *lopo* meeting house also served as a granary and the four posts supporting the floor of the loft are topped by huge wooden disks to prevent rats and mice from gaining access to the rice store. Although there are no walls, the interior of the *lopo* is kept dry by the huge roof.

Like other Atoni houses, the interior is divided. The four main house posts are referred to as *ni ainaf*, 'mother posts', but one post, at the southeast corner, is designated the *nakan*, or 'head post'. The ladder ascending to the loft is situated here.

The Atoni *lopo* (right) has a large roof which descends on all sides to below the level of the loft floor. Special ritual significance is attached to the single post, rising from the centre of the granary floor to support the apex of the roof. This is designated the *ni ainaf*, or 'mother post', of the *lopo*, and is the focus of ritual attention.

TRADITIONAL ARCHITECTURE

SUAI HOUSE

The Suai house is an elevated structure, with three different floor levels that step upwards from an outer verandah to an inner chamber with a loft overhead. These ascending levels are linked to ritual and social categories. The outside is identified with everyday activities, while the loft is where heirlooms are stored and intimate household rites are performed.

THE DAGADA LAUTEM HOUSE

The Lautem house is square in plan and consists of a box-like structure sitting on top of large horizontal trunks, which are supported by four hefty foundation posts. There is a loft above, surmounted by a high pinnacle roof, thatched with *gamuti* palm fibre. The houses of chiefs and aristocrats are larger than those of commoners and may be some four metres square and up to 11 metres in height. Traditionally, the roof was adorned with cowry and nautilus shells suspended in swags from the roof ridge. Carved wooden birds with mythological associations jut out at angles to the roof ridge which may be extended at either end as a representation of the 'ship of the dead' which carries the soul of the deceased to the afterworld — the apex of the roof is identified with ancestral spirits.

Some Dagada houses are built on masonry plinths (above), a feature which predates the arrival of the Portuguese in the 17th century and which may be an ancient survival of an earlier architectural tradition that constructed stone terraces in the manner of Polynesian marae. *The interior of the Dagada house (below) is carefully laid out with benches, sleeping platforms, storage shelves and an earthern hearth. Granaries (left) have a more typically Austronesian profile with an extended roof ridge.*

45

The Dani Compound: an Irian Settlement Pattern

The Dani of Irian Jaya do not share in the common Austronesian ancestry of most other Indonesian peoples. This distinction is very noticeable in their settlement patterns and the organisation of domestic space. The Dani do not build villages as such, but live in compounds consisting of between three to six families which are related patrilineally; the men sleep together under one roof, while their wives reside in separate huts which they share with other close female relatives.

Aerial view of a Dani compound. The rectangular structures are either pig styes or cook houses, while the larger round houses are men's houses and the smaller ones, women's houses.

Dani Settlement Patterns

The Dani are spread across the Grand Baliem valley in the rugged Jayawijaya highlands of Irian Jaya. Unlike the Austronesian-speaking peoples that make up the vast majority of Indonesia's present population, their cultural origins may be traced back to a much earlier period of human settlement in the region. They are divided into some 30 clans, each with its own recognised territory. Unlike many of their neighbours, the Dani are not slash and burn farmers, but practise a settled form of agriculture whose principal crops are taro and sweet potato. These are cultivated in well-tended gardens with raised beds and drainage ditches. Pigs provide an important source of protein and are the Dani's most valuable possession. Social status is reflected in the number of pigs a man owns and in the past pigs acted as a standard unit of economic measurement for exchanges of goods, labour and bridewealth.

The Compound

The Dani settlement consists of a residential compound, or *sili*, which is enclosed by a wooden palisade some 8 to 12 metres in height, the top of which is covered with dried grass. There is just one opening in this fence, the lower part of which is barricaded to prevent pigs and dogs from leaving the compound. The orientation of the gate follows cosmological principles which include 'facing the sunrise', 'avoiding mountain shadow', and 'backing-away from enemy territory'.

The central courtyard of the compound functions as a gathering place for *sili* members on public occasions, such as funerals, marriages and other

THE SYMBOLISM OF THE DANI MEN'S HOUSE

Much of Dani ritual life is focused on the men's house, which women are expressly forbidden from entering. Weapons and ritual objects relating to fighting are stored in the rafter space between the fireplace and the entrance. During cremation rites, if the deceased is a man, his corpse is usually kept in the men's house, sitting propped up against a side wall until it is time to place it on the funeral pyre.

❶ Antechamber: it is said that this is where ghosts sit when they come to the compound searching for food. The idea here is that if they have a place to sit, they will not be inclined to enter the interior of the men's house and disturb those who live there.

❷ Fireplace for warmth and lighting cigarettes: food is seldom cooked in the men's house.

❸ Central posts: the front two are identified as important men; the rear two as old men or youths. This reflects the seating pattern within the house: the front is reserved for warriors and important men while the old men and youths sit in the shadows at the back.

❹ Cabinet for storing ritual paraphernalia: the mandibles of pigs killed during important ceremonies are suspended beneath.

TRADITIONAL ARCHITECTURE

COOK HOUSES AND PIG STYES
The cooking shed is located near the women's houses. Its size depends on the number of families living in the *sili*: each woman has her own hearth or shares with another. It is a closed, windowless barrack-like structure, with its entrance barricaded to prevent pigs coming in, but it is a place where women socialise and men may enter during meal times.

The pig sty is similar to the cook house but is sub-divided into stalls which are occupied by a single pig or a sow with piglets. Each stall opens onto a long passageway with a door at one end for access to the building.

ritual events. There is no definite form or size for a *sili*, but they are usually rectangular in plan and may measure anything between 100 to 1,000 square metres. Sometimes a number of compounds are grouped together in clusters with connecting passages and shared fences.

During daytime the compound, or *sili*, is almost deserted save, perhaps, for a few older women and small children. The men are out hunting, mending fences or otherwise engaged in male oriented activities whilst the women are tending their fields and vegetable gardens or else collecting firewood. The women are also responsible for selling farm produce at the market, tending the pigs and keeping the house in order — there is a certain opinion that Dani women work harder than the men.

Sex and Residence

Towards the rear of the *sili* compound, but aligned with the entrance, stands the principal men's house or *honai*. This is where the head of the kin group lives, together with his unmarried sons or nearest male relatives. There may be other men's houses, depending on the number of men residing in the settlement. Each *honai* can accommodate four adults or up to eight individuals if boys are included. The main *honai*, where the head of the community resides, can usually be distinguished from the others by its superior size.

The Dani practise polygamy and each wife is provided with her own house which she may share with her closest female kin. The women's huts are called *enai* and they are located more towards the compound fence and closer to the main gate. They are usually smaller than the men's *honai*, but generally have the same form and shape.

The different sleeping arrangements for men and women are a distinctive feature of Dani society. According to the Dani, sexual intercourse is weakening and potentially dangerous. For this reason there are taboos which forbid sexual relations from about the fourth month of pregnancy until three to four years after the birth. Only when the child can walk well and is able to take care of itself may the parents resume sexual relations.

Construction Materials and Techniques

Houses can only be built by men. Both male and female houses have circular plans with diameters of between 3 to 6 metres. The walls consist of a framework made from tree branches, or rattan, which is covered on the outside with bark or rough planks, while the domed roof is thatched with bundles of dried grass. No jointing is involved, the entire structure being lashed together with rattan or bark.

The earthen floor is also covered with grass and since the walls are barely a man's height, people tend to be seated as soon as they enter the building. The door is just a simple opening which is so low (shoulder height) that one has to duck to enter. In bad weather this opening may be closed up.

The main internal feature in both men's and women's houses is a circular sleeping platform, approximately 150 centimetres off the ground. A hole in the floor of this platform provides access from below. The platform is covered with dried grass on which the occupants sleep with their feet pointing towards the entrance. Since the Baliem valley is situated at an altitude of 1,650 metres above sea level, a small fire may be lit below the sleeping platform to keep the occupants warm at night or during rainy weather.

The plan and construction of women's houses is identical to that of the men's houses, but they are smaller in size.

(Top) The outer palisade wall of the Dani compound is intended primarily for defence. It consists of a double row of sharpened stakes, reinforced with horizontal bars and lashed with rattan.

(Above) A group of women seated in the central courtyard of a Dani compound. During important rituals, when the yard is filled with people, women are expected to sit in the front half, and men in the rear.

(Below) A typical Dani settlement in the Baliem Valley with vegetable gardens laid out on the slopes behind.

47

Houses for the Dead

In a region where the house is such an important focus for the activities of the living, it is no surprise that many Indonesian peoples have a tradition of providing houses for the dead. It is a common feature of ancestor-based religions that the afterlife is perceived as an improved version of life on earth. Communities of the dead are conceived as being like the villages of the living, and tombs and mausoleums are often elaborately constructed in the form of miniature houses. In some places, the costly erection of stone tombs both ensures greater permanence, while enhancing the prestige of the deceased's descendants.

The dead are often buried in close proximity to the living: Christian graves in north Nias.

Preserving the Bones of the Dead

Indonesian funerals may be expensive and prolonged affairs, but it is through celebrating these protracted rituals that the dead are transformed into ancestors, with the power to bless their descendants with health, prosperity and fertility. Great importance is hence attached to preserving ancestral remains. The Toraja of Sulawesi, for example, have lengthy, expensive funerals which, for high-ranking individuals, may be split into two distinct phases, sometimes separated by a year or more. The dead are traditionally placed in family tomb chambers called *liang* hollowed out of huge granite boulders or cliff faces. The grave is referred to in ritual verses as: 'house without smoke, village where no fire is lit', since the afterlife is envisaged to be cold and fireless, though otherwise the same as this one.

AS IN LIFE, SO IN DEATH

In west Sumatra, Minangkabau graves traditionally employed the distinctive roof form of the *rumah gadang*, or 'great house' (see pp 26–27), with its saddle-back profile and elegant spires (left). Further to the north, the Toba Batak, up until around the 1920s, used to construct miniature wooden tomb houses (*joro*) on piles, complete in every detail including carved decorations, a hearth and an entry ladder. Today, Toba Batak graves are usually constructed in concrete to create more permanent memorials for the dead. Although a variety of Art Deco and other Modernist examples exist, the traditional house form is still commonly adopted, despite 100 years of Christian fellowship (left bottom).

Secondary rites for the dead often have a collective character. Periodically, Toraja tombs may be opened to re-wrap the bones of all those inside, at which time additional sacrifices of pig or buffalo may be made for the benefit of the deceased in the afterlife. The Ma'anyan of Kalimantan celebrate secondary rites called *idjambe*, at which the remains of a number of related persons are cremated in specially constructed coffins, and the ashes relocated in a collective mausoleum carved of ironwood, called *tambak*. In Sumatra, the Toba Batak continue to maintain an interest in secondary funeral rites at which the bones of several generations of patrilineally related ancestors will be exhumed and regrouped in a house-shaped concrete tomb, also called *tambak* or *parholian*. Even more expensive is a rite to commemorate the founding ancestors of an entire clan with the construction of an elaborate mausoleum (*tugu*). More effort nowadays seems to be spent on such monuments than on the maintenance or rebuilding of traditional houses.

Dwellings for the Dead

House-shaped graves can be found all over the Archipelago. The Ngaju of Kalimantan traditionally raised finely carved mausoleums, on tall posts, which were shaped like houses with extended roof ridges, while the Mamasa Toraja build miniature houses over burial sites. The Rotinese incorporated the dead into the house by burying them beneath the house floor; when the Dutch prohibited this practice, they made separate graves beside the houses and constructed miniature houses on top of them. In Ngada, west central Flores, female ancestors are commemorated with miniature houses erected in the central plaza. These are paired with offering posts topped by conical thatched roofs, which are dedicated to male ancestors.

Intimate Bonds

It is a feature of indigenous Indonesian religions that the living tend to maintain a relationship of some intimacy with the ancestors. Graves are often very close to houses, as in Sumba where they occupy prominent positions in the middle of the village, opposite to the houses. In both north and south Nias, tombs or stone monuments to the dead are also erected in front of houses. The shades of the ancestors may also be thought to visit the house itself. The Makassar of South Sulawesi traditionally kept an ancestral shrine in the attic; elsewhere, for example Sumba, precious and powerful heirloom objects stored in attics are closely associated with the power of the ancestors. Many peoples used to make a symbolic gesture of feeding the ancestors within the house at mealtimes, as was the case in Toraja, Toba and Tanimbar. In the latter instance, exquisitely carved ancestral altars, in stylised human form and often incorporating both male and female symbolic elements, were the centrepiece of the house. Offerings were made to the skulls of ancestors which were placed on a shelf at the top of it.

TRADITIONAL ARCHITECTURE

KENYAH MAUSOLEUMS
Kenyah charnel houses (*liang*) are always built downstream — the dead are said to be unable to return upstream to the village of living. Burial goods provide the deceased with the essentials of 'life' — sword, spear, shield, an oar, tobacco, flint and tinder, a bowl and spoon, some salt and other basic requirements — and the exterior of the mausoleum is decorated with brass gongs, Chinese jars and other indices of wealth. In the past, wooden heads, representing enemy skulls, were hung from the eaves.

Highly decorated Ngaju ossuary (sandong), central Kalimantan. The Ngaju, like their neighbours, the Ot Danum, practise 'secondary' burial when the bones of the deceased are exhumed, washed and incarcerated in house-like mausoleums. The foliage around the base of the structure symbolises the mythical tree of life while the figures above are representations of Ngaju deities.

KARO BATAK SKULL HOUSES
The Karo Batak used to build a special structure — the *geriten* or 'head-house' — in which the skulls of chiefs and important individuals would be preserved some years after their deaths. These skulls might be elaborately decorated with gold and silver and wrapped in precious cloths. These head-houses are built on a square plan with multi-tiered pyramidal roof and contain many intricate decorations and are often found in the middle of the village. The head of the deceased became the main focus of attention firstly because the head is commonly perceived in many Indonesian societies as the locus of supernatural power, evidenced by the formerly widespread practice of headhunting. Secondly the skull happens to be the most durable part of the human body. At Pematang Purba, north Sumatra, similar minature house structures can be seen on top of Simalungun Batak council houses.

WORKING IN STONE
The working of stone and erection of megaliths for the dead have a history of thousands of years in the Indonesian Archipelago. In the highlands of Sarawak stone urns may still be seen which were formerly used by the Kelabit people for the secondary placement of the bones of chiefs, in a practice believed to date back to 2500 BC. Up until their conversion to Christianity in the 1950s, they also erected huge menhirs as memorials to the dead. Comparable practices have endured among the peoples of Nias, Toba, Toraja, Central Sulawesi, Flores and Sumba. Hewing and dragging huge stones for tombs or memorials requires the organisation of a large labour force, as well as considerable resources to pay for accompanying ceremonies. It was thus an important mark of status monopolised by the aristocracy in Nias, Sumba and Toraja. These megaliths can be found anywhere near or in the villages depending on the location of the community.

The megalithic tomb of Umbu Sawolo, at Golukbalu, east Sumba. Erected in 1971, the principal grave slab weighs 80 tons and reportedly took 15,000 men 32 days to transport it into position. In addition to the intricately carved stella (detail), the grave features the distinctive roof of a traditional Sumba clan house.

❶ The upper terraces of Borobudur with their numerous Buddha statues and perforated stupas. Central Java.
❷ Besakih, the mother temple of Bali.
❸ Candi Kalasan, one of the earlier Buddhist temples.
❹ The dated temple at Candi Panataran, Blitar, East Java.
❺ Gedong Songo 9, one of the many temples found on the slopes of Mount Ungaran, Central Java.

p) Kala head from Dieng. Early Classic.

iddle) Kala head from Candi Plaosan r: Transition to the Middle Classic period.

ottom) Kala head from dated temple at nataran. East Java. Late Classic period.

p right) An 19th-century depiction of a ple at Prambanan.

RIODS OF TEMPLE CONSTRUCTION

ssic Indonesian architecture evolved ough three phases. The first or Early Classic AD 600-900) was typified by emphasis on er symmetry, monumentality, naturalistic lpture, and resemblance to Indian models. ring the Middle Classic (AD 900-1250) re were no permanent structures except for bathing places in Java. In contrast this was me of active construction in Sumatra. In the e Classic (1250-1450), the emphasis on imetry declined, and the use of architecture a framework for narrative reliefs depicting igenous and imported myths increased nificantly. Javanese architects also began to t from using andesite stone for building terials to bricks and tiles.

INDONESIA'S CLASSICAL HERITAGE

The earliest Indonesian buildings must have been made of perishable materials. Unfortunately for the architectural historian, organic materials do not survive long in the Indonesian climate. The oldest surviving Indonesian structures are those made of stone.

Indonesia's oldest stone structures were built in late prehistoric times, ± 2,000 years ago. Stone-faced terraces and associated landscape modifications for ritual purposes were constructed on mountain slopes. These terraces continued to be used through the Classic Period. In some areas of the Archipelago, these terraces are still used for religious activities.

Indonesia's Classic Period began with the erection of stone and brick temples to shelter symbols of Hindu and Buddhist deities. The oldest examples of these, dating from the beginning of the 8th century, were designed by Indonesian architects who were already familiar with working in permanent materials. Using a combination of indigenous and imported motifs and symbols, they restated prehistoric Indonesian concepts of the relationships between humans, the gods and the cosmos. The natural landscape, particularly mountains and volcanoes, was integral to their cosmological vision.

Since most structures during the Classic Period were also built of perishable materials, we possess very little data to investigate their forms. The best we can do is to study wooden structures depicted in reliefs on temples, and draw analogies with structures from more recent periods which we believe preserve building traditions from earlier times.

Few examples of Classic Period architectural forms other than temples exist. These include bathing places, and the enigmatic ruins of the Ratu Boko complex which probably served several purposes: as a royal residence and site for public rituals, and as a site for Buddhist, and later Hindu, religious activity. Remains from East Java indicate that some elite residential areas in the 14th century were built partly of brick and tile. Most architectural remains from the Classic Period are concentrated in Java, but a few sites from Sumatra, Bali and Kalimantan provide comparable data.

During the Classic Period in Indonesia, approximately 800 years long, architecture evolved in response to changes in religion, politics and the general tendency of humans to desire stylistic change. Several of the buildings of this period are considered to be part of the world's cultural heritage.

The Abode of the Gods: Architecture and Cosmology

We have only a vague understanding of prehistoric Indonesian religious concepts. Sources suggest that mountains were regarded as the places where spirits of ancestors could be contacted, their protection invoked, their potential wrath appeased with offerings, and their life-sustaining powers tapped. Indonesian inscriptions often refer to temples as mountains.

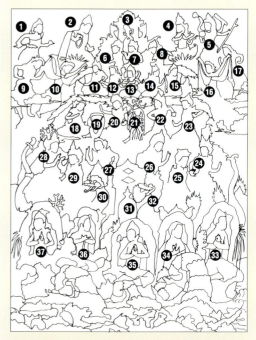

A MODERN BALINESE IMPRESSION OF MOUNT MERU AS A TEMPLE
This painting (right) depicts a selection of Hindu deities in Bali and should not be regarded as a complete representation of the entire Balinese pantheon (see page 137 for further details).

① Dewi Sri
② Dewa Budha
③ Dewa Tintya
④ Siwa Raditya
⑤ Dewi Saraswati
⑥ and ⑭ Dewa Brahma
⑦ Dewa Ismara
⑧ Dewa Wisnu
⑨ Widya Dara
⑩ Widya Dari
⑪ Dewa Wisnu
⑫ Dewa Mahadewa
⑬ Dewa Guru (Siwa)
⑮ Iswara
⑯ and ⑰ apsara and apsari (heavenly beings)
⑱ and ⑳ dewa (gods)
⑲ purnaghata (pot of plenty)
㉑ kalpataru (wishing tree)
㉒ and ㉓ dewi (goddesses)
㉔ Dewa Maha Dewa
㉕ Dewi Maya
㉖ Dewa Brahma
㉗ Dewa Iswara
㉘ Wisnu
㉙ Dewi Uma
㉚ and ㉜ naga (dragon)
㉛ amirta (elixir of immortality)
㉝ Resi Waraspati
㉞ Resi Budha
㉟ Resi Anggara
㊱ Resi Somo
㊲ Resi Reditya

The three main temples at Candi Lara Jonggrang, Prambanan, Central Java.

Temple Design
The basis of Indonesian Classic temple design was the desire to create a replica of the mountain at the centre of the universe where the spirits of the gods could be induced to descend into a statue or *lingga* housed in a cave-like chamber.

The earliest Classic Indonesian architecture consists of Hindu shrines erected high on volcanoes in central Java. Both physically and symbolically, these structures rested on the belief that mountains were supernaturally powerful places. Soon after the ruling elite started building in stone, construction sites began to spread to the lowlands. This expansion may have stemmed from a combination of motives: the desire to make religious sites more accessible to the general population, and the ruling elite's recognition that association with divine power could significantly enhance their own temporal authority.

The keben *fruit-shaped motif and the bell-shaped gourd were popular decorations for wall tops in the mid- to late 9th century.*

The Mountain as a Symbol
Several basic principles underlying the form assumed by the Indonesian temple were indigenous beliefs in the supreme power residing in ancestors and mountains. Although Indian religion and architecture played a supplementary role supplying new motifs and shapes to restate previously existing concepts, Indian theories of symmetry as a fundamental component of the universal order significantly augmented prehistoric Indonesian concepts. 'Classic' art emphasises symmetry and precise ordering of elements, each with a designated place in the overall composition. As far as we can determine, these concepts were not important to prehistoric Indonesian architects. Thus 'prehistoric' can be equated with 'Preclassic' Indonesian art and architecture. There is evidence that Indonesians perceived that the universe was divided into four quarters, but the combination of this idea with a philosophy and divine order seems to have been a novelty.

Candi Jawi   Candi Mulungan   Candi Kalasan   Candi Tugurejo

STUPA
The stupa is a special Buddhist form. It consists of three parts: a body, usually bell-shaped; a container for a relic, usually square; and a spire. According to Buddhist scripture, after cremation Buddha's bones were buried under eight such shrines in north India. In other contexts, stupas are used to house relics, or simply as symbols of Buddha. Free-standing stupas in Indonesia are rare; usually they were used as part of the roofs of other structures.

Candi Sumberawan

Candi Plaosan

Sources of Early Indonesian Stone Architecture

Architecture in permanent materials began to appear in Indonesia at about the same time as the first designs for stone structures were being formulated in India. In both areas the earliest buildings were intended for religious purposes, to house icons. These icons, either anthropomorphic statues or, in the case of temples dedicated to the god Siva, the lingga or phallus, were perceived as receptacles for the spirits of the gods, who were ritually invoked to descend into them by prayer and offerings. In both Indian and Indonesian cultures only religious specialists were allowed to enter the central sanctuaries.

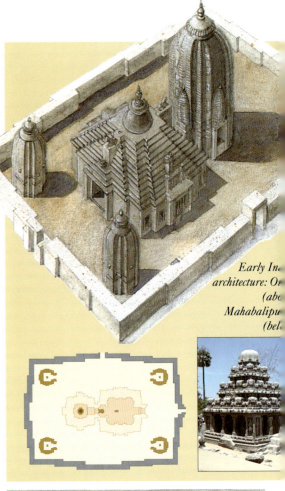

Early In[dian] architecture: Or[issa] (abo[ve]) Mahabalipu[ram] (bel[ow])

Stone Temples and Sacred Caves

The central requirement for Indonesian and Indian designers of temples was to furnish a space closed off from the outer world, in which the priests could present offerings, offer prayers, and communicate with the gods when they descended to earth and took up residence in their icons, undisturbed by profane influences. The temples were not intended as spaces to accommodate large groups of worshippers. In both India and Indonesia no traces of the wooden forebears which must have preceded the earliest stone buildings remain.

In India, natural caves were sometimes used as places of worship. In other instances, solid rock was carved into caves with ceilings replicating wooden structures. At Mahabalipuram, south India, complete three-dimensional replicas of structures traditionally built of perishable materials were carved from stone. In Indonesia, however, we have no such information to help us reconstruct the possible nature of the earliest sanctuaries built of perishable materials. A few cave sites were artificially excavated in Indonesia, but they were very simple structures. Artificial cave sites from the Classic period include Lawang, Silumbu, and Abang, near Purworejo; two caves at Ratu Boko; and a small cave nearby at Candi Abang.

The earliest stone edifices from India from about the 5th century comprise small sanctuaries probably intended to house *lingga*. They were essentially squat rectangles. One of their major definitive traits was the pillared front porch. The use of pillars and columns, usually highly decorated, has remained a typical element of Indian religious architecture ever since. Some have detected in this a connection with the art of Gandhara, in what is now northern Pakistan. Gandharan art preserves numerous elements of Hellenistic art, which emphasises the use of columns and pillars.

Pillars and columns are not found in the earliest Indonesian stone temples, which date from the early 8th century. It is however possible that pillars did exist in earlier wooden buildings. The oldest surviving permanent structures in Indonesia are Hindu temple complexes on the Dieng Plateau and at Gedong Songo. At both sites the dominant architectural form is the *candi*, a stone-walled room surmounted by a tiered roof, and raised on a plinth or basement. The entrances are formed by small narrow vestibules with walls rather than pillared porches, an Indonesian trait perhaps based on prehistoric wooden structure, perhaps also connected with a greater emphasis on the secrecy of the rituals conducted inside the *candi*.

Timber Antecents

We can gain an impression of the early wooden architecture of Indonesia from one of the reliefs at Borobudur (first gallery, eastern face, northern wing, upper register). The building portrayed here seems to

»»*A painting of the temple ruins of the Prambanan area by Dessin de Barclay.*

(Below) Relief of a wooden structure with supporting 'caryatids' on Borobudur. (Below right) An Indian temple with external pillars.

INDONESIA'S CLASSICAL HERITAGE

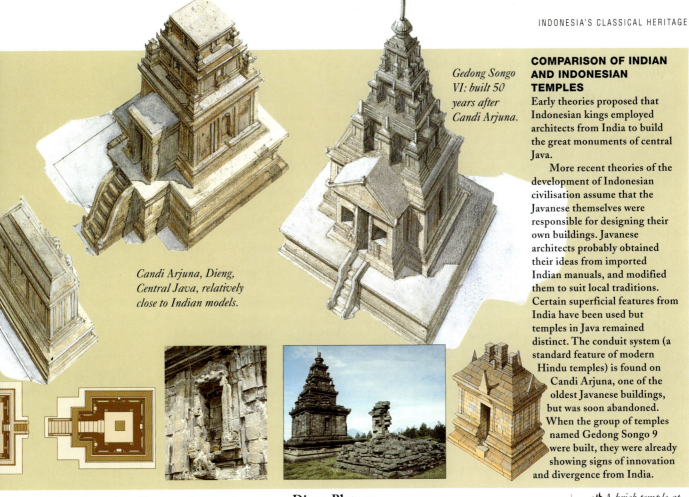

Candi Arjuna, Dieng, Central Java, relatively close to Indian models.

Gedong Songo VI: built 50 years after Candi Arjuna.

COMPARISON OF INDIAN AND INDONESIAN TEMPLES

Early theories proposed that Indonesian kings employed architects from India to build the great monuments of central Java.

More recent theories of the development of Indonesian civilisation assume that the Javanese themselves were responsible for designing their own buildings. Javanese architects probably obtained their ideas from imported Indian manuals, and modified them to suit local traditions. Certain superficial features from India have been used but temples in Java remained distinct. The conduit system (a standard feature of modern Hindu temples) is found on Candi Arjuna, one of the oldest Javanese buildings, but was soon abandoned. When the group of temples named Gedong Songo 9 were built, they were already showing signs of innovation and divergence from India.

have employed an external load-bearing structure, with caryatid-like supports in the form of rampant animals. This design closely resembles similar structures in south India (4th to 9th centuries), but by the time the architects of Java began to build in stone, local architectural techniques had already begun to diverge from Indian models. While the Javanese continued to employ external load-bearing structures, they abandoned the use of animal figures as supports and replaced them with columns; this stage can also be identified in the reliefs. When the Javanese adopted stone as a building material, an external load-bearing structure became redundant, and the columns and supports were transformed into decorative elements on the external walls.

Thus, although the earliest Javanese temples seem to have employed columns, whether this was an indigenous or imported practice is still a matter for debate. Traditional dwellings in much of Indonesia were raised on columns. If the domestic dwellings shown on Borobudur's reliefs depict the Javanese landscape of about AD 800, it can be inferred that Javanese houses of that time were erected on columns and employed a stressed roofbeam technique now mainly associated with the Batak and Minangkabau of Sumatra, and the Toraja of Sulawesi. The use of columns on early religious structures may thus have stemmed from prehistoric Indonesian custom.

Dieng Plateau

The earliest Javanese buildings, found on the Dieng Plateau, date from the early 8th century. The most important group of structures consists of four temples facing west, now called the Arjuna group. Archaeological excavations have established that Candi Arjuna and Candi Semar opposite it were built in an initial period of construction around AD 750. Candi Arjuna consists of a square chamber built over a pit containing a ritual foundation deposit. A short vestibule provided access to the inner chamber which once housed a *lingga*. A slight depression carved into the stone received libations of water poured over the *lingga* during rituals and conducted it to supplicants outside through a conduit. This arrangement, which is a standard feature of modern Hindu temples in India, was abandoned in subsequent Indonesian temples of the same type.

A brick temple at Bhitargaon, Orissa, India.

(Centre and below) The form of Candi Bima has sometimes been interpreted as the expression of influence from Orissa. It remained in use for several centuries, during which it was extensively remodelled, possibly as a result of conversion from a Hindu to a Buddhist sanctuary.

55

Indonesian Methods of Building with Stone

Early Indian religious sanctuaries at Mahabalipuram and other sites were sculpted from solid rock as an iconographic representation of the sacred Mount Meru, which in mythology is identified as the home of the gods. The subsequent tradition of Hindu architecture, both in India and overseas in Southeast Asia, can be seen as a practical compromise between the desire to reconstruct this legendary mountain and the physical limitations of working in stone.

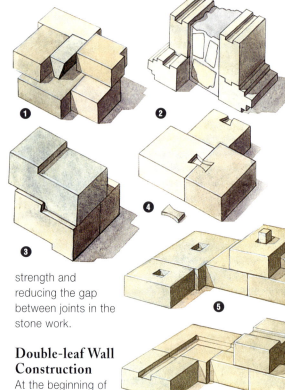

❶ *Stone wedges driven between blocks to increase the compactness of the joints.*
❷ *The double-leaf wall method with rubble infill.*
❸ *Interlocking stone courses at Borobudur.*
❹ *A method for pinning adjacent blocks together.*
❺ *Using mortise and tenon joints.*
❻ *and* ❼ *Mitre-joints for overlapping stone course.*

Reinforced Joints

In Indonesia, there were no important attempts to imitate Indian buildings built entirely by carving them from solid rock. Instead walls were constructed '*à joint vif*', that is stone courses placed one on top of the other without any binding material. In the earliest period, for example the Hindu monuments at Dieng, in Central Java, in the 8th century, the strength of these joints was reinforced by cutting a section out of individual blocks of stone to create a kind of tongue and groove configuration which interlocked with neighbouring blocks in both the horizontal and vertical directions. At 8th-century Buddhist sites, such as Candi Sewu in Central Java, wedges were driven in between the stone blocks, thus pushing the elements on either side outwards towards the corners of the building, giving each course great strength and reducing the gap between joints in the stone work.

Double-leaf Wall Construction

At the beginning of the 9th century, Javanese master builders adopted the Indian technique of double-leaf stone walls. Java is the only region of Southeast Asia where this method of construction is

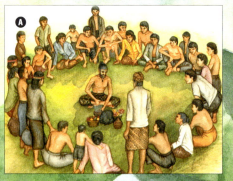

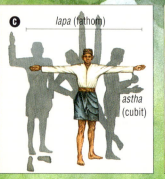

lapa (fathom)
astha (cubit)

SEQUENCE OF TEMPLE CONSTRUCTION
Ⓐ A ritual is first held in the middle of the compound. A priest chants prayers over the sacred stone.
Ⓑ A stick is planted in the middle of the complex. The crowd gathers around in a circle.
Ⓒ Measurements for the building of the temple or temples are taken from the body dimensions of the chief 'architect'.
Ⓓ A square outline is derived using cardinal points.
Ⓔ Stones are laid along the axes designating the boundaries of the temple complex.

LAYING OUT A TEMPLE
A stick is planted into the ground and markings are made at the east and west points created by the shadow of the stick during sunrise and sunset respectively. A line is drawn across linking these two points. Another line running perpendicular to the above forms the north-south axis. A square outline is formed which constitutes the area of the temple compound. Nine stone-markers are next planted; four at the cardinal points and the others at equal distance away from these points along the outline of the compound.

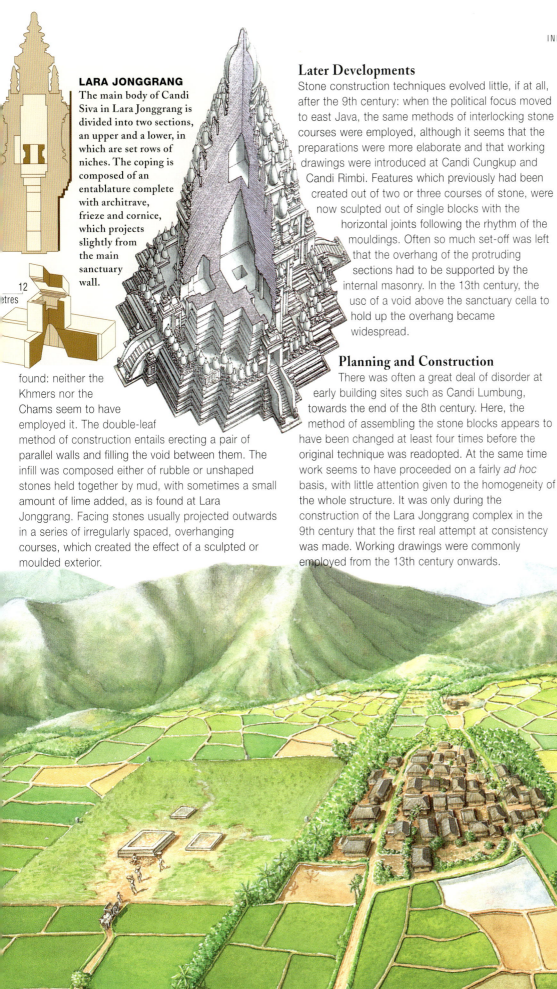

LARA JONGGRANG
The main body of Candi Siva in Lara Jonggrang is divided into two sections, an upper and a lower, in which are set rows of niches. The coping is composed of an entablature complete with architrave, frieze and cornice, which projects slightly from the main sanctuary wall.

found: neither the Khmers nor the Chams seem to have employed it. The double-leaf method of construction entails erecting a pair of parallel walls and filling the void between them. The infill was composed either of rubble or unshaped stones held together by mud, with sometimes a small amount of lime added, as is found at Lara Jonggrang. Facing stones usually projected outwards in a series of irregularly spaced, overhanging courses, which created the effect of a sculpted or moulded exterior.

Later Developments

Stone construction techniques evolved little, if at all, after the 9th century: when the political focus moved to east Java, the same methods of interlocking stone courses were employed, although it seems that the preparations were more elaborate and that working drawings were introduced at Candi Cungkup and Candi Rimbi. Features which previously had been created out of two or three courses of stone, were now sculpted out of single blocks with the horizontal joints following the rhythm of the mouldings. Often so much set-off was left that the overhang of the protruding sections had to be supported by the internal masonry. In the 13th century, the use of a void above the sanctuary cella to hold up the overhang became widespread.

Planning and Construction

There was often a great deal of disorder at early building sites such as Candi Lumbung, towards the end of the 8th century. Here, the method of assembling the stone blocks appears to have been changed at least four times before the original technique was readopted. At the same time work seems to have proceeded on a fairly *ad hoc* basis, with little attention given to the homogeneity of the whole structure. It was only during the construction of the Lara Jonggrang complex in the 9th century that the first real attempt at consistency was made. Working drawings were commonly employed from the 13th century onwards.

INDONESIA'S CLASSICAL HERITAGE

«« *(Top diagram) Shrine for the marker of the centre of the Lara Jonggrang complex, probably also erected for use in rituals. (Bottom diagram) Stone box at the apex of the cella of a subsidiary chapel, probably for holding some kind of offering.*

TEMPLE-FOUNDING RITUAL
It was on December 27, AD 902, a small crowd gathered around a rice field near the edge of a forest in Central Java. On that day a local nobleman was sponsoring a ceremony to inaugurate the construction of a new temple. Such gatherings were relatively common in ancient Java in the 9th century, when several stone edifices were erected.

The ceremonies conducted were often recorded in writing on stone (*piagem*), or plates of silver or copper. The ceremony of December 902 was recorded by a scribe on a copper plate which has been preserved.

The ceremony followed a standard format. First the noble sponsoring the event distributed presents to all the people that had come. Next the participants decorated themselves with flowers and paint. A sacred stone was set in the centre of the future temple compound. The people then sat in a circle around the stone and a priest intoned curses against anyone who would dare disturb the peace of the village. Thereupon began a celebration which probably took longer than the ritual itself.

Perspective Effects in Javanese Temple Architecture

The architects who designed and built the great Hindu and Buddhist temples of eastern and central Java were masters of perspective effects. They manipulated changes in scale and the positioning of architectural elements to create an illusion of greater mass and stature.

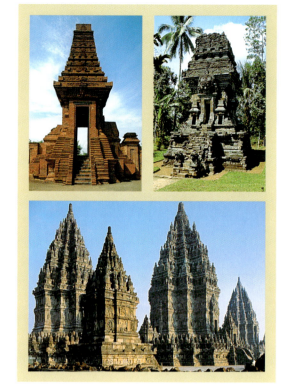

Antefixes are attached to the main wall of a candi *to give the impression that the monument is taller than it actually is.*

(Top left, clockwise) Candi Bajangratu, and Candi Kidal, East Java. Candi Lara Jonggrang, Central Java.

The Javanese temples were designed so that when viewed from certain locations they would appear much taller than they really are. These points can be reconstructed by extending the lines of sight to their points of convergence.

Mount Meru and the Abode of the Gods

Javanese sanctuaries, or *candi*, dedicated to the worship of Siva or Visnu, were identified with the deity's own abode and in this capacity provided a ritual focal point for acts of worship and religious ceremonies. Indian mythology identifies this dwelling place of the gods as a natural cave on Mount Meru, the mystical mountain situated at the centre of the Hindu universe, or else as a flying palace in orbit about this mountain. Obviously no human construction could ever equal or even approach the vastness of Mount Meru itself, but the architectural version had to appear majestic enough to be a persuasive representation of its legendary counterpart. To achieve this effect, all possible means, including the purely visual, were employed to make these man-made edifices seem larger than they actually were. The manipulation of perspective was developed with this end in mind.

The Illusion of Height

The superstructure or roof of a sanctuary is multi-tiered, being composed of a number of stepped storeys. There are numerous variations on this general plan, but each temple represents a different example of the same principle, namely the artificial enhancement of diminishing perspective. The laws of perspective state that elements of identical height, when vertically stacked at regular intervals, will appear to decrease in size in proportion to their distance above the observer. If these elements are actually reduced in height with each ascending level, then each element will seem to be higher than it really is and the structure as a whole will appear taller. For example, if the interval between the rungs of a ladder are gradually reduced from bottom to top, the ladder will seem taller than it is in reality.

The temples of the Dieng Plateau and Gedong Songo make use of this effect of diminishing vertical perspective, and this tendency is stronger still at Prambanan and in the later temples of East Java. Devotees, on entering the sanctuary, were confronted by an abstract image consisting of familiar architectural elements, some reminiscent of structures built of wood. Their representation here, on a grand scale, enlarged even to a disproportionate degree, was well suited to embodying the symbolic universe set out in sacred texts and ritual, even in the absence of any direct reference to this symbolic dimension in the actual architecture itself.

Candi Lara Jonggrang

The ornamentation of the numerous sanctuaries which make up the temple complex at Prambanan, can be divided into five separate sections or levels. First, there is the main body of the edifice, which is itself divided into two sections by a broad band. The second section consists of the first of three stepped storeys that comprise the roof. Its base reproduces that of the main body of the structure, but on a smaller scale (for example in c*andi apit,* 0.75 metres as opposed to 1.45 metres), and above this, after a row of triangular ornaments called antefixes, one finds carved elements directly attached to the main wall of the sanctuary, creating the effect that the monument rises in the background behind them. This wall is topped by a full-length cornice. The third section is constituted by the second of the stepped storeys of the roof. At this level, the effect of a rapid

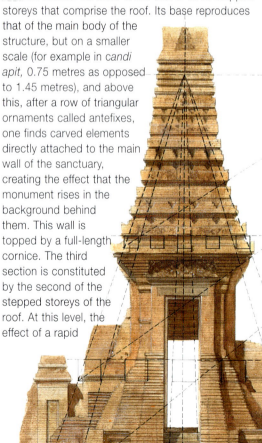

INDONESIA'S CLASSICAL HERITAGE

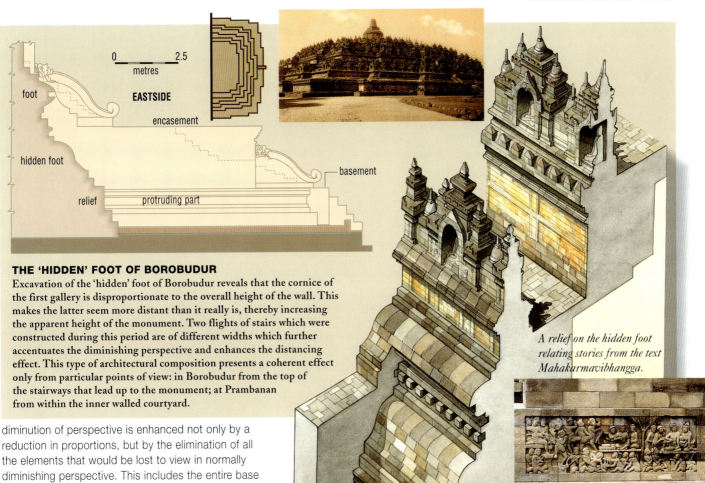

THE 'HIDDEN' FOOT OF BOROBUDUR
Excavation of the 'hidden' foot of Borobudur reveals that the cornice of the first gallery is disproportionate to the overall height of the wall. This makes the latter seem more distant than it really is, thereby increasing the apparent height of the monument. Two flights of stairs which were constructed during this period are of different widths which further accentuates the diminishing perspective and enhances the distancing effect. This type of architectural composition presents a coherent effect only from particular points of view: in Borobudur from the top of the stairways that lead up to the monument; at Prambanan from within the inner walled courtyard.

A relief on the hidden foot relating stories from the text Mahakarmavibhangga.

diminution of perspective is enhanced not only by a reduction in proportions, but by the elimination of all the elements that would be lost to view in normally diminishing perspective. This includes the entire base and a considerable portion of the section above which is decorated with figures. The latter, in this instance, is reduced to a single band bearing a line of antefixes while the cornice of the main wall of the sanctuary is also considerably lightened. The fourth level consists of the third and smallest of the roof storeys. This may repeat, in its essentials, the level below, but in some instances may be eliminated altogether, as in the case of *candi apit*. The fifth and final section of the building is constituted by the crown which repeats elements which have already appeared at lower levels, but which are reproduced here on a reduced scale — 1.25 metres compared to 1.75 metres in the case of *candi apit*.

This latter section, its apparent height increased by the artificially diminished perspective of the lower sections, should actually be smaller than it is, if it had been designed in proportion to the main body of the structure. On the contrary, however, it is considerably more substantial than it should be and seems even larger given that no part of it clearly marks the change of scale. This strategy, which might be thought to interrupt the continuity of the effect of perspective, serves instead to emphasise the summit of the edifice.

Borobudur
In the initial stages of the construction of Borobudur, the master builders incorporated perspective effects which operated not only in the vertical plane but also on the horizontal. This first version was left incomplete, but when work halted the mouldings of the foundation and the cornice of the retaining wall of the second gallery had already been built, and a start had been made on the retaining wall of the third gallery. Given the enormous scale of this undertaking — Borobudur at this point formed a gigantic square with sides 90 metres long — it would hardly have been feasible to make the upper levels in proportion to the base, and for this reason the architects incorporated certain manipulations of perspective into their design.

MOULDING AND ARTIFICIAL HEIGHT
A comparison of the temple mouldings of an east Javanese *candi*, Candi Jago, (left) and a central Javanese *candi*, Candi Mendut (right).

The East Javanese architects attempted to exaggerate the apparent height of the candi even more than the Central Javanese.

(Above top) The temples from the Arjuna group on Dieng Plateau.

(Above) Candi Jago, a Buddhist shrine. Late 13th century. For comparison of use of perspective, see diagram at left.

59

Ornamentation of Classic Javanese Stonework

An apsara. *The Javanese images of these heavenly maidens are decidedly demure in comparison with their voluptuous counterparts in India.*

Ganesha — often found on the Hindu Javanese temples on the east or west side.

The lion is a common symbol of Buddha. Its position on this Buddhist edifice Candi Ngawen is rare; it may be a reminder of an earlier practice of carving animal-shaped pillars in wooden buildings.

The Javanese artists had a wide range of ornamental designs at their disposal to adorn their temples. These motifs were selected from a vocabulary of patterns in South Asia, and further elaborated in their Javanese environment. They were also combined to form compositions; certain motifs were regularly found in particular locations and groupings on temples. The motifs expressed complex messages about the divine nature of the structures; they were not randomly organised decorations. They were subtly different from the message which they expressed in India. Many of these motifs consist of things which the Javanese, whether Hindu or Buddhists, believed were found in heaven, as well as other more abstract motifs such as naturalistic and geometric designs.

Various Kinds of Ornaments

The most common kind of ornamentation used in Javanese temples is the antefix. They are triangular elements which were carved in many variations. They were used as decorations for the tops of walls and cornices. Another form of ornaments in the same category were the *tumpal*, which were also triangular in shape and especially popular in east Java.

On relief panels or niches, we can often find the *kalpataru* or 'wishing tree' which was used as a motif of heaven in central Java. Another floral symbol is the *purnaghata* or the pot of plenty, often shown with flowering plants growing from them.

Other common symbols include *kendi* or ewers which were used as containers of holy water in rituals and to symbolise the elixir of immortality, and *kinnara* which are heavenly musicians, usually female, half-human, half-bird.

At the Siva complex of Lara Jonggrang, Prambanan, elaborate compositions of lions in niches with various animals adorn the bases of the three main shrines. Elsewhere in Java, motifs of imaginary animals are also depicted on temple bases. They may have been symbolic of the wild jungles on the slopes of Mount Meru.

ANTEFIXES FROM THE MAINWALLS OF BOROBUDUR
1. First gallery
2. Second gallery
3. Third gallery
4. Fourth gallery

KALA HEADS
These demonic images were very important in India and Cambodia as well as in Java Bali. They were often place

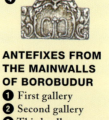

GEOMETRIC MOTIFS
A number of these motifs may have been derived from patterns used on Javanese cloth. Some have suggested that they depict temple hangings. There are two main types of motifs; the naturalistic forms which usually represent forests and animals, and abstract and geometrical representations of floral motifs.

above niches for statues and over doorways. In Java and Bali they were given greater emphasis than elsewhere. They evolved several stylistic phases. Their symbolism is controversial: some believe they represent the demon Time who stole the elixir of immortality, while others note that they are frequently referred to as Banaspati, 'Lord of the Jungle'. (Left to right) *Kala* from Candi Lumbung, *kala* from Borobudur, *kala* from Candi Jago, and *kala* from Candi Singasari. The *kala* became more stylised with time.

PILASTERS

Large quantities of these imitation pillars were carved in many forms on most Javanese buildings. They may have been meant to suggest that the stone buildings were palaces, which in Java would have been built of wood with many pillars. There may have been numerous wooden temples such as those that are represented on the temple reliefs of Borobudur, Candi Lara Jonggrang and a number of Late Classic period Javanese temples. Stone pillar bases have also been found which may have been used to hold intricately carved wooden pillars which might have been used to support a decorated wooden roof.

Makara.
These were fanciful composite animals with elephant's trunks, fish scales, lion's paws and deer horns. They were usually used as markers at the foot of staircases in central Java and Sumatra. Combined with kala, *they often formed the borders of statuary niches.*

YONI AND LINGGA

The *lingga* and *yoni* are both symbols representing the Hindu god Siva and his consort Parvati. The *yoni* can be highly decorative such as the ones featured which are taken from Central Java. The early Siva-*lingga* is usually very plain and geometrical but in the Late Classic period, it became more stylised and elaborated.

INDONESIA'S CLASSICAL HERITAGE

61

Hindu Architecture of Central Java

The Gedong Songo ('Nine Buildings') temples built in the mid-8th century represent a consolidation and standardisation of Hindu architecture succeeding the period of experimentation which took place on the Dieng Plateau. The Gedong Songo design established a formula which was so successful that it remained in use, with numerous variations, for the extraordinarily long period of 600 years.

Map showing the location of Hindu temples in Central Java.

↗ *(Top) Candi Lara Jonggrang, Prambanan. (Middle) Candi Puntadewa and Sembadra, Dieng. (Bottom) Candi Selogriyo.*

(Below) The Gedong Songo buildings share the same Hindu inspiration as the temples of Dieng, and date from approximately the same period, around the mid-8th century (though possibly a little later than Candi Arjuna).

CRUCIFORM PLAN
A type of architecture which distinguishes Dieng and Gedong Songo can be found at other important temples such as Candi Siva, Prambanan and Candi Selogriyo which have similar cruciform ground plans.

The Temple Precincts

Gedong Songo is located high on the slope of Mount Ungaran, an extinct volcano in north central Java. There are in fact more than nine buildings here; the number 9 in Java is purely symbolic of a propitious unit, and is a modern name. We do not know what the ancient name for the complex may have been. The Gedong Songo temples are placed on terraces on the upper slope of the mountain, with a glorious view of a huge swath of central Java. From there one can see the whole range of peaks from Mt. Perahu, where the Dieng Plateau is located, in the west, to Mt. Lawu in the east. This view may have been one of the main factors which led the ancient Javanese to select this location for the site of a religious complex.

The temples flank a ravine through which flows a stream of water volcanically heated almost to boiling point. This natural feature probably formed another factor which attracted the attention of the ancient Javanese, who might have associated hot springs and other volcanic features with supernatural forces.

The Gedong Songo temples are distinguished from one another by differences in internal plan. The three principal temples in Group III face west. The central temple, dedicated to Siva, is square, with an entrance porch. Niches set into the exteriors of the other three walls contain statues of Agastya, Ganesha and Durga. This is the first appearance of an iconographic triad which became virtually obligatory for the designers of all Siva temples in Java for the next six centuries.

A smaller temple north of this edifice is dedicated to Visnu. The temple which once stood on the south end was probably dedicated to Brahma. The provision of three temples for the Hindu trinity prefigures the layout of the Siva complex of Lara Jonggrang. Another small structure facing the central temple dedicated to Siva resembles Candi Semar at Dieng and may have contained a statue of Nandin, the bull, who represents his vehicle.

Candi Lara Jonggrang

After a period of Buddhist dominance in central Java from about AD 780 to 830 during which no important Hindu monuments were built, Hinduism experienced a resurgence, culminating in the construction of a huge complex dedicated to Siva, now called Candi Lara Jonggrang. The complex was consecrated in 856, a date given in an inscription translated by the epigrapher J.G. de Casparis. The complex was probably associated with a town of some size, and an extensive irrigation system, according to the inscription, but neither exists today.

This vast ensemble consists of three walled courtyards set on rising terraces. The two inner courtyards are concentric and precisely oriented toward the east, but the outermost is differently aligned, probably reflecting the layout of the town with which the temple was associated.

ARCHITECTURAL MOTIFS OF HINDUISM
The parrot first appears around the time when Lara Jonggrang was began in AD 835. It became very popular in later architecture such as Candi Ijo. The lion in a niche also appears quite prominently at Lara Jonggrang but its popularity failed to spread to other sites. The twin door guardians of Nandiswara and Mahakala first appeared on Gedong 9 and remained popular ever since. Unusual decorations on the exteriors of Hindu shrines include a Ganesha on a *yoni* at Candi Gebang and the enigmatic figures of bearded ascetics from Candi Morangan.

The ground plan of the complex was established by setting out a number of reference points. These reference points were commemorated by nine stone markers on the upper terrace, over each of which was built a small shrine topped by a *lingga*. Perhaps the markers were preserved to facilitate future expansions and repairs.

The terraces at Lara Jonggrang are built of artificially heaped-up earth. Eight major sanctuaries occupy the upper terrace. The three principal structures, cruciform in plan, are dedicated to the trinity of Visnu, Brahma and Siva. Opposite each is a smaller temple for the vehicle, or mount, of the deity. Two other structures called *candi apit* stand at the north and south entrances to this complex.

Candi Siva's stone balustrade is carved on the inner wall with bas-reliefs illustrating the first part of the Ramayana. Candi Brahma bears bas-reliefs illustrating the conclusion of the Ramayana while the reliefs on Candi Visnu depict the playful youth of Visnu's incarnation as Krisna. The two *candi apit* were among the first archaeological monuments in Java to be reconstructed. Their appearance resembles the other temples, but on a smaller scale. Their functions are unknown.

The four lower terraces of the middle courtyard contain 224 smaller sanctuaries or *candi perwara*. These can be divided into two types. Those at the corners have two doors, while the rest have one door. This configuration was probably an idealised representation of the kingdom as a mandala.

CANDI MERAK AND ITS CONSTRUCTION
A cross-section of Candi Merak showing the location of the statuary base for the main statue in the structure. The temple has never been rebuilt except on paper; the ruins are too fragmentary to permit restoration which would meet conditions of anastylosis (see p. 81), the drawing at right shows the temple as if restored. The drawings at left show various segments of the temple which have undergone reconstruction.

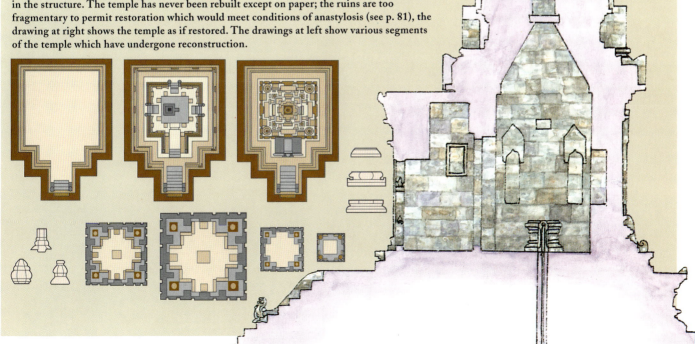

Candi Borobudur

Candi Borobudur occupies a unique position in the architecture of the Hindu-Buddhist era. It differs from contemporary structures of the late 8th and early 9th century in that it does not consist of an enclosed sanctuary set on a basement, or plinth, but instead constitutes a massive stepped pyramid of superimposed terraces of diminishing width, surmounted by a huge bell-shaped stupa.

(Above) The upper terraces of Borobudur which consists of numerous stupas.

(Below) An artist's impression of the building of Borobudur. Stone blocks from Borobudur were taken from the boulders that lined the Progo river nearby.

Geography and Design

Candi Borobudur stands on an elongated natural hill. The original peaked ridge of the hill was levelled to create an artificial plateau. The monument stands at the southeastern end of this plateau, and encases the summit of the hill which was apparently left intact. Additional soil filling was required for levelling the surface, since the hilltop was not large enough to serve as a core for the entire structure. The monument rises approximately 34 metres above the surrounding Kedu Plain. A level area on a projecting spur at the northwestern end of the hill provided a site for a monastery.

The base, body, and superstructure of Borobudur can be clearly distinguished from one another due to fundamental differences in their design. The base is about four metres in height and forms a square with sides 113 metres long; the sides are not simple straight lines, but have projections called redents. With its width, the base gives the impression that it is a massive terrace encompassing the main edifice.

SPLITTING BOULDERS
A fire is built on the stone where the chiselled marks are and when the stone gets very hot, water is thrown onto the fire and stone. Due to sudden contraction, the stone will split. Another technique is to put wooden wedges into the holes and then wet them, this causes the wood to expand pushing the rock apart.

The body of the monument consists of another five terraces, superimposed one upon the other. Each is four metres narrower than the terrace beneath it, and of decreasing height as well. Balustrades (the term is not architecturally accurate, but its application to this feature at Borobudur has become standard practice) along the outer edges of each terrace convert them into narrow galleries or corridors with walls ornamented with bas-relief carvings depicting Buddhist doctrines and scenes from the life of Gautama Buddha.

The uppermost part of the monument is distinguishable from the rectangular terraces on which it sits. This top section consists of three concentric platforms (squares with rounded corners), each of which supports a ring of perforated stupas. These stupas are surmounted by the huge dome at the centre of the monument. In its present state it soars into the sky to a height of nearly 35 metres above the plateau. Originally it would have been much taller yet; the stone umbrellas which once rose above the dome have been shattered by lightning.

1. Bukit Menoreh
2. Desa Segaran (village)
3. Desa Jowahan (village)
4. Candi Pawon (temple)
5. Candi Banon (temple), of which only two bricks remain
7. Desa Maitan (village)
8. Desa Brongsongan

INDONESIA'S CLASSICAL HERITAGE

Monk chiselling the story title of the relief panel.

The master using a piece of charcoal to draw the scene on the panel.

An apprentice chiselled out the characters and figures.

The master carved the finer details on the figures such as their jewelleries and clothing.

Next white plaster was applied over the panel.

The relief was finally painted in pastel colours.

Candi Borobudur has an entrance on each of the four sides of the monument. These have all been treated identically in architectural terms. In this respect no single side can be readily identified as the 'front' of the building, and it is only by reading the narrative reliefs which adorn the galleries of the terraces that one can discern that the main entrance is located in the middle of the east elevation.

Access to the upper part of the monument is provided by stairways situated in the middle of each side of the pyramid, leading from the surface of the plateau all the way to the base of the main stupa.

One Concept or Two?

Candi Borobudur's unique design has invited some scholars to suggest that significant design changes were made during construction. The most plausible conclusion, based on Dumarçay's analysis, is that Borobudur is the result of a single plan. That Borobudur was conceived as a stepped pyramid of ten ascending stages coincides with J.G. de Casparis' hypothesis that the monument was meant to symbolise the kings of the Sailendra dynasty on one hand, and to glorify their Buddhist religion on the other. Buddhist scriptures teach that Buddhahood can only be attained after passing through ten stages of bodhisattvahood, and by coincidence the reigning Sailendra king happened to be the tenth in his dynasty.

An inaccurate elevation view of Borobudur taken from the Leemans monograph.

(Below) The height of the upper galleries was reduced increasingly so as to make the structure look taller than it actually is.

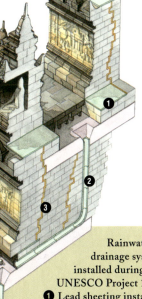

Rainwater drainage system installed during the UNESCO Project 1973-82.
❶ Lead sheeting installed in 1973-82 to prevent rainwater from percolating through the stones and eroding the soil beneath the monument.
❷ Plastic drainage pipes.
❸ Araldite tar for water proofing.

Buddhist Architecture of Central Java

The Sailendra kings and queens who reigned between approximately AD 780 and 830 sponsored the construction of massive shrines dedicated to Mahayana deities. The succeeding line of rulers were more inclined to Hinduism, but contributed to the erection of Buddhist sanctuaries as well; the best known are Candi Sari and Candi Plaosan. Despite its relatively brief history, the Buddhist architecture of central Java underwent many renovations, making its history complex and difficult to disentangle.

Dwarapala (door guardian) at the entrance to Candi Plaosan, Central Java.

Candi Kalasan

The first known Buddhist shrine in Indonesia was erected at the site known as Candi Kalasan, where an inscription dated AD 778 has been found. The original temple had a square groundplan and stood on a basement resembling the approximately contemporary structures on the Dieng Plateau. This building existed for only a brief period before it was rebuilt on a cruciform plan.

Candi Sewu

Archaeological excavations have made it possible to reconstruct the rituals conducted in conjunction with the complex's founding. First an enormous pit was dug and filled with layers of sand and pebbles. On a layer of sand eight centimetres below ground level, a theogonic mandala was laid out, the corners of the mandala are marked by small boundary stones. Deities are represented by one of their attributes: a musical instrument modelled in clay represents the Tara of music, while a Chinese bowl containing wood and charcoal represents the Tara of incense. The term Tara describes manifestations of the consort of the bodhisattva (enlightening being) Avalokitesvara. On top of this mandala a brick altar was built which was perhaps used in rites associated with the laying of the temple's foundations. Over this altar a pedestal was erected for the main statue of the complex. After these preliminary rituals the construction of the temple itself began.

Candi Sewu was remodelled a number of times. The first stage of construction began around AD 778. The original temple had one central chamber and four smaller cellae. This shrine was surrounded by 244 subsidiary open-sided temples. In the second phase, beginning around AD 790, the complex was completely redesigned. This was probably linked to a profound change in the Buddhist religion of Java resulting from the adoption of the worship of the five Jina or 'Conqueror' Buddhas. As at Borobudur, statues representing the five deities were installed: Aksobhya on the east, Ratnasambahava on the south, Amitabha on the west, and Amoghasiddhi on the north. In the central cella stood a statue of the supreme Buddha Vairocana. Side chambers were joined to the central sanctuary while doors closed off the pre-existing passageways meant for circumambulation. This work was conducted in a comparatively brief period.

In the third stage, carried out at a more leisurely pace, the approaches to the sanctuary were remodelled. This phase, which also took place in other Buddhist structures of central Java, was not completed until about AD 840. As a result, the statues of the divinities, which had formerly been visible from outside, were now hidden, probably as a result of changes in ritual procedures.

The last stage involved further modification of the iconography of Candi Sewu. This does not seem to have been the result of a well-defined plan, and was never completed.

Candi Sari and Candi Plaosan

These complexes were built after the re-emergence of a Hindu elite

(Below) Niches flanked by heavenly figures such as apsaras *and* gandarwas *reinforced the symbolic depiction of temples as heavenly mountains at Candi Sari, Central Java. Much of the sanctuary has now disappeared.*

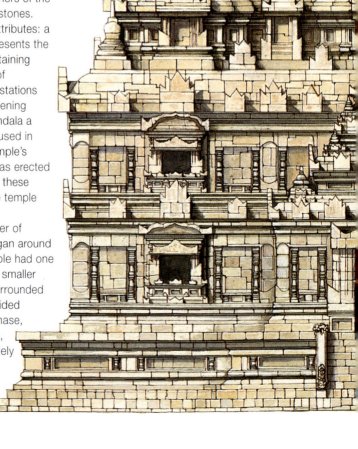

INDONESIA'S CLASSICAL HERITAGE

FRONT FAÇADE OF CANDI SAJIWAN

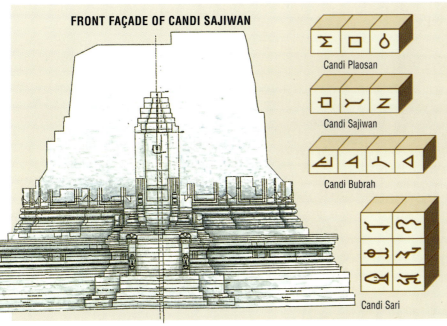

STONE MARKERS
Certain stones of many Central Javanese Buddhist shrines have been found carved with markings. Their significance is unknown; they may have served to identify stones contributed by villages or donors.

in AD 832. The two complexes closely resembled each other; they appear to have been modelled on wooden structures like those depicted in reliefs at Borobudur. Both have three cellas on a lower storey and another three on an upper floor, reached by a wooden staircase in the interior. Both are remarkable for the richness of their exterior decoration.

Candi Plaosan is better preserved than Candi Sari. It was built between AD 830 and 850 during the reign of a ruler known as Rakai Garung, on the site of an older temple. The complex was once surrounded by a moat, now filled with silt. This is the only known instance of this practice in central Java; however later temples in east Java such as Candi Jawi were furnished with similar moats.

Candi Plaosan consists of two complexes. Plaosan Kidul (Kidul = south in Javanese) was a major shrine surrounded by two concentric rectangles of temples and stupas. Little of this complex remains. Plaosan Lor (Lor = north) is better preserved. On the far north of the site is a courtyard with remains of a square stone base for a wooden roof, long vanished.

CANDI PLAOSAN LOR
At this complex, built in the mid-9th century, the two main temples have a rectangular plan, with porch and staircase on the west. A broad band runs around the exterior dividing the temple body into two levels. This horizontality was reinforced by two rows of windows, originally barred with wood. Both levels are richly decorated with carvings. The roof of the temple and the porch bear stupas.
1. Stone base for wooden pavilion
2. , 3. Two-storeyed shrines (restored)
4. Subsidiary chapels surrounding 1.
5. Wall enclosing 2. and 3.
6. Subsidiary chapels
7. Row of stupas
8. , 9. *Dwarapala* statues
10. Winding moat
11. Plaosan Kidul shrine
12. Subsidiary chapels

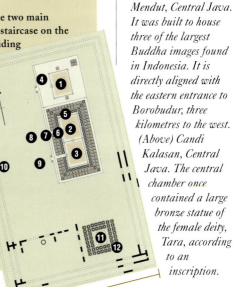

(Above top) Candi Mendut, Central Java. It was built to house three of the largest Buddha images found in Indonesia. It is directly aligned with the eastern entrance to Borobudur, three kilometres to the west. (Above) Candi Kalasan, Central Java. The central chamber once contained a large bronze statue of the female deity, Tara, according to an inscription.

Stone Architecture of East Java

Buildings constructed from permanent materials reappeared in east Java in the 13th century. The resumption of the practice of building in stone coincided with the emergence of the kingdom of Singasari, and the evolution of new interpretations of Hindu and Buddhist doctrine in the light of indigenous Javanese philosophy. None of the new structures was as large as the major monuments of Central Java.

(Above) The distribution of Late Classic stone temples in east Java. These include temples ranging from Singasari to early Majapahit period.

Temple Types and Functions

Despite considerable political turbulence, a kingdom named Singasari consolidated its control over strategic areas of Java in 1222 and by 1275 extended its power over parts of Sumatra. Soon after that, Singasari initiated a vigorous programme of building stone temples.

Most temples in east Java seem to have served to honour people of the ruling class after their death. East Javanese religion, whether clothed in Buddhist or Hindu garb, focused on deliverance (*moksha*) as a state in which the soul was reunited with a deity from whom it had temporarily become detached. The architecture seems to have been designed to accommodate these ceremonies.

Candi Kidal

This shrine dedicated to Visnu was completed around 1260. It was enclosed within a nearly square walled courtyard (21 x 22 metres). The groundplan was laid out in a manner similar to those of central Javanese complexes; excavations have unearthed small *lingga* at the corners of the site which marked the reference points used in construction.

The courtyard has four gateways aligned with the temple. The main sanctuary contained a single cella with a doorway on the west side. The superstructure consists of three receding stories of decreasing proportions. The base bears central medallions depicting episodes from the Garudeya, a Hindu text which relates a quest for the elixir of immortality.

The surface of the courtyard is slightly lower than the surrounding area. The floor may have been watertight and the courtyard may occasionally have been flooded with water to create a shallow pool, as is sometimes found in India.

EVOLUTION OR INNOVATION?

East Javanese temples exhibit a number of features which first appeared in central Java, but which subsequently have been developed further. These include: increased asymmetry in the groundplans of temple complexes; wooden superstructures; temple complexes occupying several terraces built into a mountainside; frequent use of narrative reliefs; and double-leaf walls. Perspective effects designed to increase the apparent height of temple roofs reached exaggerated proportions, whereas the actual height of monuments diminished.

Narrative reliefs depicted purely Javanese texts as well as Buddhist and Hindu scriptures. The style of carving deviated radically from the naturalistic high relief of central Java: instead east Javanese artists carved stylised two-dimensional forms reminiscent of leather shadow puppets. Statuary also depicted deities with visages which possibly portray the features of the rulers commemorated in the shrines. Monumental gateways of the split and lintel forms appear.

Other Sites

Other temples of the same period generally resemble Candi Kidal, but with differences in the base. Candi Jago has a particularly massive foundation consisting of several levels which are carved with narrative reliefs illustrating mainly Buddhist texts. The single cella, which is almost completely destroyed, housed a complex iconography of esoteric Buddhist statues and was equipped with sophisticated facilities to enable the statues to be ceremonially bathed.

Candi Singasari, which has a cruciform plan, houses statuary of the same type as that at Lara Jonggrang. The main icon here was probably a Siva *lingga*, but the three subsidiary cellae contained images of Durga, Agastya and Ganesha, facing the customary directions. The reference points marking the temple complex of Singasari were statues of the guardian deities of the relevant directions not *lingga*.

The Majapahit Era

Singasari was succeeded by its daughter kingdom Majapahit in 1294. The most important stone temples of the Majapahit period were built at Panataran. A sanctuary dedicated to Ganesha bears a date corresponding to 1369. The groundplan of the complex seemingly lacks an overall pattern. The principal activity here seems to have been the periodic construction of new structures within the same complex, suggesting that the site may have had a special status. The Nagarakrtagama, a court poem composed in 1365, records a royal visit to Panataran, indicating that the site may have served as a state temple. The main structure is located at the far west of the complex, furthest from the main entrance on the east.

Candi Surawana and Candi Tegurwangi are similar temples located near each other, in the vicinity of modern Pare, between Kediri and Trowulan. The only remnants of both are high bases; the superstructures were apparently built of wood. Both were oriented to the west, and were decorated with reliefs depicting texts from a variety of sources. They were probably built to honour deceased members of the east Javanese elite.

CANDI MOULDINGS AND PERSPECTIVE EFFECTS

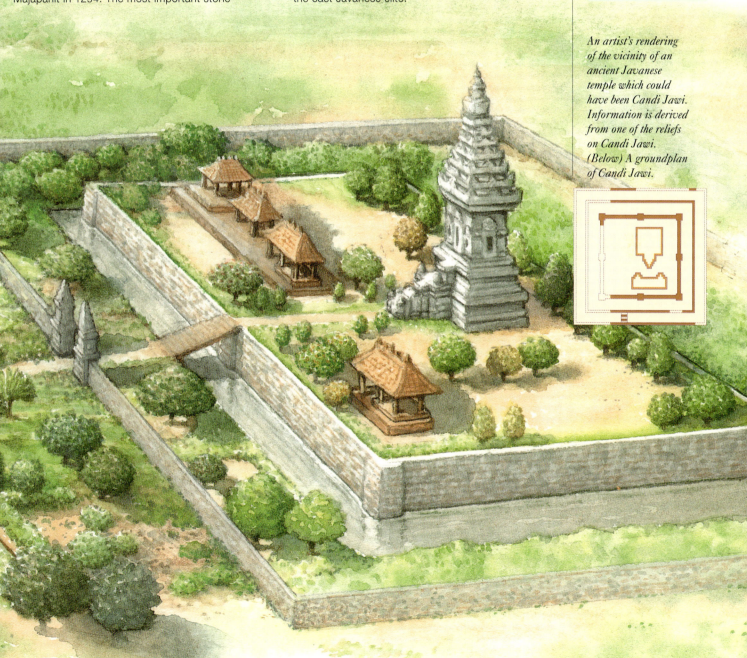

An artist's rendering of the vicinity of an ancient Javanese temple which could have been Candi Jawi. Information is derived from one of the reliefs on Candi Jawi. (Below) A groundplan of Candi Jawi.

Brick Architecture of Majapahit

Majapahit succeeded Singasari in 1294 as the centre of political power in Java. Its capital, identified with the site of Trowulan in East Java, was a major urban centre and focus of a political sphere of influence which encompassed most of the Indonesian Archipelago. Brick replaced stone as the main material for constructing permanent architecture soon after Majapahit's founding, although some stone monuments were also erected.

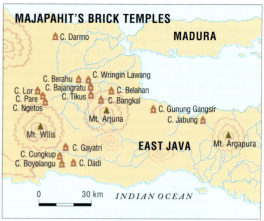

↗ *Map showing the distribution of brick architecture in the region of East Java.*

» *Candi Lor overgrown by roots of a* waringin *tree.*

(Below top) Gunung Gangsir, a brick structure near Porong, consists of a two-storied basement and body. Controversy over its dating persists. (Bottom) Candi Berahu, a Hindu shrine, has been restored several times.

Architecture of the Metropolitan Area

The principal site of the Majapahit era, and probably the location of the royal capital, is located in the vicinity of the modern village of Trowulan, in the hinterland of east Java. A huge number of ruins, still incompletely mapped, are spread over an area of at least 100 square kilometres. Many of these ruins comprise sections of walls which probably formed the boundaries of enclosures or compounds entered by gateways which were major structures in their own right. Candi Bajangratu and Candi Wringin Lawang are the major surviving examples.

The capital was undoubtedly the site of a large and dense population. Much of this, Indonesia's first major city, as we may justifiably call it, comprised many brick structures both sacred and secular. Unfortunately the bricks from the ruins of Trowulan have been quarried for decades, and the process is still continuing in the late 1990s.

The Nagarakrtagama, a poem written in 1365, is unique for its narrative depiction of conditions in 14th-century Java. The poet, Mpu Prapanca, describes the palace as "that royal compound, wonderful, its wall is red brick, going round, thick, high" (Canto 8, stanza 1, translated by Pigeaud). A Chinese author of the same period tells us that the royal citadel was surrounded by a wall 30 feet high and 100 feet long, pierced by double gates. The Nagarakrtagama records that the northern portal had iron doors "ornamented with figures". Other structures in the palace included *bale* (small pavilions), *mandapa* (pillared halls), *witana* (large halls), multi-storied buildings for Hindu and Buddhist clergy, structures for offerings, gateways, and streets lined on both sides by houses.

Standing architecture at Trowulan is now limited to a few brick buildings. Candi Berahu is a Hindu shrine which has been restored several times since its 14th-century foundation. It remains impressive due to its height, but is otherwise quite plain; few of its original features, and no decorative elements whatsoever, are still extant. The site of Sumurupas (Candi Kedaton) is difficult to interpret. It consists of two large brick foundations and the remains of several smaller structures, all of which may have been altered to an unknown extent in recent times. Sumurupas is still used as a place of meditation, as are several other sites of Trowulan which have been substantially built over or incorporated into newer structures. Menak Jingga, now a grass-covered mound, was built of a combination of brick and stone. Narrative reliefs and terracotta models from this site and other contemporary east Javanese locations reveal the former existence of a wide range of building types constructed on stone bases with plinths or floor which may have been made of brick, and a roof supported on wooden columns.

Brick Structures Outside the Capital

At Candi Pari, near Porong, Late-Classical Javanese architecture can be seen at its most inventive. This edifice bears a date corresponding to 1371 carved on the lintel over its entrance, situated in the west. The interior consists of a square cella. The statue of the principal deity, now vanished, once stood against the sanctuary's eastern wall. The interior was illuminated by two high windows in each side wall.

The ornamentation above the entrance represents the roof of a rice granary. Such granaries came under the protection of the rice goddess Dewi Sri, consort of Visnu. This motif here indicates that the sanctuary was dedicated to him. The most exceptional aspect of Candi Pari is however its roof, consisting of three stepped storeys of diminishing dimensions, separated by antefixes. The meticulous workmanship makes the exaggeration of perspective entirely coherent; most probably the builders were assisted by a preliminary design which allowed them to visualise in advance how the result would look.

INDONESIA'S CLASSICAL HERITAGE

THREE TYPES OF BRICK ARCHITECTURE

Civic architecture in Majapahit included temples, gateways and pools. Although we have no written information about any of them, archaeology suggests that some of these ruins served public purposes.

Gateways, of two types, gave access to urban areas. Surviving examples include Bajangratu and Wringin Lawang in Majapahit's former capital, and Candi Darmo, a separate site. Wringin Lawang is the oldest known example of the split gate, a form which is characteristic of Balinese architecture.

Bathing pools and reservoirs provided water to the urban population. Some reservoirs were built upstream, just outside the urban area. An example of the reservoir form is the Segaran which is an extensive brick-lined tank.

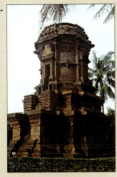

GATEWAY — BAJANGRATU

The oldest known example of the *paduraksa* gate is Bajangratu. It comprises a narrow doorway with a threshold with round holes for doorposts which show that a double-leaf door once existed here. This indicates that the gate may have served to restrict access to an enclosed area. It is surmounted by a soaring roof intricately carved and resembling the roof of a temple.

BATHING PLACE — CANDI TIKUS

Candi Tikus was built as an ornate bathing place. At the centre of its main pool is a large symbolic reconstruction of Mount Meru from which water spurted through carved stone spouts shaped like lotus buds and *makara*. It was built on the southeast corner of the city. It is not known whether it was for public or special use.

TEMPLE — CANDI JABUNG

Candi Jabung stands beside the modern road (perhaps also an ancient route) leading from Majapahit's capital to the eastern tip of Java. Candi Jabung, dated 1354, was intended for Buddhist worship. It stands on a very tall cruciform base divided into three tiers, with a flight of steps ascending the west side. The sanctuary is circular on the exterior, octagonal within. The external decoration consists of false doors surmounted by *kala* heads.

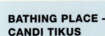

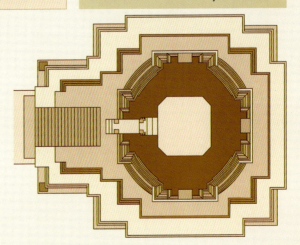

Architecture in Ancient Javanese Inscriptions

It can be assumed that the range of Indonesian house types found in the past would have been at least as rich as is the case in the Archipelago today. Unfortunately, since in premodern times even the dwellings of the king and upper classes, although undoubtedly highly ornate, were built entirely of perishable materials, they have vanished without trace. Written sources however give us important information on some components of early house forms in Java.

KEMUNCAK
Fragments of clay objects which may have been roof decorations have been found in abundance in Trowulan. The practice of using such roof ornaments is still known from Bali and examples can also be found in such Javanese structures as the Kasepuhan Palace at Cirebon. These roof finials are made of terracotta clay and appear in all shapes and forms. They are usually referred as *kemuncak*s.

Relief from a Majapahit period temple in East Java. The relief is now in the collection of the Archaeological Service Museum in Trowulan, East Java.

Written Evidence
Inscriptional evidence concerning architecture in Indonesia is only found within the *corpus* of Old Javanese inscriptions between the 10th and 14th centuries. The earliest mention of architectural matters was in the reign of King Sindok in the 10th century. The next references appeared during the 11th-century rule of King Airlangga. After this comes the Kadiri period of the 12th century, the Singhasari period of the 13th century and Majapahit at the end of the 13th and 14th centuries.

Architectural data is found in the king's bestowal of a grant to a person having special merits. The grant consists of special rights regarding several things, such as wearing special clothing, growing special kinds of plants, and owning a house with some special traits.

Inscriptions from the earliest period mention only three special traits of a privileged person's house (see table). The fringe suspended from the eaves at the front part of a house is often observable in depictions of houses in reliefs on the walls of East Javanese temples. During the reign of King Airlangga, seven kinds of architectural privileges were

THE STREETS OF TROWULAN
The *Nagarakrtagama*, a court poem written in 1365, describes the houses of the palace retainers as having "carved wooden pillars, well-arranged...the bases are brick, red, fitted with raised work, select, ornamented with figures. Spread, to be sure, are the products of the potters, used as roof tops of those houses, superior" (Canto 11, stanza 2). Such houses as these illustrated here would have represented a new use of architectural material in Indonesia. Before the 14th century, no dwellings, even palaces, are known to have been built of permanent materials.

given. However the richest variety of bestowals is found in inscriptions of the Kadiri period. It has 20 items in the list, including all the three items in the Sindok inscriptions, and all the seven items in the Airlangga inscriptions.

The increasing variety of special traits for the houses of the privileged from time to time also demonstrates evolution in design. Those architectural innovations have first arisen within the royal palace. Only after those had been well-developed, were they then distributed to other parties who were given privileges by the king. The right to special architectural traits had always been formulated in the inscriptions as something solicited from below. Initially privileges were only given by the king to low-ranking nobilities (during the Sindok period) or to religious personages who had close relations with the king (during Sindok and Airlangga periods). Only in the Kadiri period were those symbols of excellence then distributed to the village leaders.

Archaeological Remains

Systematic excavations at Trowulan, the probable site of Majapahit's capital in the 14th century, have uncovered remains of numerous structures which possessed brick floors and foundations for walls. There is nothing to indicate that these structures were meant for religious purposes, and the association of the floors with large amounts of pottery and other domestic-type refuse makes it seems highly probable that these were part of dwelling areas.

It is now known that several extensive complexes with brick floors and wall foundations, and tile roofs, occupied the site of Trowulan during the 14th century. Unfortunately, much of the site has been severely disturbed and the rest is rapidly vanishing.

SINDOK (10TH C)	(1) *palangka binubut* (wooden seat smoothed with a lathe), (2) *ringring bananten* (fringe made of fine and silky material), (3) *salu* (large bench attached to one or more sides of the wall in a verandah)
AIRLANGGA (11TH C)	(1) *palangka binubut* (wooden seat smoothed with a lathe), (2) *ringring bananten* (fringe made of fine and silky material), (3) *palungan asahab/ atutup bananten* (litter covered by silken cloth), (4) *payung apagut* (a pair of decorative umbrellas installed in the front verandah), (5) *patarana pananten* (cushions wrapped in silk), (6) *suraga/tilam panaten* (silken mattress), (7) *bale inantun* (open hall at the back of the house)
KADIRI (12TH C)	all the items from the earlier two periods plus: (1) *waruga u tengah* (open hall in the middle of the house), (2) *umah apapan* (house with wooden floor), (3) *umah wedung tempak* (?), (4) *saka wwalu/inasta* (eight pillars), (5) *parwata bukur* (mountain-like structure), (6) *bukur i tengah* (mountain-like structure in the middle courtyard), (7) *wuwung awingka* (terracotta decoration on roof ridge), (8) *witana* (separate open hall), (9) *watangan* (courtyard for tournament play), (10) *lesung kuning* (yellow trough), (11) *kayu kuning* (yellow wood [trough]), (12) *bagañjing* (small building for reading)
SINGHASARI (13TH C)	in addition to the items listed above in the three earlier periods, the list includes: (1) *abañwa-abañwa* (pleasure water works), (2) *kamale/kembang kuner/galuguh* (names of special plants to be put in front or at sides of the house)
MAJAPAHIT (14TH C)	includes all the items listed above, plus one new item: (1) *sahab/awarana bananten* (silk drapery)

(Below) An artist's rendering of a street in Trowulan, the ancient capital of the 14th-century kingdom of Majapahit.

Terraced Temple Sites

The oldest surviving examples of manmade structures in Indonesia, some of which may date from over 2,000 years ago, are not 'buildings'; they are modifications of the landscape, or, terraces cut into hillsides, arranged like giant stairs. If the main building material was earth, the secondary material used was stone: facings for the vertical 'risers' of the terraces, paving for paths and stairways, and free-standing monoliths.

(Top) Menhirs of the Bori Toraja, south Sulawesi.

(Above) Candi Yudha, a Hindu sanctuary built on the slopes of Mount Penanggungan, East Java.

Early Terraced Sites and Megalithic Culture

Early writers on Indonesia of whom R. von Heine-Geldern was most influential argued that there had been at least two phases of megalithic culture in Indonesia, correlated with migrations from the Asian mainland. Terracing and menhirs were believed to belong to the earlier phase, dated to the Neolithic era. This approach was consonant with the Diffusionist school of thought, which operated under the assumption that Southeast Asia had been a cultural backwater, responding to external stimuli rather than actively pursuing cultural innovation.

This interpretation of prehistoric landscape architecture in Indonesia has now been largely abandoned, due partly to changed perceptions of the role played by Indonesians in developing their own culture, and partly to the fact that most terraced sites which are thought to date to the prehistoric era give evidence of use in more recent times. It is impossible to form firm conclusions regarding the age of these sites which have undergone modifications since they were first built.

POLYNESIAN *MARAE* STRUCTURES

The term marae is part of the vocabulary of ancient Polynesian language. It designates a public place reserved for the social and religious activities of the community. It is also an intermediate area between the group's own territory and the external world. Other frequently associated structures include those used by priests, for ancestors and for reunion. They were found at the time of European conquest in several parts of Polynesia. They resemble Indonesian terraced sites which suggests that they had a common origin in prehistoric Austronesian religion. (Right) *Marae* from Tahiti.

❶ raised stone
❷ fine pavement
❸ non-paved
❹ coarse pavement
❺ raised stones

Punden Berundak

That at least some of these sites, in Indonesian termed *punden berundak*, date from prehistory is highly probable, in view of the existence of similar structures in Polynesia. The *marae* of the western Pacific are almost certainly the architectural expression of the same cultural beliefs as the Indonesian *punden berundak*. Both island realms were populated by Austronesian speakers who began to occupy both Indonesia and the islands of the Pacific 5,000 to 7,000 years ago. 'Punden' is a Javanese word literally meaning 'respected, honoured'. Today it is often applied to a particular place near a village, often on a hill, associated with spirits of the village founders. Sometimes Islamic-style funerary monuments have been erected on them.

'Berundak' means 'terraced'. The best-preserved examples are found in the highlands of West Java. One of the largest sites, Gunung Padang was brought to light in 1979. The site, on a hilltop 885

PREHISTORIC *PUNDEN BERUNDAK*

The most active *punden* dating from preIslamic times is probably Kosala, West Java, still in use by the Badui people who rejected Islam when it penetrated west Java in the 16th century. The site was used by the 19th-century Badui and is presently a sacred area in the Badui territory.
❶ Large flat stones such as this are laid around the complex. ❷ Stone faced terraces. ❸ Standing stone. ❹ Pavement made up of rectangular flat stones.

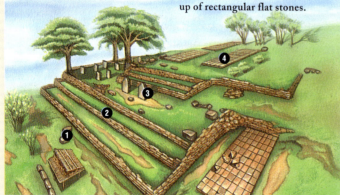

EARLY CLASSIC TERRACED S[ITES]

The terraced sanctuary forms a thre[ad] of continuity linking the prehistoric phase with the Indic, and also the e[arly] Islamic era. An important site in ce[ntral] Java is Kraton Ratu Boko ('King Bo[ko's] Palace'). The entrance to the comple[x is] erected on a plateau divided into th[ree] terraces ❶, ❷ and ❸. ❹ Two gatew[ays] with 5 doors and an upper one with [3] doors ❺ give access to an upper leve[l] with remains of a pool ❻, a structur[e] perhaps meant for burnt offerings ❼ and pillar bases for wooden roofs ❽

metres high, comprises five terraces, the largest of which measures 28 x 40 metres. Gunung Padang is unusual because it utilises thousands of blocks of basalt, either naturally columnar-formed or intentionally split. Excavations on the site in 1982 by Dra. Bintarti of the National Research Centre for Archaeology uncovered plain earthenware pottery. No evidence of burials has been discovered. The site was probably a centre of worship in which the monoliths were identified as containers for the souls of the ancestors.

The site is aligned along a northwest-southeast axis, apparently determined by local topography. No attempt to orient it toward a compass direction or significant visible landmarks such as Mt. Karuhan ('Mount of the Ancestors') is discernible. Gunung Padang seems to have escaped disturbance by recent occupation, unlike other terraced sites in Java where Islamic graves have been erected or where ceremonial activities are still conducted.

Other important *punden berundak* in west Java include Arca Domas, with nine terraces, also located in the Badui area; and Lemah Duhur, with five terraces at 1,000 metres above sea level. Although some recent graves have been erected here, the site seems otherwise well preserved

Other areas where *punden berundak* are well-developed include east Java, Bali, south Sulawesi, south Sumatra, and Nias. In South Sumatra's Pasemah region, Dr. Haris Sukendar recognised a type called 'terrace graves', a combination of *punden berundak* and burials which may be preIslamic. In Nias, terraced structures and menhirs are still used.

Terraced Sites of the Late Classic Period

Later Classic-period sites based on the *punden berundak* are found on numerous Javanese mountains, including Lawu, Muria, Penanggungan,

Arjuna, Welirang and Argapura. Almost all of these examples were in use between AD 1000 and 1500. Dr. Hariani Santiko has questioned the assumption that these structures descend from prehistoric roots, suggesting that they may instead be symbols of Mount Sumeru. It may be possible to reconcile the two interpretations; for the Javanese Mt Sumeru could easily have been incorporated into pre-existing belief in sacred mountains.

Balinese *punden berundak* are numerous. Major sites include Penebel, Tenganan, Selulung, Kintamani and Sembiran. Miniature *punden berundak* which are still used in contemporary worship can also be found in two *pura dalem* in Sanur. One of Bali's most important temples, Pura Besakih, can be seen as a *punden berundak*.

The major problem for scholars interested in understanding the symbolism of the Indonesian *punden berundak* and its influence on historic architecture is that of dating. No early (i.e. proto-historic) dates have yet been confirmed for any component of a *punden berundak*. This obstacle must be surmounted for research to make further progress. At present it is impossible to chart the stages in the evolution of this form of landscape architecture during its lifetime of over 2,000 years.

(Above left) Candi Ceto, a terraced temple site on the slopes of Mount Lawu, Central Java. (Right) Remains of a terraced site on Mount Argapura.

(Below) An intricately carved stone relief from Candi Sukuh, Central Java.

LATE CLASSIC TERRACED SITES
The most famous terraced monument of the Late Classic period is Candi Sukuh on the slopes of Mount Lawu, Central Java. This complex consists of three terraces ❶, ❷ and ❸ the largest of which supports ❹ a truncated pyramid. Inscriptions found on *garuda* statues date the site to the mid-15th century ❺.

TERRACED SITES OF THE INDONESIAN ARCHIPELAGO

■ within a wide area
◆ mountain sites

TERRACED SITES IN INDONESIA
❶ Nias: terraced structures (*aerosali*) with menhirs (*behu*) are still used for village meetings and new structures are built for burials.
❷ Pasemah: 'terrace graves' — a combination of pre-Islamic *punden berundak* and burial.
❸ West Java (Badui): Gunung Padang, Arca Domas, Lemah Duhur and Kosala. The terraces at Gunung Padang are complemented by alignments of standing monoliths, a mortar and grinding stones.
❹ Mount Lawu: Candi Sukuh and Candi Ceto.
❺ Mount Welirang.
❻ Mount Argapura.
❼ Bali: Penebel, Tenganan, Selulung, Kintamani, Sembiran and Besakih.
❽ Mount Muria.
❾ Mount Penanggungan: over 80 sites have been identified.
❿ South Sulawesi.

Brick Temples of Sumatra

Sumatran architects of the Classical era largely eschewed the use of stone. The only surviving examples of their work are executed in brick. In Sumatra's damp climate and rank vegetation, this material has deteriorated severely. Human action has been even more destructive than natural forces and has caused the disappearance of an unknown but surely appreciable number of structures.

(Above) One of the restored temples at Muara Jambi.

Brick structures at Palembang

I-Ching, a Chinese Buddhist monk who visited Sriwijaya in the late 7th century, mentioned that large Buddhist monasteries were established in Sumatra; a 14th-century Chinese traveller reported that Palembang possessed many brick pagodas. Today, little evidence of these remains: 7th-century inscriptions, Buddhist statuary and votive tablets have been found at Palembang, but no brick monuments survive. However, at Geding Sura, east of the modern city, a royal Muslim graveyard occupies a site with at least six foundations of brick structures with decorations resembling that of 14th-century Java. At Temple II, the bricks encase an older structure of stone, while at nearby Candi Angsoka, now also a Muslim grave site, fragments of a Classical temple including terracotta *kala* and lion heads have been found.

Research in the 1980s at Seguntang Hill, west of the city, led to the discovery of scattered bricks of an ancient type. Some are rectangular, but others have curved sides suggesting that they once formed parts of stupa. As early as 1930, the Dutch archaeologist F. D. K. Bosch recorded that many brick fragments were found while noting that Candi Angsoka and Seguntang Hill had been quarried for brick by the local Public Works Department for several years.

Excavations at Tanahabang, upstream from Palembang, which began in 1991, have uncovered foundations of nine brick *candi*. These structures probably date from the 9th to 10th centuries and were Sivaitic, as indicated by numerous statue fragments. The site is contemporaneous with the golden age of Sriwijaya and may well have been within that kingdom's sphere of influence. Other architectural sites in the Sumatran hinterland have been discovered at Muara Takus, Padang Lawas, Batusangkar and Sungai Langsat. These can be dated by associated statuary, inscriptions and various other means, to the 12th to 14th centuries,

MUARA TAKUS

At Muara Takus, the main surviving monument is a tall slender stupa, Candi Mahligai. This is flanked by other stupa foundations which were restored in the 1980s. All were made of brick with some stone decorations. The site can be dated, from short inscriptions, to the 11th to 12th centuries. The complex was originally enclosed within a brick wall, 74 metres square, and an earthen rampart over two kilometres long, which was open on one side. Some of the bricks from this wall were inscribed with religious diagrams.

❶ Candi Tua
❷ Candi Bungsu
❸ Candi Mahligai
❹ Candi Palangka
❺ One metre high brick wall
❻ Monasteries
❼ Earthen wall rampart
❽ Brick platform
❾ Kampar river
❿ Village houses
⓫ Unidentified feature
⓬ Brick foundation

The brick structures have been restored to different degrees. The locations of the monastery and village are merely suggested; there is no archaeological evidence for their existence.

INDONESIA'S CLASSICAL HERITAGE

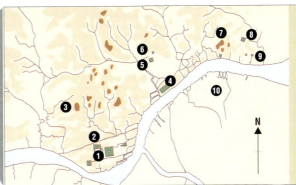

when Sriwijaya had been eclipsed by the kingdom of Melayu. Only Sungai Langsat, however, can be definitely linked to Melayu.

Muara Takus
Several structures at the largest stupa complex of Muara Takus, probably dating from the 11th century, bear indications that they were enlarged at a period subsequent to their original construction which suggests a relatively long period of use.

Bricks from the complex's walls are inscribed with religious diagrams which included *mandala*-like patterns (squares, circles or triangles with images or symbols of deities). *Vajra* (thunderbolt) motifs were also used; this indicates the popularity of esoteric Vajrayana Buddhism in both Sumatra and Java during the Middle Classic era.

Padang Lawas
At Padang Lawas, at least 25 brick temple complexes are spread over an area of 100 square kilometres. The shrines were largely devoted to esoteric Buddhism, and were built between the 11th and 13th centuries. Three of the shrines used the term *bahal* in their names: in Nepal, this word denotes two-storeyed temples of the Vajrayana school. The ruins at Padang Lawas provide no evidence that the area ever supported a dense population. Probably these sites owed their existence to their location at strategic nodes on inland trade routes.

Muara Jambi
Muara Jambi, which probably dates from the 11th to 13th centuries, is the only site in Sumatra where relatively well-preserved Classic period brick structures can be correlated with historical data. Melayu, which had already existed by the early 7th century, had its political and cultural centre along the Batanghari River. By about 1080, Melayu succeeded Sriwijaya as the dominant polity in Sumatra. The site at Muara Jambi consists of 12 structures, parts of which still stand, and at least 21 unexcavated mounds of brick and soil. The structures were all Buddhist shrines.

Other Sumatran sites
More brick foundations were found in the 1970s at Kota Cina and Tanjung Anom in north Sumatra. These were associated with both Hindu and Buddhist statuary. Kota Cina was an active maritime trading centre in the 12th and 13th centuries, as is indicated by large amounts of broken Chinese ceramics. Tanjung Anom was briefly occupied in the 14th and 15th centuries.

(Left) A brick from the wall surrounding Muara Takus inscribed with mandala diagrams and vajra symbols.

(Above left) The temple ruins at Pulo.

(Above right) Ornamental frieze of dancing figures, from the base of Bahal I, Padang Lawas.

Candi Mahligai, a brick and sandstone stupa, has the unusual form of a tower rather than the bell-shape which typifies Buddhist architecture.

(Below) Candi Biaro Bahal III, Padang Lawas, Sumatra. This 12th-century structure has been much restored.

Artificial Caves and Rock-cut Temples

The ascetic hermit living in a cave was a highly respected figure in ancient Indonesia. In the 14th-century court of Majapahit three principal religious groups were acknowledged: the Hindus, the Buddhists and the rsi or ascetic hermits. Hinduism and Buddhism also held hermits in high esteem; the gods themselves were envisioned as living in caves on Mount Meru. Cave and mountain symbolism forms a continuous thread running through Indonesian art and architecture from prehistory to the contemporary period.

(Right top) Goa Gajah is famous for the demonic head which overhangs the entrance to the cave. Some have argued that this face really depicts the witch Calon Arang of Balinese mythology.

(Right below) A kala head depicted on the gateway to the Selomangleng cave in East Java. Two artificial caves in the East Java area have the name Selomangleng. One is located near modern Kediri; and this one is located about 50 kilometres further south, near Tulungagung.

(Right) Candi at Gunung Kawi. This set of five temple façades are similar to Javanese temples of the 9th century but may have been carved in the 11th century.

(Below right) The cloister of Gunung Kawi consists of a central building with a rectangular plan, a gallery and a set of chambers, all carved from solid rock. In addition, a large number of niches possibly meant for meditation stretches away downstream.

Sumatra

In north Sumatra, small artificial caves called *batu umang* (*batu* = 'rock', *umang* = 'fairy') pose an enigma. Local legend assigns responsibility for their creation to non-human agents. One site at Lau Garut, in the hinterland of the Karo area, is flanked by carvings of ships. The ship often functions as a symbol of the journey of the soul after death, and north Sumatrans traditionally deposited the bones of their ancestors in ossuaries. The chambers in *batu umang* are usually of small dimensions, perhaps two metres long, one metre wide and of similar height. They may have served either as ossuaries or as meditation locations.

Kalimantan

In east Kalimantan a group of natural caves at Mount Kombeng, Muara Kaman, were found to contain a number of statues of Hindu deities. They resemble Javanese sculptures of the 8th and 9th centuries. It has not yet been established whether the images were actively worshipped in the caves, or whether they were merely deposited there for safe-keeping.

Central Java

Central Java, the centre of architectural development during the early Classic, contains a number of cave sites. A group of three natural caves on a small island in the middle of Telaga Warna, 'Coloured Lake', on the Dieng Plateau, near Candi Bima, are now in use as meditation spots. One of these was associated with an inscription from the early 13th century. This inscription, the only one dating after 919 to be found in central Java, has given rise to a number of unsolved questions regarding the continued use of sites in this region after the transfer of the centre of Javanese civilisation to east Java.

In August 1979 a survey team formed by the chief of Donorejo village, Purworejo Regency, discovered a pair of 22 carat gold statues in the

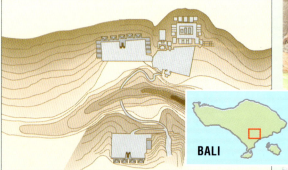

GUNUNG KAWI, BALI

Gunung Kawi, 'Poet Mountain', is situated in a deep limestone gorge on the banks of the sacred Pakerisan River. This site consists of meditation chambers, a hermitage or cloister, and huge temple façades. An inscription over one of these façades reads 'haji lumah ing jalu', 'the king buried in Jalu'; it has been argued that this refers to King Anak Wungsu (1050-1077), brother of King Airlangga of Java. In the base of each of these façades is a niche into which once fitted a stone deposit box like those found in the pits beneath Javanese temples. These have all been looted.

Seplawan limestone hills. The statues were found about 500 metres from the cave's mouth, on an 'altar' or natural flat surface about four metres above the cave floor. They were accompanied by other objects of gold and semi-precious stones, bronze and silver urns, ladles, crowns and seeds, possibly of millet. The statues portray a male holding a female's right hand with his left. Both wear cloth decorated with floral designs, are sheltered by parasols, and have halos behind their heads.

Royal gardens in 18th-century Java, at Taman Sari, Yogyakarta, and Sunyaragi, Cirebon, included numerous complex artificial caves. This analogy may help to explain the existence of artificial caves at the Ratu Boko site, on the Siva Plateau overlooking the plain in which lie the major early Classic temple complexes of Lara Jonggrang, Sewu and Plaosan.

East Java

East Java possesses three major artificial caves. Two have the same name: Selomangleng; the third, named Bottle Cave, lies near the summit of Mount Penanggungan, a peak which played an extremely important role in Javanese society for a period of 500 years. Bottle Cave is not large, but a terracotta horse's head in Majapahit style found inside it, plus its location near the mountain's summit, imply that the cave was important to the practice of the ascetics who constructed it.

Bali

The use of religious structures hewn from solid rock was most elaborated in Bali. One of the best-known sites is Goa Gajah, 'Elephant Cave'. This site may have been mentioned in the 14th-century *Nagarakrtagama* poem of the Majapahit court, which refers to a Mahayana Buddhist sanctuary there. It is possible however that the poem actually refers to another complex of ruins located a few metres away; some boulders fallen into the bed of a stream bear carvings of stupas.

An artist's rendering of the building of Gunung Kawi during the late 10th century. The first two candis on the left of the cliff were probably carved first and the remaining three were completed at a later date. Debris from the site was dumped into the Pakerisan river.

Conservation and Reconstruction

To restore or not to restore? This has been a question which historians and architects have hotly debated for over a hundred years. In the 1920s, when government-supported restoration of Indonesian historical monuments was debated, there were three schools of thought. One advocated the stabilisation of monuments, for one could never be sure that a restoration of monuments to their 'original glory' was accurate. The second school wanted to embellish the restorations and make the buildings look as good as new partly in order to attract the tourists who were already beginning to visit Southeast Asia. The third school emerged victorious. Their motto was moderation, their goal to create a scientific mode of restoration in which reconstruction would take place only when firm data existed to guide the hand of the restorer.

(Top) One of the temple in the Lara Jonggrang complex, Prambanan, Central Java.

»»Restoration workers collecting the scattered pieces of stone around the site and gather them together in a section of the compound where the stone will be divided into their respective groups.

The Early Restorers

The first restorations of Indonesian monuments were carried out by the Indonesian monarchs themselves. The 1365 poem Nagarakrtagama mentions that King Hayam Wuruk of Majapahit gave funds to restore old collapsed religious structures. Archaeological evidence of ancient reconstruction is found at many Javanese and Sumatran sites. Borobudur, Kalasan, Sewu and the Mahligai stupa of Muara Takus are only a few examples.

The Latter Conservators

C.G.C. Reinwardt established a commission to identify, collect and conserve ancient artifacts in 1822. In the middle years of the 19th century slow progress was made in studying ancient Indonesian buildings. In 1840 a regulation called for a list of antiquities to be made. In 1855 a law required that any discoveries of objects of potential antiquarian value had to be reported to the government. In 1885 J.W. Ijzerman, a railway engineer, established the Archaeological Association of Yogyakarta. That same year he discovered the hidden foot of Borobudur; he also cleared temple rooms at Prambanan.

Ijzerman's successor, Groneman, cleared more of Prambanan. In 1889 he had all loose stones from the site piled up in one spot, but kept no record of where they originated from. A Dutch scholar later called this "archaeological murder on a grand scale". Other Dutch scholars negatively compared the situation in Indonesia with the achievements of the French in Indochina. In 1901 a Commission in Netherlands India for Archaeological Research on Java and Madura was formed. This Commission inaugurated the first official restorations of Indonesian monuments. Its work was continued after 1913 by the Archaeological Service. After independence, in the mid-1970's a separate department called the Directorate for the Conservation and Protection of the National Heritage, under the Directorate General of Culture, was established for this purpose.

One of the Commission's first acts was to restore the sites of Pawon and Mendut, near Borobudur. In 1907 Borobudur became the

EARLY IMPRESSIONS OF ANCIENT RUINS
Some European artists of the 19th century delighted in depicting ancient Javanese ruins in a romantic style which often exaggerated their size and proportion. (From below left, clockwise): Ruins at a Central Javanese temple, Candi Sewu; Candi Lara Jonggrang, gateway at Borobudur; ruins at Arca Domas, *dwarapala* at the entrance leading to Borobudur; and ruins at Macan Putih.

INDONESIA'S CLASSICAL HERITAGE

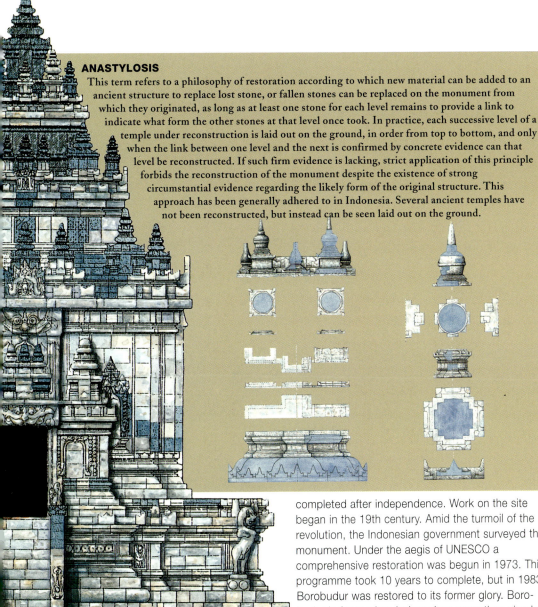

ANASTYLOSIS
This term refers to a philosophy of restoration according to which new material can be added to an ancient structure to replace lost stone, or fallen stones can be replaced on the monument from which they originated, as long as at least one stone for each level remains to provide a link to indicate what form the other stones at that level once took. In practice, each successive level of a temple under reconstruction is laid out on the ground, in order from top to bottom, and only when the link between one level and the next is confirmed by concrete evidence can that level be reconstructed. If such firm evidence is lacking, strict application of this principle forbids the reconstruction of the monument despite the existence of strong circumstantial evidence regarding the likely form of the original structure. This approach has been generally adhered to in Indonesia. Several ancient temples have not been reconstructed, but instead can be seen laid out on the ground.

(Above) The caryatid lion motif found on one of the temples in the Candi Ngawen complex. The complex originally consisted of three main shrines dedicated to the worship of the Hindu Trinity gods: Siva, Visnu and Brahma.

« A reconstruction drawing of Candi Ngawen by Perquinn, 1927. The stones coloured in blue represented the missing blocks.

object of a four-year project. In 1915 to 1918 a few important structures at the Panataran complex in East Java were rebuilt.

In the late 1920s and 1930s a number of important restoration projects were conducted: Kalasan (1926-1929), Ngawen II (1925-1927), Badut (1925-1926), Merak (partially restored; 1925-1926), Sari (1929-1930), and a subsidiary temple of Sewu (1928).

In the 1930s work slowed down, principally because of the Depression. Nevertheless work continued at Mt. Penanggungan, where Kendalisodo was completed in 1936-1939. Candi Gebang was rebuilt during the same period. At Candi Jawi, the foot and upper portion were reconstructed separately in 1938, but as the connection between them could not be found, the two parts lay side by side for decades. At an early Islamic shrine, Sendang Duwur, a gateway was restored in 1939-1940.

At Prambanan, one of the side chapels was restored in 1930-33 while the Siva Temple was only completed on 20 December 1953. The Brahma and Visnu temples were completed in the 1980s.

The restoration of Borobudur is an excellent example of a conservation project which began during the colonial era but was expanded and completed after independence. Work on the site began in the 19th century. Amid the turmoil of the revolution, the Indonesian government surveyed the monument. Under the aegis of UNESCO a comprehensive restoration was begun in 1973. This programme took 10 years to complete, but in 1983 Borobudur was restored to its former glory. Borobudur is for modern Indonesians more than simply a monument of outstanding historical interest; it is a *pusaka*, an artifact of great cultural significance.

The Indonesian government has assigned a high priority to conservation and restoration of ancient monuments. At the close of the 20th century many important sites from the Classic, Islamic and colonial periods in central Java have been reconstructed. Much work has also been conducted on other islands at such sites as Padang Lawas, Muara Jambi and Muara Takus, Sumatra; and in the islands of the eastern archipelago, including mosques and colonial forts in Maluku and Sulawesi. Indonesian scholars have exploited new technical innovations and materials which enable them to execute much more elaborate restorations than were possible during the colonial era. Indonesian experts are now called upon to participate in restoration projects in other countries, the most recent example being at Angkor in Cambodia.

(Below top) Candi Mendut before restoration.
(Bottom) The site of the Lara Jonggrang complex was scattered with stone blocks which came from the 400 shrines in the complex.

(Above) Masjid Agung, the Grand Mosque in Yogyakarta, Central Java.

(Left) A mosque in the Padang area, West Sumatra. The multi-tiered roof is a quintessential feature of Indonesian Islamic architecture. In front of the mosque stands a Minangkabau rice-barn — typically traditional building types continued to coexist alongside new architectural forms.

(Top right) Traditionally, gra… were situated in close proxim… the houses of the living in mar… parts of the Archipelago.

(Middle right) The palace of t… Raja of Goa, Makassar. In ce… to the kraton of Java, with th… complexes of courtyards, gar… and pavilions, palaces in som… of Indonesia were often no m… than enlarged and more opule… versions of ordinary houses.

(Below) The Grand Mosque in Banda Aceh was designed by an Italian architect and built by the Dutch between 1879-1881 to replace the earlier Masjid Agung, which was destroyed during the Aceh Wars. Whereas the original structure featured a multi-tiered roof, the new version, with its onion-shaped domes, is clearly modelled on Moghul Indian architecture.

CITIES, MOSQUES AND PALACES

(above) The palace of the Sultan of Kutai, east [Kali]mantan. The Norwegian explorer and [adv]enturer, Carl Bock, described the Sultan's [pala]ce in 1879 as "a large square, wooden [buil]ding, approached through a long covered [cour]tyard, with two openings for doorways [a]nd covered with corrugated galvanized [ir]on roof". He added that it "looked for all [th]e world like a Methodist chapel".

Our oldest concrete evidence for these three important architectural phenomena dates from the early Islamic period. The waning influence of Majapahit in the late 15th century was balanced by the ascendancy of Islamic polities in Indonesia, most notably the powerful Muslim state of Demak which gained control over many ports along the northern coastline of Java. The new religion introduced a novel building type, namely the mosque, and with it, the cemetery. Islam expressly forbids cremation which had been the principal means of disposing its dead during the Classic era. No doubt there were other architectural innovations at this time — for example, in the design of palaces and the layout of cities — but the scanty remains from the Majapahit capital at Trowulan makes it difficult to assess these changes.

Islam spread through the Archipelago by assimilation, trade and military conquest. Initially the coastal areas were the main centres of Islamic influence. It was not until the 17th century that the greater part of the Archipelago came under Muslim control. The gradual spread of Islam does not seem to have greatly affected the vernacular architecture of the region and traditional house types conforming to a basic Austronesian morphology continued to coexist alongside new architectural forms in much of the Archipelago.

Muslim trading ports formed the principal focus of architectural innovation and urban development at this time; elsewhere, agrarian communities continued to conform to the mandala-type spatial arrangement of the Hindu-Buddhist era. The extent to which the royal palaces, or *kraton*, of the early Islamic period followed the conventions of the Majapahit era is uncertain in that little historical evidence remains from this time — present-day palaces in Yogyakarta, Surakarta, Cirebon, Deli, Ternate and other parts of the Archipelago are not more than about 200 years old. Nevertheless, it seems likely that many traditional elements are preserved, even in these later structures, at least in terms of layout and the arrangement of space. While the mosque replaced the *candi* as the focal point of religious life, traditional construction techniques and design concepts continued to be employed. The location of the tomb of a founding father behind the mosque reveals the survival of an ancient Austronesian tradition of reverence for one's ancestors, as does the idea of placing a cemetery on top of a hill as at Imogiri in Java and also in Gorontaro. The enclosure of the mosque within a walled precinct, on the other hand, stems from Indonesia's Hindu-Buddhist past.

The Genesis of an Urban Tradition

The emergence of an urban way of life marks an important transition in the history of Indonesian architecture. Given that the vernacular architecture of the region consists largely of wooden structures, it is by no means easy to pinpoint a precise date for this event.

(Top right) A early 19th-century watercolour painting of the river port at Banjarmasin, Kalimantan.
(Right) A 1905 map showing the territorial boundaries of the Balinese kingdoms.

(Below) The ports in the vicinity of modern Banda Aceh for centuries formed important links between India and other coastal ports of the Indonesian Archipelago.

Linguistic Evidence

Geographer Paul Wheatley has linked the emergence of an urban tradition in Southeast Asia to the time when the term *negara* (from Sanskrit *nagara*, signifying both the residence of the ruler and the area under his control) first began to be widely used in the region. According to Wheatley, the inception of urbanism in Southeast Asia was due to foreign influences from India and China. However, more recent theories of urbanisation have attributed responsibility for the complex of social, economic and demographic patterns associated with the city to indigenous factors.

The present-day meaning of *negara* in Bahasa Indonesia is 'state' or 'nation'. According to the *Nawanatya*, a 14th-century book of court etiquette composed in the kingdom of Majapahit, it described a situation whereby one could reach a neighbouring settlement without having to cross irrigated rice fields or other types of farm land. The implication is that a number of interconnected settlements existed, possibly separated from the agricultural community and perhaps representing a discrete and integrated social unit. The semantic shift in the meaning of the

term *negara* towards the concept of statehood may have reflected an incorporation of these village conglomerates into a larger polity.

The term *kota*, and its cognates *khita* or *kuta*, also provide us with important evidence of the early urbanisation. Hindi in derivation, *kota* originally described a walled settlement or fort, but subsequently came to designate an urban centre, and now embraces the concept of the city or metropolis.

In Malaysia, the Persian word *bandar*, 'legalised trading port', is used to translate the English word

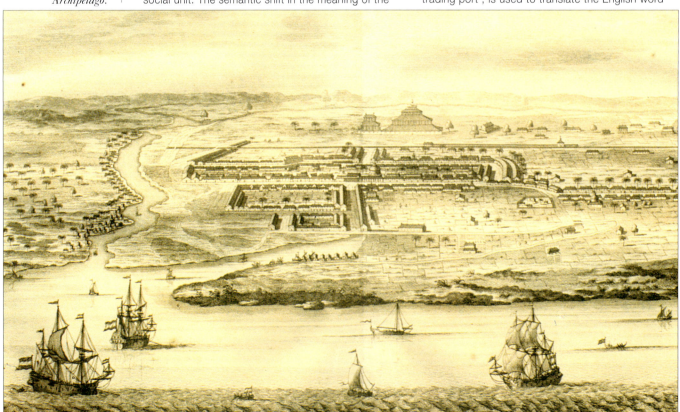

'city'. Linguistics would therefore seem to suggest at least two different antecedents for the modern pattern of urban life: the fort and the port.

Evidence of Early Cities

The oldest evidence of large densely-populated areas in Indonesia, where a multitude of economic, religious and administrative activities were conducted, dates only as far back as the late 11th century AD. It must be concluded that the earliest Indonesian kingdoms, such as Tarumanegara and Mataram in Java, Kutai in Kalimantan, and Sriwijaya in Sumatra, were capable of ruling large areas and constructing large monuments such as Borobudur without requiring the settlement pattern associated with urbanisation. This is not unprecedented. Other centres of important development such as the Khmer of Angkor (Cambodia) also seem to have succeeded in establishing civilisations without the need for cities. Large ceremonial complexes require large labour forces, but like Angkor they were probably built by mobilising the rural population during the slack seasons of the agricultural cycle.

When cities did arise in the early second millennium AD, they seem to have been of two types: the trading port with access to international maritime routes, and the administrative centre of prosperous agrarian zones. Densely-populated ports may have existed much earlier, as in the case of Sriwijaya/Palembang. The *Ying-yai Sheng-lan*, a Chinese account of the early 15th century, states that at Palembang, "Only the dwellings of the highest officers are on the banks of the river, the people live scattered about on bamboo rafts tied to a root of a tree or a post, moving on the tidal stream". Evidence for such impermanent 'settlements' will be extremely difficult to recover, due to the fact that their remains are buried deeply under alluvial sediment.

Muslims from the Near East, India and even China, probably made up a significant proportion of early urban populations in the region. Muslim quarters were important constituents of early Indonesian cities, especially in Java. Islam encouraged the growth of cities wherever it spread. These immigrants from China and the Indian Ocean probably played a crucial role in the emergence of urban settlement patterns in Indonesia.

The Trading Port

Another factor which no doubt led to the growth of the first true cities in Indonesia was the general expansion of Asian maritime trade in the 13th and 14th centuries. Geographically, Indonesia was strategically placed. It also provided many important commodities, especially pepper, cloves, nutmeg and a wide variety of other local products. Indonesians had been the main carriers of this trade since the beginning of the first millennium AD, and they continued in this capacity until the Europeans arrived on the scene in the 16th century.

The Agrarian Polity

By the 14th century, at least one other type of urban site had also emerged: the hinterland administrative centre. This type of site is as yet represented by a single known example: Trowulan, the likely capital of Majapahit, east Java. It was actually linked to maritime trade despite its location several days' journey from the coast. Unfortunately we do not possess detailed knowledge of the spatial layout of any early Indonesian city.

The main reason for Trowulan's existence, however, was probably due to its dual role as the administrative centre of Indonesia's largest ancient kingdom and as producer of textiles and a wide range of manufactured items of clay and metal for local consumption. It was probably in reference to Trowulan that the citation for the 14th-century *Nawanatya* was written. It is impossible to settle the debate regarding the origin of the later Javanese royal capitals, or to analyse the importance of design versus unplanned growth in their evolution. The search for answers to these question remains an important challenge.

(Above) A bronze temple lamp uncovered in Kota Cina, 'Chinese fortified settlement', a busy port of the 12th-13th centuries, north Sumatra.

(Left) Timber houses raised on stilts were probably a common feature of early Indonesian trading centres.

(Bottom) Homes like these, built on floating bamboo rafts are probably very similar to the type of dwellings which can be found crowding the mouth and tributaries of the Musi river during the height of Sriwijaya's suzerainty.

Architecture of the Early Islamic Period

When Islam arrived in Indonesia, it did not cause a revolution in building styles. Instead, the architecture of the transitional period (14th-16th centuries) reflected new ideas and influences from a variety of sources but retained fundamental traits from previous eras. Just as Indian ideas had been filtered through an Indonesian screen, so too with Islam and its attendant architectural forms.

The Banten minaret has a gateway derived from the Classic candi *grafted onto a tower of Moghul Indian pattern.*

↗ *The* menara *at Kudus, a pre-Islamic brick temple, which has been converted into a drumtower.*

The Advent of Islam

Islam did not take Indonesia by storm, but spread gradually during the 14th and 15th centuries, and it was largely confined to ports in Aceh and northeast Sumatra and along the northern coastline of Java. Few Indic monuments had been built in this coastal zone, so there was little geographical overlap between old and new traditions in the earliest phase of Islamic architecture. However one prominent example of a structure which may have been built in the Classical style and then converted for use in the services of Islam is the Kudus Tower. Although it is unknown whether this building was originally erected by Hindus or early Muslims, the structure clearly incorporates a number of Indic elements such as niches for statues.

Continuities of Form and Decoration

Examples of architectural forms developed in the Late Classic which strongly influenced early Islamic architecture include multi-tiered roofs, two types of ceremonial gateway — the split portal and the lintel gate — and a variety of decorative elements such as elaborate clay finials for roof peaks (usually termed *memolo* or *mustoko*). The wing motif which appears on early Islamic gateways is probably derived both from late preIslamic references to Garuda, in connection with his search for the elixir of immortality, and earlier Indic *makara* shapes. Similarly, the theme of a hermit's pavilion set on a mountain side, which appears in early Islamic palaces (the Kasepuhan at Cirebon) and tombs (Sendang Duwur), can readily be linked to the theme of Mount Meru as the home of the gods. No doubt many other continuities between the Hindu-Buddhist and early Islamic periods once existed, but much of the architecture of this period was executed in wood. No pre-Islamic examples have survived while only a few early Islamic structures are still extant.

The Oldest Islamic Structures

Although the Great Mosque of Demak is generally considered the oldest mosque in Indonesia, it is by no means certain this is the most ancient structure in the region erected by a Muslim architect. The honour may belong instead to parts of the Kasepuhan, or 'Elder', royal palace in Cirebon. A chronogram on a gateway leading to the *sitinggil* (a raised area at the northern end of the palace complex where rulers held audiences) can be read as the Saka equivalent of AD 1454. Although there is some evidence that Sivaite Hindu statues were once associated with this structure, tradition asserts that the rulers of Cirebon had already converted to Islam by the mid-15th century. The early Islamic palaces retain many features of pre-Islamic architecture. The Kasepuhan palace is particularly interesting because it was probably begun in the late pre-Islamic period, and continued

AN EARLY ISLAMIC PALACE
The layout of the Kasepuhan palace conforms to that of most other Javanese *kraton*: the palace faces a public square (*alun-alun*), with a great mosque on the west and a marketplace on the north. The Kasepuhan planners may have been the first to establish this configuration, although it might have already existed elsewhere in the preIslamic period. No pre-Islamic Indonesian palaces have yet been reconstructed.

1. Sitinggil
2. Provisions house
3. Gapura
4. New gate
5. Prayer house
6. Drum house
7. Carriage house
8. Sripenganti
9. Tunjuk
10. Pendopo Jinem
11. Small prayer house
12. Pendopo
13. Jinem ardem
14. Palace wall

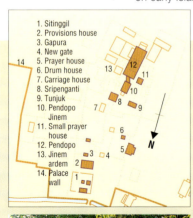

(Extreme left) Gateway to the sitinggil, *dated AD 1454 by a chronogram.*

(Left) Gateway to Pendopo Jinem symbolising the entrance to a hermit cave.

(Above) The megamendung *(clouds and rain) motifs on Cirebonese batik reflect Chinese influence. Similar details can be found on the Kasepuhan gateway (left).*

CITIES, MOSQUES AND PALACES

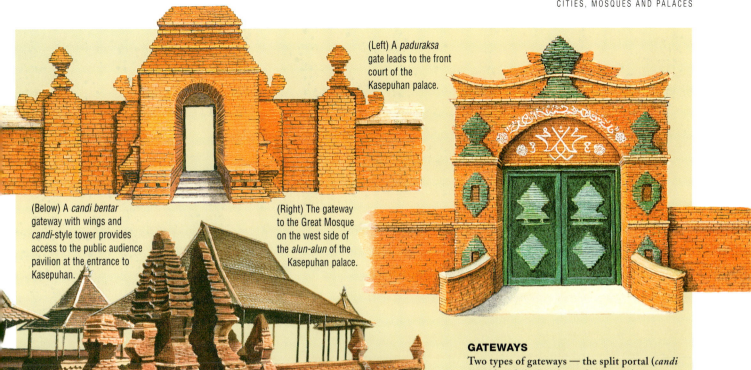

(Left) A *paduraksa* gate leads to the front court of the Kasepuhan palace.

(Below) A *candi bentar* gateway with wings and *candi*-style tower provides access to the public audience pavilion at the entrance to Kasepuhan.

(Right) The gateway to the Great Mosque on the west side of the *alun-alun* of the Kasepuhan palace.

GATEWAYS
Two types of gateways — the split portal (*candi bentar*) and the lintel gate (*paduraksa*) were adopted from Late Classic architecture by early Islamic architects.

to grow during the entire transitional era. The complex thus contains clues to the stages of the process through which Islam gradually become incorporated into Indonesian architecture.

Hermit Caves and Floating Pavilions

The history of the older parts of the Kasepuhan complex is not well documented, but the unique style of the main entrance to the residential part of the palace compound provides some clues that its probable date of construction was perhaps not long after the *sitinggil* in the mid-15th century. The entrance façade is covered with white plaster reminiscent of the *vajralepa* or 'diamond plaster' used on pre-Islamic Javanese temples. It is intended to represent a hermit's cave on a mountain side, an idea which is communicated by a combination of symbolic devices. The most striking of these is the motif called *megamendung* (lit. 'clouds and rain') which also occurs in local batik. *Megamendung* motifs are found both above the doorway and next to its foot, indicating that the entire edifice should be conceived as floating on clouds or standing on the upper slopes of Mount Meru; the curved corners framing the gateway are a stylistic convention to symbolise that the door is the entrance to a cave. In front of the door stands a miniature mountain approximately 50 centimetres high, constructed of brick and covered with unpainted plaster. This medium is also used in the Cirebon palace gardens to represent a rocky mountainous landscape. Like the cloud pattern, this decorative technique can be traced to Chinese antecedents. The doorway was probably constructed at some time during the Ming dynasty (1368-1643). Porcelain tiles inserted in the gate and other parts of the palace complex date from a later period, after the introduction of Dutch influence. These may have replaced older ceramics; most of the plates in the façade of the Kudus Tower date from Dutch times, except for one 15th-century Vietnamese plate which may be part of the original structure. Vietnamese wall tiles are also found on the front of the Masjid Demak.

Fragments of similar tiles have been discovered at Trowulan, probable site of the capital of Majapahit. Their use may reflect Islamic influence inspired by the decorative wall tiles used in many early Islamic structures in west and central Asia. Next to the Kasepuhan palace are the remains of an ornamental garden, the Pakungwati. One of the principal features of this unrestored garden is a Sumur Upas (poison well). A similarly-named well is found at the site of the Kedaton (Place of the Lord) at Trowulan. Although no firm evidence exists, it seems possible that in both instances, water drawn from the well was used for the Indonesian ritual of sealing oaths by drinking 'imprecation water'.

JAVA

(Above) *Ceramic plates are inserted as decorations on the walls of the pavilion in the* sitinggil *of the Kanoman palace in Cirebon, West Java.*

«*Ceramic objects such as this blue and white colonial-period plate can be found on the walls of the* menara *of the mosque in Kudus. They served to emulate the Islamic tiles that can be found in central Asian mosques.*

87

Early Muslim Places of Worship

Active trade links between Southeast Asia and the Near East date back to at least the 5th century. The teachings of the 7th-century prophet Muhammad only became implanted in the Indonesian Archipelago in the late 13th century, probably after the decisive conquest of much of India by Muslims. The exterior forms of the early Javanese mosques clearly reveal a debt to pre-Islamic Indonesian architectural forms.

The minaret in Banten, West Java.

(Above) A simplified version of the multi-tiered roof used for meru *towers in modern Balinese temples was adopted by early Muslim architects in Indonesia.*

(Below) The royal mosque on the west side of the alun-alun *at Yogyakarta exemplifies the character of the traditional Indonesian mosque.*

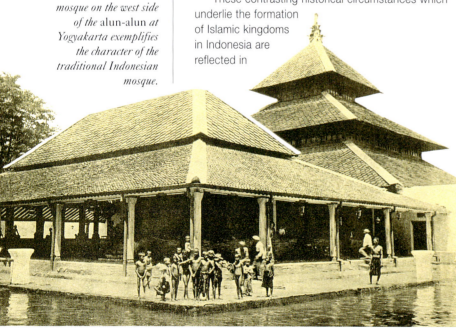

The Emergence of Islamic Kingdoms

Traveller's reports indicate that Muslims resided in the northwestern part of Sumatra as early as AD 674, although there is no evidence that large scale conversions took place at that time. Between the late 13th and mid-15th centuries Islam spread along the Malacca Straits to Java and beyond, giving rise to the first independent Islamic kingdoms in Indonesia.

The spread of Islam through the Indonesian Archipelago can be divided into three distinct historical processes, each linked to a different pattern of development. The establishment of early Islamic states in north Sumatra reflected the emergence of entirely new polities rather than the subjugation or conversion of existing kingdoms. In Java, however, Muslim rulers succeeded to the political power base of Hindu kings. The new political elite did not completely revolutionise the ideology nor the outward symbolic displays of the older rulers; rather, they maintained a high degree of continuity with the past while consolidating the transfer of power and extending the dominion of the earlier Hindu polities. Finally, in eastern Indonesia (Borneo, Sulawesi and Maluku) where established rulers simply converted to Islam, there was no significant change in the state's constitution.

These contrasting historical circumstances which underlie the formation of Islamic kingdoms in Indonesia are reflected in architectural differences between different parts of the Archipelago. In Sumatra, mosques do not occupy a significant position in terms of their spatial relation to the palace of the ruler; rather, the mosque itself provides the focus for a wider area which includes the palace complex. In Java, on the other hand, there is a strong relationship between mosque and the ruler's palace, even when they are located some distance away from each other. This is particularly significant in the case of great mosques (*masjid agung*) of Java which are situated within, or attached to, the palace complex. In Sulawesi, however, conversion to Islam may have simply involved the appropriation of existing religious buildings to serve as mosques.

Early Mosques

It is unfortunate that none of the earliest Islamic structures in Sumatra survived. This is in contrast to Java where several early Islamic buildings still remain, many of them in their original condition.

During the Classical Era, centres of Hindu and Buddhist thought and innovation existed in various parts of Indonesia, particularly in Sumatra and Java, but Islamic learning came from overseas, most notably Persia, Transoxiana, and India, at the height of Sufism. In these circumstances, it is perhaps not surprising that many indigenous and Hindu-Buddhist architectural elements continued to persist in buildings of the early Islamic period. This heterogeneity of influences makes Islamic architecture in Indonesia interesting to study.

Influences from the pre-Islamic era are clearly evident in many Islamic buildings in Indonesia, from Java to Sumatra, Nusa Tenggara and Maluku. This common architectural heritage reflects the close

MINARETS

The minaret was not originally an integral part of the Indonesian mosque. The great mosque at Demak, for example, employs a very simple structure of recent origin for this purpose, while the Kudus tower is not used as a minaret, but rather is the place where the *bedug* — a huge drum which in Indonesia is beaten as a preamble to the summons to prayer — is kept. Indeed, the Kudus tower may originally have been constructed expressly for this purpose. Drumtowers called *kul-kul* are integral components of contemporary Balinese temples. One *kul-kul*, at the Pura Penataran Sasih at Pejeng, contains a bronze drum approximately 2,000 years old. This suggests that these towers may be of prehistoric Indonesian origin, kept alive through the Hindu-Buddhist period and persisting in the Islamic era of Indonesian civilisation.

CITIES, MOSQUES AND PALACES

*A stone plaque on Mantingan mosque near Jepara. It depicts a hermitage with a pavilion (*pendopo*) and split gateways (*candi bentar*).*

cemeteries are another common element of these mosques as is also the case for the earliest great mosques in Sulawesi and Kalimantan. The formal appearance of the latter, however, differs markedly from early mosques in other parts of Indonesia due to the singular manner in which Islam was introduced to these areas, namely by proselytisation and conversion of the rulers.

Soko Tunggal and *Soko Guru*

The multi-tiered roofs of early Indonesian mosques continue a roof-building tradition used in religious buildings of the pre-Islamic period, as can be seen from east Javanese temple reliefs of the 13th and 14th centuries. The *meru* roof found in Balinese temples today descends from the same era. The origin of the style is unknown; it may be much older than the 13th century. The basic idea of the *meru* roof is the same as the multi-storeyed pagodas of north Asian Buddhist structures, adapted to a timber medium of construction.

The principal architectural device in the *meru* roof is the group of four pillars, known in Javanese as *soko guru*, which support the uppermost tier of the roof in one continuous sweep from the ground level. This method of construction requires the availability of very large trees. It was, however, a custom in Java to make the pillar on the northeast, of smaller pieces of wood held together with metal bands; this pillar is called the *soko tatal*. The symbolism of this practice is unknown.

A second form of structure adopted for some early mosques is the *soko tunggal* (*tunggal* = sole, solitary). As the name implies, the roof in this type of structure is supported by a single central pillar. Its origin would seem to be the smaller structures found in east Javanese temple reliefs, perhaps used for meditation by small groups or individual ascetics. Examples of such structures are found in the Kraton Kasepuhan; the grave of Sunan Bonang, Tuban, east Java; and a small village mosque near Yogyakarta.

political relationship that existed between Muslim rulers in these areas. Shared features include the tripartite division of buildings into a base, main body and superstructure; centralised plans; multi-tiered roofs; an outer colonnade or peristyle; an additional terrace at the front of the building; a walled courtyard with entrance gate; minarets; and an associated cemetery within the mosque precincts or at least in close proximity.

Most of the earliest mosques in Java, from the great mosques in palace complexes to humble village mosques, typically include several, if not all, of these features, particularly the employment of a double or triple tiered roof, while the earliest mosques in Sumatra also share many of the same attributes. Contemporary mosques from Nusa Tenggara and Maluku, however, lack a peristyle, terrace, courtyard and gate, but retain the multi-tiered roof and centralised ground plan of Javanese mosques. Integrated

«« A mosque in Surabaya with twin minarets.

The soko tunggal *of a mosque in central Java.*

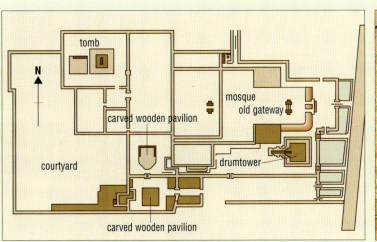

MASJID KUDUS
Beside and behind the Kudus mosque, which was largely rebuilt in the 20th century, is a series of walled courtyards and gateways, remnants of an earlier set of structures which can only be partially reconstructed. At Kudus the main cemetery is associated with the royal mosque, as is also the case at Banten, but there is no fixed association between mosques and tombs.

Palace and City

The term kraton *(the Javanese word for palace) refers to the seat of the ruler (*ratu *— at the level of king or prince), and is widely used in many parts of Indonesia including Sumatra, Java, Kalimantan, Sumbawa, Sulawesi and Maluku.* Kraton *have played an important role in the political symbolism of the state. In Java, for example, the* kraton, *rather than the territory, defined a kingdom's geographical image.*

The gateway to the north entrance to the palace of Surakarta. The alun-alun *to the north is traditionally a place where persons who wish to settle unresolved differences would gather in the shade while they wait to see the ruler.*

Centre and Periphery

The ultimate authority in the *kraton* rested with the Sultan (or *Susuhunan*, 'Exalted One', in Surakarta), who was believed to possess a cosmic energy known as *wahyu* (heaven sent fortune). The possession of this quality was reflected in the fertility of land and the absence of natural disasters. In this scheme of things, power, both spiritual and temporal, was conceived as being located at the centre, becoming more diffuse towards the periphery. During the period of the Islamic kingdom of Mataram's rule over central Java (16th-18th centuries), a distinction was made between an 'inner' and an 'outer' world, constituted respectively, by the palace (often referred to as the *dalem*, 'inside') on the one hand, and the surrounding fields and forests, on the other. The inner world was identified with all that is civilised, refined and sacred, while the outer world was conceived as wild, rough and profane: power, like purity, resided at the centre, within the walls of the palace complex.

Sacred Mountains and Axial Layouts

In Java, the layout of the *kraton* precincts and surrounding town was determined by cosmological precepts. The ground plan constituted a spatial metaphor for the spiritual and temporal authority of the ruler, and state ceremonies, which were closely linked to this geography, reinforced these ideas. Most *kraton* and their associated towns and cities are located on a plain served by at least one river and its tributaries. In Java, Sumatra, Sumbawa and Ternate, the *kraton* is typically backed by a sacred mountain. In Java this relationship between *kraton* and mountain was emphasised by positioning all the buildings in the palace complex on an axis with this sacred mountain.

The Surakarta *Kraton* and City

The *kraton*, its public squares (*alun-alun*), state mosque and market place have all played a fundamental role in defining the topography and character of Indonesian towns. At the centre lay the palace precincts with the *alun-alun* providing a place for public gatherings, state ceremonies, and recreational activities. The mosque was the centre of religious life and also served as a judiciary in matters of religious significance. The market place provided the economic focus of the community, with specialist markets defining the character of the local economy and 'weekly' market days (according to the Javanese five day cycle) setting the pattern for commerce and trade. These elements established a distinctive urban infrastructure the influence of which continues to be felt to this day.

THE BALINESE PALACE

Balinese palaces resembled the *kraton* of Java in some respects, particularly the reliance on the pavilion as a common built form, but differed significantly in other ways. For example, where the Javanese palaces were built along a north-south axis, the Balinese palaces were approximately square in plan, a symmetry which stemmed from the express intention of constructing palaces according to mandalas described in architectural manuals such as the *Hasta Kosali*. These manuals may have been derived from 14th-century Java, but were modified by the Balinese over time.

The layout of Ubud was one of the most symmetrical of Indonesian palaces. Eight courtyards delineated by walls surrounded a ninth at the centre, which was where the king lived. Each of the other courts had a specific function. For example, the courtyard to the northeast corner was devoted to religious structures, while the public audience hall was to the northwest. The latter was built as a *bale kambang* (floating pavilion).

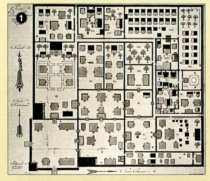

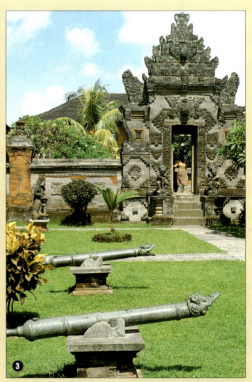

❶ *Layout of the former palace of Denpasar.*
❷ *A pendapa in the Lingsar garden, Cakranegara palace on West Lombok.*
❸ *The Bali museum in Denpasar.*

CITIES, MOSQUES AND PALACES

1. northern *alun-alun*
2. Pagelaran gate
3. *sitinggil*
4. Brojonolo gate
5. Mandungan courtyard
6. Ponconiti pavilion
7. Srimanganti gate
8. Trajumas pavilion
9. Srimanganti pavilion
10. Donopratopo gateway
11. Plataran courtyard
12. Kencono pavilion
13. Proboyekso pavilion
14. Manis pavilion
15. Sultan's quarters
16. Gedong Kuning

THE YOGYAKARTA *KRATON*
Although the *kraton* is the seat of royal power, many *kraton* are not particularly imposing structures in terms of their scale and general appearance. The concept of power and sovereignty is expressed instead through ideas of order and alignment as exemplified in the cases of Yogyakarta and Surakarta.

Founded in 1756 by the first Sultan of Yogyakarta, Hamengkubuwono I, the Yogyakarta Kraton consists of a series of courtyards and gates which are aligned along a north-south axis drawn between Mount Merapi in the north and the Indian Ocean to the south. The *kraton* is centred on the main reception hall — the Kencono pavilion — which is the only building in the complex that faces east, all the others facing north or south. In this respect, the Kencono pavilion creates a second, east-west axis which fixes the palace complex in space, and indeed in relation to the universe as a whole.

The sea has an ambivalent status: on one hand, the treacherous waters of the Southern Ocean is conceived as a place of danger and death, but on the other hand, it is also the abode of the goddess Ratu Lara Kidul with whom the Sultan is said to be on intimate terms. These ideas are reflected in the way the palace is organised in spatial terms.

According to the sociologist Selo Soemardjan, Yogyakarta's city plan can be seen as a spatial metaphor for the social stratification of traditional Javanese society. The Sultan and his immediate family are situated at the centre, surrounded by the aristocracy who reside within the palace walls. Beyond this live those who have regular dealings with the court. Finally in the countryside, there lives the rural population.

The Mosque as a Sacred Space

Islam instructs believers that no material things should be considered sacred. The Qur'an contains few regulations regarding the form which mosques should take. Nevertheless, the architecture of the mosque encloses a space which believers consider hallowed. The physical aspects of early Indonesian mosques were determined by a combination of Islamic and indigenous ideas about the form which sacred buildings should take.

Elements of the Demak Mosque:
1. *mustoko/memo*
2. *multi-tiered roof*
3. *mihrab*
4. *soko guru tatal*
5. *soko guru*
6. *serambi*

The Basic Form of the Mosque
The mosque is conceived as a place where groups of people meet regularly to pray. It is the receptacle for the group prayer. In addition to being large enough to accommodate the local Muslim community, the mosque has to conform to a few other requirements. Its entrance must be on the side away from Mekkah; in Indonesia, this means on the east or southeast. The side opposite the entrance should be a wall with a mark giving the direction of the Ka'abah in Mekkah. This direction is called *kiblat*, and the marker is the *mihrab*. Worshippers in the mosque orient themselves with their heads in this direction, which in Indonesia is west-northwest.

The Qur'an contains no special instructions for the architectural form of the building itself. The Indonesian architects were free to interpret these basic requirements in accord with their own preexisting ideas. They had no exact indigenous parallels on which to draw; communal prayer in pre-Islamic Indonesia, if it existed, would have been conducted in open courtyards as it still is in Bali today. However we have no firm evidence that large public prayers were conducted in ancient Indonesia. No virtue was attributed to such acts; rather, the ideal was that individuals would meditate and pray in private, even in isolation. Thus the introduction of the mosque and the idea of large communal prayer groups were new in Indonesian society.

(Above) In Demak ancient wooden doors are ornately carved with makara-*like beasts and stupa-shaped silhouettes.*

(Below) Roof finial on a mosque, Gresik, East Java.
(Bottom) Stone plaques at Mantingan mosque, Jepara.

The Interior of the Mosque
Early Indonesian mosques were built of wood rather than brick or stone. Their designers drew upon millennia of experience and customs related to the use of this material. Imported influences had little or no role to play here. Although Islam came to Indonesia from the Near East, and the first indigenous Muslim communities included many people from South Asia and China, early mosque architecture in Indonesia emphasised certain basic local traditions.

The oldest surviving Indonesian mosques are quite large. They were in most cases closely associated with palaces. These large structures make especially prominent use of immense pillars to support their multi-storied roofs. Significantly pillars also play a prominent role in preIslamic Indonesian house construction. Palaces in early literature are sometimes glorified as having a thousand pillars. Special rituals are conducted in many parts of Indonesia when the main pillars of houses are erected. In western Sumba, the upper roof of the house is supported by four major columns like the *soko guru* of the early Javanese mosque, to which they are explicitly compared by Sumbanese builders. In Sumbanese rituals the front right-hand column at the centre of the house acts as a kind of conduit through which the power of the ancestral spirits is drawn from heaven to earth. In other parts of Indonesia such as Simalungun, north Sumatra, tradition states that slaves were placed alive into a

CITIES, MOSQUES AND PALACES

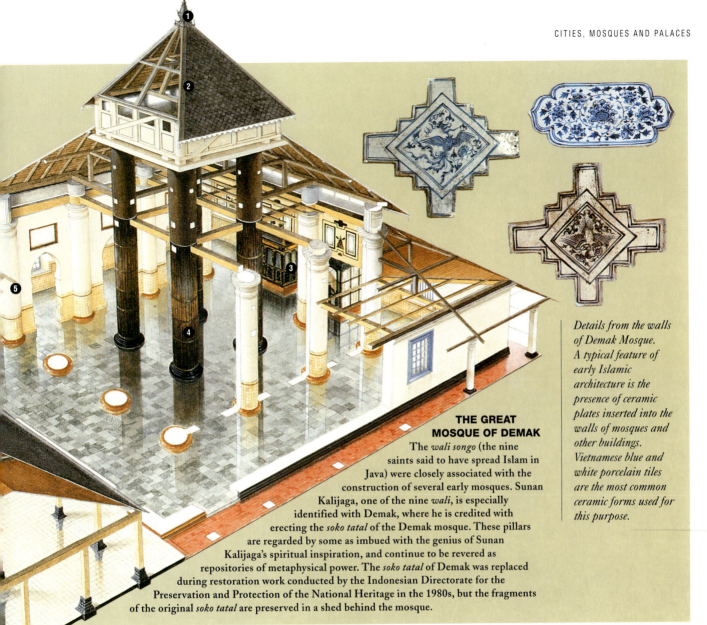

THE GREAT MOSQUE OF DEMAK

The *wali songo* (the nine saints said to have spread Islam in Java) were closely associated with the construction of several early mosques. Sunan Kalijaga, one of the nine *wali*, is especially identified with Demak, where he is credited with erecting the *soko tatal* of the Demak mosque. These pillars are regarded by some as imbued with the genius of Sunan Kalijaga's spiritual inspiration, and continue to be revered as repositories of metaphysical power. The *soko tatal* of Demak was replaced during restoration work conducted by the Indonesian Directorate for the Preservation and Protection of the National Heritage in the 1980s, but the fragments of the original *soko tatal* are preserved in a shed behind the mosque.

Details from the walls of Demak Mosque. A typical feature of early Islamic architecture is the presence of ceramic plates inserted into the walls of mosques and other buildings. Vietnamese blue and white porcelain tiles are the most common ceramic forms used for this purpose.

pit and then buried beneath the main house pillar in order to give it strength.

In Java, one of the most striking features of the interiors of the oldest mosques is the set of four huge pillars, *soko guru*. The northeastern pillar in several mosques is called the *soko tatal*, literally splintered pillar, and made of pieces of wood held together with metal bands. This pillar is located at the front right-hand side of the entrance, and thus corresponds to the special Sumbanese column.

Javanese tradition accords a direct role in the construction of several of the earliest mosques to the *wali songo*, the Nine Saints said to have spread Islam through Java. These *wali* are especially associated with the *soko tatal*. In the Great Mosque of the Kasepuhan Palace, Cirebon, the *soko tatal* is said to be the handiwork of Sunan Kalijaga.

The Exterior

Multi-tiered roofs date back to structures found in preIslamic temple reliefs, and are directly related to modern Balinese *meru*-roofs. The peaks of the mosques are decorated with pottery finials called *mustoko* or *memolo*. F.D.K. Bosch, a Dutch scholar, compared them to the *brahmamula*, container of the essence of divine unity in Hindu cosmogony.

The *serambi* (roofed porch) is another important addition to Indonesian mosques. These features are normally found on the east side, where the entrance is located. The exteriors of the east walls of the early mosques are in several instances decorated with elaborate ornamentation — at Mantingan, this consists of carved stone plaques. At Kudus, the *serambi* entirely encases an earlier brick gateway of *paduraksa* form.

Furthermore the earliest mosques had doors of double-leaf design, identical to those of pre-Islamic Javanese temples and modern Balinese residential quarters.

The kiblat *marker in Indonesian mosques often assumes greater architectural importance than is necessitated by the Qur'an. In many instances it is highly decorated. In Demak and Cirebon it is a deep cave-like recess large enough to receive a human. The Cirebon mihrab (left) is decorated with carved lotuses and other non-Islamic symbols such as a Majapahit-style sunburst and stylised* makara.

95

Regional Mosques: Tradition and Eclecticism

The oldest surviving mosques in Indonesia are found in Java. Javanese merchants and teachers were influential in spreading Islam to other parts of Indonesia, especially the eastern archipelago. Javanese influence was particularly strong in Maluku, due to the intensive spice trade. The multi-storied roof, commonly thought to have been a Javanese innovation, is found from Aceh to Ambon. Many local mosque-building traditions arose in Indonesia, however, some with little or no Javanese influence.

A general feature of mosque architecture is the decorative use of ceramics: the interior of the Masjid Jamik, Madura.

(Above) A map showing the spread of Islam throughout the Indonesian Archipelago.

Maluku

Islam came to Maluku in the late 15th century via Java. Its strongest impact was felt in the twin spice-growing islands of Ternate and Tidore. These small but wealthy islands, which had already been political rivals for centuries, became centres of Islamic societies. Ternate is dominated by the volcanic cone of Mount Gamalama. The Sultan's Mosque lies on the volcano's eastern slope, near the ancient harbour. According to legend a royal ancestor, Syek Jafar Sadek, is buried at the mountain's summit. Circumambulation of the mountain played an important part in the court rituals. The Sultan's Mosque was a prominent feature in the kingdom, and attracted the attention of many early European visitors. The mosque was completely restored in the 1970s. It stands on a masonry base, and has a five-tiered roof supported on 16 columns. Four main columns like *soko guru* support the uppermost roof at the corners, where it flares to a slightly reduced pitch. This feature is also found in mosques as far away as Palembang, Sumatra. Hooded rectangular openings between the tiers provide ventilation and light. This facility probably provided the tiered roof with a popularity quite separate from its symbolism.

An outer array of columns supports the lower edge of the second roof, and the upper edge of the third, by means of attached purlins. The lowest roof rests on the plastered brick perimeter walls. This feature is also found in many of the oldest Javanese mosques. Upper and lower edges of the intermediate roofs are supported by horizontal ties attached to the columns or walls. Some of the masonry base dates from the early 18th century, but comparison with 19th-century prints shows that the recently restored roof tiers are not as lofty as they once were. The mosque is associated with pools of water, now lined with cement. Worshippers must wash with pure water, *air wudlu*, before entering the mosque to pray and this requires the provision of pools of water near a mosque to serve such purposes. A uniquely Indonesian trait is the addition of an elaborate pool, such as that at Banten, with the most developed examples being found in Sumatra. The royal mosque of Tidore is similar to Ternate's in many respects,

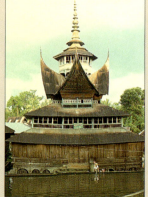

MINANGKABAU STYLE MOSQUES

Indonesian mosques often incorporate local features and elements in their design. In West Sumatra, mosques frequently employ the local Minangkabau 'horned' roof profile and are richly ornamented with traditional woodcarvings (above left). The same technique may also be employed for other Islamic structures such as this small *surau*, or prayer house, which is slightly less rich in appearance (above right). The mosque at Air Tiris (left) is a particularly good example of local carving skills with its intricately detailed wooden panels.

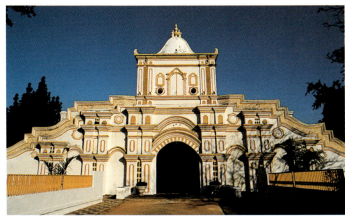

(Left) The gateway to the Masjid Raya in Sumenep, Madura, is a typical example of structures that exemplify Portuguese characteristics. Mosques in Sri Lanka have similar features.

(Below) Masjid Prasasti in Ambon — an example of an early Malukan mosque.

except the roof is simpler, though still supported by four principal columns. The associated octagonal pool is, however, of great interest. It is situated in a pavilion on the south side of the *serambi* and is supplied with water via a channel sculpted in the form of a *makara* which harks back to the symbolism of pre-Islamic Java.

Sumatra

The royal mosque of Aceh was a centre of armed resistance to the Dutch in the 1870s, and therefore was destroyed in battle. Early prints show it as a structure with wide hipped roofs similar to those of a mosque still standing in the 17th-century citadel of Sultan Iskandar Muda (1607-1636), at Indrapuri, 20 kilometres to the south. In west Sumatra, three- and five-tiered mosque roofs are supported on ranks of concentric columns, often focussing on a towering central support which reaches the apex of the building. Old mosques in Palembang, Banjarmasin and Pontianak in Kalimantan have similar roof designs and possibly are related to other examples from peninsular Malaysia. Some of these Minangkabau mosques are built on islands in artificial ponds, analogous to the *bale kambang*. In other examples, such as that at Air Tiris, the traditional elaboration of Sumatran woodcarving has been allowed full expression.

Near Eastern Influences

Domes, pointed arches and other surface embellishments, well-known features of Islamic architecture in central, south and southwest Asia, did not appear in Indonesia until the 19th century, when ironically they were introduced through Dutch influence over local rulers. Indonesian scholars gradually became familiar with these alien forms as they began to visit Islamic centres in Egypt and India. After the establishment of the Republic of Indonesia, many older mosques built in traditional style were renovated and small domes were added to their square hipped roofs. An example from eastern Ambon demonstrates a hybrid form which conserves some of the elegance of the original building. Probably it was built in imitation of similar modifications made to the main mosque in the regional capital nearby. Since the 1970s the appropriateness of traditional buildings has been politically acknowledged, and some layered hipped forms have been reinstated. President Soeharto contributed to this trend during the 1980s by instigating the Amal Bakti Muslim Pancasila Foundation which subsidised the erection of small mosques in less prosperous communities. The standardised design of these buildings includes three hipped roofs above a square prayer hall, with proportions reminiscent of the Great Mosque of Demak.

JAVANESE INFLUENCES

A main characteristic of early mosques in Sumatra and elsewhere in the Archipelago outside of the island of Java is the multi-tiered roof. Adopted as a common feature of mosques in Java, the form was used all over the Archipelago where a sizeable Muslim community was beginning to form in ports and other coastal cities. There was however no standard number of tiers or levels. This form of roof can be found in the mosque in Palembang and Padang in Sumatra (left top and bottom); and in Ternate, Maluku (above).

EUROPEAN-INDIAN FEATURES

Domes, pointed arches and other features representative of Near Eastern Islamic architecture began to make their presence felt with the coming of the Dutch. Examples include the mosques at Penyengat (left), Kotaraja (top) and Tanjung Pura (above).

Taman: an Earthly Paradise

The earliest Indonesian reference to a garden is found on a South Sumatran inscription of the late 7th century, from the site of Talang Tuwo, in which a ruler of Sriwijaya records the construction of a garden, and signifies his wish that the merit of this act be shared among all living creatures. Nothing of this early garden now remains.

Early Gardens
The oldest surviving gardens are those built by Javanese royalty and sultans namely Panembahan Krapyak, Sultan Agung of Mataram, Sultan Ageng Tirtyasa of Banten and Iskandar Tani of Aceh. A second, more recent group, dates from the middle of the 18th century: Sriwedari, c. 1743, Sunyaragi, c. 1741 and Taman Sari, c. 1758. Others, more recent (19th and 20th century) show that the rulers of Java, Bali and Lombok remained faithful to old tradition until the beginning of the Republican era.

(Below) The gunungan *(artificial rock-mountain) erected in Aceh in mid-17th century. Artificial mountains were standard features of many royal gardens in Indonesia.*

Gardens in Javanese Texts
Some of the most important insights regarding Indonesian perceptions of gardens can be obtained from ancient Javanese literature. Gardens appear in pre-Islamic texts as important scenes of action and symbols of a higher plane of existence in which humans, gods, and nature are united.

Gardens appear in all early Javanese literary genres, for instance, in the *wayang kulit*, where a garden named Sriwedari appears. In general, as the French scholar Denys Lombard concludes, the garden in Javanese thought juxtaposes symbols of two fundamental elements: earth and water. From these two complementary principles all the elements of garden design emanate.

(Above) The pool in the Narmada garden in West Lombok. After restoration, the garden has been turned into a tourist attraction and the pool is now used as a public swimming pool. The little house left of the pool shelters the sacred spring; the terraced hills symbolise the mountains.

Gardens of Java
In Cirebon, behind the main buildings of the Kasepuhan and Kanoman palaces, are found ruined gardens with artificial hills and pools. The site of Sunyaragi, outside the original city, consists of artificial hills with complicated interior passages, an artificial mountain (*gunungan*) with a seat for a sultan on top, and other labyrinthine structures. According to the Cirebon Chronicle, this garden was constructed in 1741.

The famous Taman Sari ('Perfumed Garden') was laid out during the time of the first Sultan of Yogyakarta, Hamengkubuwono I, who had built the first palace, in 1758. It comprises a series of courtyards organised on an east-west axis, and a series of pools. The largest, Segaran (literally 'sea')

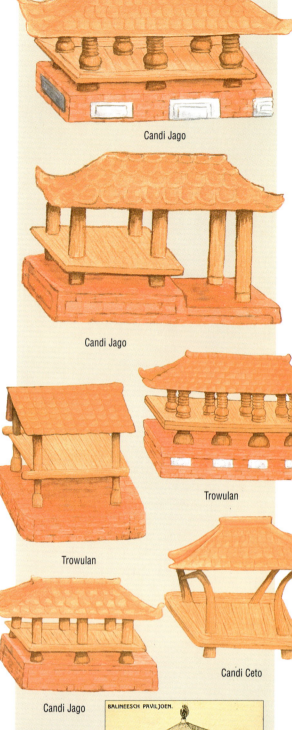

Candi Jago

Candi Jago

Trowulan

Trowulan

Candi Ceto

Candi Jago

PAVILIONS
Balai or *pendapa* could be designed as small highly decorated structures providing intimacy for courting couples, or as large areas providing space for public gatherings. Indonesian gardens made use of a mixture of pavilions of different types, distinguished by the number of their pillars and conformation of their roofs. Temple reliefs and literary sources of the 13th and 14th centuries from East Java prominently depict pavilions in the temple compounds and gardens.

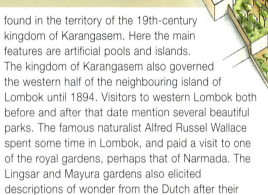

TAMAN SARI — 'PERFUMED GARDEN'
1. Segaran Pool
2. Keranga Island
3. Sumur Gumuling
4. Guards' Pavilion
5. Umbul Winangun
6. Gopok-gopok Building
7. West Gate
8. Gayitowati Pool

was enormous and contained an island with a multi-storied building on it. It could be reached either by boat or by two underwater passageways. One of these also led to an enigmatic cylindrical structure several stories high with internal galleries. The sultan sometimes sat in a tower in the midst of the Umbul Winangun, supposedly watching his wives bathe. Many courtyards were planted with decorative trees and flowers. In the Yogyakarta area other old garden residences built subsequently can also be found, at Ambarwinangun (in the west) and Ambarrukmo (east of the city).

The gardens of Java include the remains of Tasik Ardi ('Sea and Mountain') in Banten. The main features here are a large pool about 200 metres square, once lined with brick, in the midst of which is an artificial island where once stood a two-storey high stone pavillion and a landing for boats. It was probably built by Sultan Ageng who reigned during the second half of the 17th century.

Gardens Outside Java

Important gardens were also built in Sumatra, in particular the Taman Ghairah of Aceh, of the early 17th century, but little of it survives. Similar gardens are found in various parts of southern and southeastern Bali. The best known and preserved are found in the territory of the 19th-century kingdom of Karangasem. Here the main features are artificial pools and islands. The kingdom of Karangasem also governed the western half of the neighbouring island of Lombok until 1894. Visitors to western Lombok both before and after that date mention several beautiful parks. The famous naturalist Alfred Russel Wallace spent some time in Lombok, and paid a visit to one of the royal gardens, perhaps that of Narmada. The Lingsar and Mayura gardens also elicited descriptions of wonder from the Dutch after their conquest of the island.

The practice of garden building was mainly if not exclusively the province of royalty and, in the preIslamic period, of the Hindu and Buddhist religious establishments. With the disappearance of the nobility in 1945, the gardens themselves began to vanish too. Archaeologists have restored some, notably the Sunyaragi in Cirebon and Narmada and Mayura in Lombok. Perhaps others will be similarly rescued before all vestiges of them disappear.

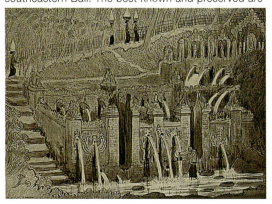

(Extreme left) An old document depicting a bathing place at Sawan, Bali.

(Left) The balai kambang *(floating pavilion) in the garden at Klungkung, Bali. The Hall of Justice is in the background.*

Muslim Tombs and Cemeteries

Conversion to Islam re-introduced funerary architecture to many parts of the Indonesian Archipelago in places where the prehistoric practice of interring the dead had long disappeared after several centuries of Hindu and Buddhist influence. In the the case of the latter religions, cremation is the preferred method of disposing of the dead, but the Muslim religion stipulates that the deceased should be buried in a grave or tomb (kubur or makam).

Burials and Islam

The customs associated with burial in orthodox Islam emphasise simplicity and equality of all people before God. Elaborate funerals and burial structures are expressly forbidden in the Qur'an. In reality, however, these injunctions against expending resources on monuments to the dead have often been disregarded. One of the world's greatest architectural treasures, the Taj Mahal in India, is an Islamic tomb. It is not surprising that similar compromises between religious purity and human preference were made in Indonesia. Political factors have often been responsible for the construction of monuments far in excess of what strict adherence to faith would allow.

The oldest traces of Islam in Indonesia are tombstones. Individual graves of Muslims dating from the period before the conversions of Indonesians have been found in Sumatra and Java; it is believed that these were isolated graves of foreign Muslim immigrants, probably traders; they were found in association with port sites in such places as Barus and Gresik. The earliest tombstone which is generally accepted as that of an Indonesian convert is that of Malik al-Saleh, ruler of the port of Samudra, on the north coast of Aceh, Sumatra. This king is mentioned by Marco Polo, who resided in Samudra for several months in 1293. A number of the earliest tombstones in Sumatra and Java were imported from Cambay, near Gujarat, northwestern India. This circumstance provides important evidence that the Gujarati merchants were one of the important sources for early Indonesian Islam. A particularly well-preserved example of this type of tomb is that of Malik Ibrahim, who died in 1419 in Gresik, east Java.

Tombs are sometimes located next to mosques, but there is no fixed rule about this. Often they are situated on vacant land outside the village. Graves are never found in Indonesian palaces.

Madurese tombstones form a local variant of early north coastal Javanese funerary art. Motifs in Madura and north Java are usually floral and very ornate.

The tomb of Malik Ibrahim, d. AD 1419, Gresik, was imported from Cambay, in Gujarat, Northwest India.

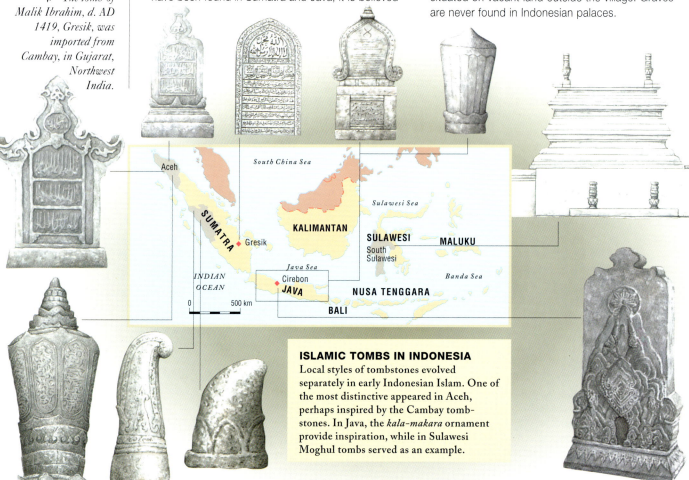

ISLAMIC TOMBS IN INDONESIA
Local styles of tombstones evolved separately in early Indonesian Islam. One of the most distinctive appeared in Aceh, perhaps inspired by the Cambay tombstones. In Java, the *kala-makara* ornament provide inspiration, while in Sulawesi Moghul tombs served as an example.

Indigenous Tombstones

The Cambayan form of tombstone did not become widespread in Indonesia. Instead, two indigenous designs provided the model for many of the earliest Muslim graves. One of these originated in Aceh, north Sumatra, and is usually known as the Batu Aceh (Acehnese stone). This type consists of several variants. One of the two most characteristic forms is the rectangular block imitating a building, inscribed with stylised Qur'anic verses and surmounted with projecting curved motifs often called 'wings'. The other common form is called the 'club'. This type of burial marker was used for people of consequence in Sumatra, the nearby islands of Riau, and the Malay Peninsula in the 15th through 17th centuries.

An Early Javanese Cemetery

The other main inspiration for early burial monuments was used in east Java by the late 14th century. The oldest evidence that a significant number of Javanese had been converted to Islam consists of a group of graves in the village of Tralaya. This site, near Trowulan, probably formed part of the huge capital of the kingdom of Majapahit, overlord of much of Indonesia during the 14th and 15th centuries. These graves have an outline inspired by the *kala-makara* ornament of earlier Classic-period Javanese art. One face of the stones is sculpted with Qur'anic verses; the other bears variations on a design based on the Majapahit sunburst motif. The stones bear no names, but they do have dates, which are given in Javanese numerals and the Javanese *Saka* era rather than the Islamic Hijrah era.

Neither the earliest Batu Aceh or the Tralaya tombs are associated with any other architectural remains. More elaborate burial complexes only began to evolve in the 16th century. Several of these large complexes are important pilgrimage sites.

The Wali Songo Group

The *wali songo* ('Nine Saints') are credited in Javanese popular belief with the conversion of Java to Islam. In reality the number nine is simply a figure traditionally invested with supernatural significance; the list of names accounted as being among the *wali* varies from place to place.

The important pilgrimage places among the tomb complexes include: Gunung Jati, near Cirebon; Kudus; Muria, near Semarang; Bonang, Tuban; Giri, near Surabaya; and Kalijaga.

The practice of *ziarah*, religious pilgrimage to a tomb of a holy man, is common in Indonesia. In Malay the term *keramat*, probably derived from the Arabic *keramah*, 'blessed, happy', is used to refer to the place itself which is the object of the pilgrimage. Orthodox Islam denies the possibility that the living may communicate with the dead or derive any benefits from praying to their souls, but does allow people to visit these tombs, honour them for the values which those buried there embodied, and meditate to instill in the living a firmer resolve to live a proper life. Traditional Javanese mysticism emphasises the possibility of unity of all sentient beings, and it is likely that some visitors harbour the ambition of achieving some form of mystical union with the spirit of the holy person.

The tomb complexes are sometimes built on flat ground, but others were erected on terraces cut into hillsides, in a manner derived from the preIslamic sanctuaries of the 14th and 15th centuries and prehistoric Indonesian traditions connected with invocations to the ancestors. Walls and gateways form important markers of areas with different levels of access. The layouts and some of the architectural motifs bear some similarities to Balinese temples.

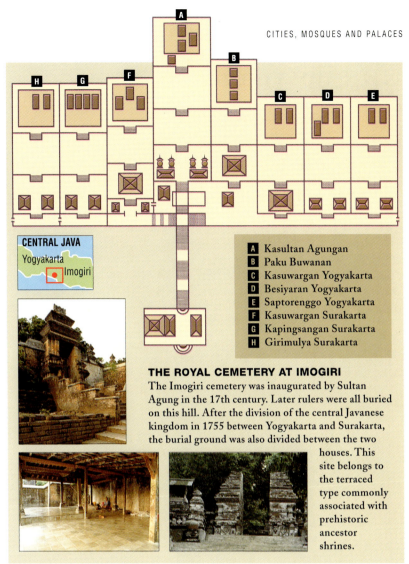

A Kasultan Agungan
B Paku Buwanan
C Kasuwargan Yogyakarta
D Besiyaran Yogyakarta
E Saptorenggo Yogyakarta
F Kasuwargan Surakarta
G Kapingsangan Surakarta
H Girimulya Surakarta

THE ROYAL CEMETERY AT IMOGIRI

The Imogiri cemetery was inaugurated by Sultan Agung in the 17th century. Later rulers were all buried on this hill. After the division of the central Javanese kingdom in 1755 between Yogyakarta and Surakarta, the burial ground was also divided between the two houses. This site belongs to the terraced type commonly associated with prehistoric ancestor shrines.

«« The oldest gravestones of Muslim Javanese are found at Tralaya, a village situated near Trowulan, the former capital of the 14th-15th century kingdom of Majapahit.

The sites of Sendang Duwur (left) and Tembayat are not accounted tombs of walis, but they are of particular artistic significance, and belong to the same general style and time period. The Sendang Duwur tomb complex in northeast Java, early 16th century, boasts a gateway famous for its exaggerated wing motifs or a paduraksa (lintel gateway).

Cities of the Pesisir

The pesisir, or north coast of Java, has historically presented a striking contrast to the society of the interior. Where the hinterland usually consisted of a strongly ritualised court with elaborate ceremonial architecture based upon the revenue from a dense agricultural population, the north coast has long been characterised by a series of cosmopolitan trading ports more outward looking than inward-centred. This difference in outlook resulted in constant tension and in the late 17th century the cruel Amangkurat destroyed many of these ports in order to consolidate his own power. The Dutch, however, stepped into the gap and during the Dutch colonial period a historiographic image of Java was constructed which concentrated solely on the hinterland courts. This is, however, an injustice as during the 14th through 16th centuries, the pesisir had already been a thoroughly Indonesian zone of development, characterised by a specific set of architectural manifestations.

(Top) The gateway to the Masjid Jamik in Sumenep, Madura. (Below) The Muslim mausoleum at Gresik, East Java.

Banten

This port in northwest Java became the most prosperous trading centre in the Archipelago after the fall of Demak in the mid-16th century. Banten had been a secondary port in the kingdom of Sunda Pajajaran when the Portuguese arrived in 1511, the main port being Sunda Kelapa, later renamed Jayakarta (modern Jakarta). A site 12 kilometres inland, Banten Girang ('Upstream Banten') shows that a fortified centre with access to Chinese, Thai and Vietnamese ceramics had existed since the 14th century. Perhaps Banten was already active at that time.

About 1527 Banten was seized by a Muslim force from Demak and Cirebon and became the centre of a new Islamic kingdom. After Demak's decline when its sultan died in 1546, Banten rapidly became the main connecting node which provided pepper and Malukan spices to the oceanic traffic going to India and China. Banten managed to hold its own against growing Dutch power in Jayakarta until 1682 when a civil war broke out and the Dutch intervened. For over a century Banten was a prosperous and powerful city, and the main urban centre where the new Islamic culture of Java evolved.

Early European attention to Banten ensured that it would be better documented than any other Indonesian city of this age. The city was laid out in accordance with precepts imported from Java rather than mirroring local Sundanese ideas. The city in 1596 housed roughly 100,000 people. It was walled, and transport within the city was mainly by water: rivers and canals. The area within the wall was divided into a northern and a southern half. Only Indonesians were allowed to live within the city wall; foreigners were located outside, with foreign Muslims on the northeast, foreign non-Muslims on the west, both along the shore. The northern section contained the residential compounds of the elite. One exception was the compound of the *shahbandar* or the harbour master, located on the eastern side of the *alun-alun*. On the south side was the palace, Surosowan; and on the west, the Grand Mosque.

Like other Javanese cities, Banten was dominated by a north-south axis. This ceremonial way began at the palace gate and ran along the side of the *alun-alun*, then across a river by a bridge and terminated at the river mouth. The internal structure of the city was marked by a division into residential quarters, each under the sway of a particular

(Above top) The multi-tiered roof of the Grand Mosque at Banten, West Java.

(Above) The tradition of carving intricate designs on the roof beams, pillars and walls of Kudus houses probably perpetuates a tradition developed in Indonesia much earlier.

CITIES, MOSQUES AND PALACES

A city plan of the Banten coastal port showing the location of the market, palace and mosque. The Banten mosque is represented as the largest structure in the entire city, on the west (right) side of the main square.

Fort Speelwijk was built after 1682 at the mouth of the Banten river.

nobleman. The foreign communities similarly each had their own leaders. A Dutch map of the city's site made in the late 19th century also shows the probable existence of quarters where the population engaged in a common craft such as pottery making.

Jayakarta
Modern-day Jakarta obtained its name when the Muslim forces from Demak and Cirebon captured the Hindu port of Sunda Kelapa in the early 16th century and renamed it Jayakarta, or 'Victory City'. The Tugu inscription and other archaeological evidence indicate that it may already have been an important centre as early as the 5th century. The city layout closely resembled Banten until it was conquered by the Dutch in 1619.

Semarang
The site of modern Semarang was occupied by the late pre-Islamic period. Although many artifacts such as statues of Hindu deities have been discovered, unfortunately no clear idea of the date of the site's first occupation can be established. It was an important centre by the time of the Zheng He voyages of the early 15th century, as indicated by the famous Gedung Batu temple there: an eclectic complex combining Javanese, Chinese and Islamic elements in honour of this Yunnanese Muslim eunuch admiral.

Demak, Kudus and Jepara
These neighbouring cities along the north coast of Java were all important trading ports in the early 16th century. Archaeological evidence suggests that all these cities were already occupied in the late pre-Islamic period, but more detailed information is not yet available. Archaeological surveys in the Rembang area show that Chinese porcelain of the 13th century is widespread in the area. This suggests that the region around Mount Muria was an important trading zone by Majapahit times. When Europeans arrived in the 16th century, Jepara in particular was a thriving port. It was, however, devastated by the callous Amangkurat of Mataram in the late 17th century during his campaign against the *pesisir* which he feared might break away and challenge his authority by becoming centres of commerce and political power.

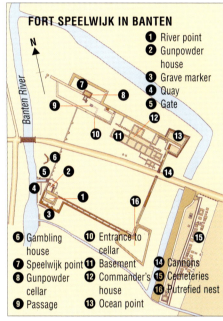

FORT SPEELWIJK IN BANTEN
1. River point
2. Gunpowder house
3. Grave marker
4. Quay
5. Gate
6. Gambling house
7. Speelwijk point
8. Gunpowder cellar
9. Passage
10. Entrance to cellar
11. Basement
12. Commander's house
13. Ocean point
14. Cannons
15. Cemeteries
16. Putrefied nest

BANTEN *TIYAMAH*
This building in 17th-century Dutch style was erected at the order of Sultan Haji of Banten and designed by a Dutchman, J.L. Cardeel, who converted to Islam, became a member of the Banten court with the title Pangeran Wiraguna, and designed this building which stands on the southwest side of the Grand Mosque. It is still used as a centre for Islamic education. Its name, *Tiyamah*, is Arabic.

"Batavia, formerly known as Jacatra, 5.600 miles away from Amsterdam and 12 miles from Bantam (Banten) in Java has been built by the Dutch and is considered impregnable, having resisted five sieges by the Javanese kings. Its roadstead is considered the safest in the world and therefore extraordinary because every morning at 10 o'clock, a south wind develops which conducts the boats into town; and in the evening at 10 o'clock a north wind develops which leads the boats back out into the sea. In this harbour all East Indian treasures of the Dutch company accumulate and 12,000 men along with 50 ships are always being maintained." (After publication by Homann Heirs Nuremberg).

ARCHITECTURE OF THE 17TH TO 19TH CENTURIES

Early Dutch settlements in the 17th century were generally *intra-muros* that is to say, within walled defences to protect them from attack by other European trade rivals and native revolt. The fort was both a military base and a centre of commerce and administration. It typically included a governor's residence, officers' quarters, barracks, warehouses, offices, a chapel or church, and the houses of European merchants. The fort was usually located along the waterfront of a coastal or riverine port that was the focus of mercantile activities and maritime trade.

As the Dutch became more securely established in the region, towns grew up beyond the walls of the fort. In the 18th century, the most important urban centres were Batavia, Semarang and Ujung Pandang. Over time, city centres became congested and wealthier merchants and other men of influence began to build their residences on the outskirts of town and in the surrounding countryside. One of the few surviving examples of these country houses is the National Archives building in Jakarta. This was formerly the home of Reiner de Klerk before he became the Dutch Governor General. Completed in 1760, the house is perfectly symmetrical and once had a large formal garden laid out in the European manner. Doors, windows and ornamentation also follow Dutch designs, but Indonesian and tropical influences can be discerned in the wide eaves and single hipped roof over the main part of the house.

Some Dutch buildings in Indonesia are entirely European in their conception, the Protestant Church in the old city centre of Semarang being one such example. Built between 1778 and 1814, the church is remarkable for its eclectic use of different classical elements. Especially noteworthy is the octagonal plan of the nave and surrounding arcade which are surmounted by a magnificent Byzantine dome or cupola; the main entrance is distinguished by a pedimented portico flanked by a pair of Baroque bell towers.

The 19th century saw a growing appreciation of indigenous architectural forms. The magnificent Tawang railway station in Semarang, which was built in 1864, provides an interesting example of a harmonious assimilation of eastern and western ideas. Although European classicism is the prevailing influence, a traditional Javanese element appears in the form of four columns supporting the domed central part of the hall. These draw their inspiration from the *soko guru*, or principal posts, which support the upper, pyramidal roof (*joglo*) of a traditional Javanese *pendapa*.

Map of Batavia in 1655.

Town Formation in 19th-Century Java

The ground plan of many Indonesian towns and cities, especially in Java, was originally laid down during the colonial era. Initially the Dutch and other European powers were content simply to establish fortified trading posts, but later, when the Dutch came to extend their rule over much of Java and other parts of the Archipelago, they tended to adapt themselves to the native model of urban settlement whose political symbolism, in relation to the palace of the ruler, they consciously exploited to endorse their own authority.

The Residency at Bojong (Semarang) in the 1880s.

By the time Batavia became the main VOC fort in Java, the Dutch had already established their presence in other parts of the Indonesian Archipelago. Fort Rotterdam was built at Makassar (now Ujung Pandang) by the Dutch in the 1670s. The fort became the centre of Dutch power in South Sulawesi.

Fortified Trading Settlements

A nation of seafarers and merchants, Holland established one of the first multinational companies, the Vereenigde Oost-Indische Compagnie (VOC), or Dutch East India Company in 1602, with a view to seizing control of the highly profitable spice trade in Asia. Trading posts were established in Maluku and Banda and exclusive commercial treaties negotiated with local rulers. Initially, Dutch settlements consisted simply of a warehouse and some basic accommodation for the chief merchant (*opperkoopsman*) and his staff, but turbulent relations with the native population and European rivals soon required fortification and a degree of self-sufficiency for these settlements.

In 1619, Batavia (previously named Jayakarta and Sunda Kelapa) became the VOC stronghold in the East and this signalled the arrival of the Dutch as a major political and economic presence in the Archipelago. Batavia competed successfully with other Javanese entrepôt city ports like Banten, Cirebon and Demak, and in the next 100 years the Dutch continued to establish strategic posts at Semarang, Surabaya and other locations.

The 19th-Century Colonial Town

At the end of the 18th century the Dutch East India Company suffered severe losses and eventually went

bankrupt owing to personal pocket lining by company officials. After a continuous spate of political changes that arose out of the Napoleonic Wars, the VOC administration of the Netherlands Indies was replaced by a colonial government answerable to Holland in 1800. Whereas VOC interests in the region had been purely commercial, the new colonial government was also seeking territorial power. A more systematic exploitation of the Archipelago was introduced which extended to inland regions as well as the coastal areas. Beginning in Java, the colonial administration introduced a system of residencies under the jurisdiction of a Dutch resident. These were subdivided into regencies governed by a *bupati* or local Javanese noble. With this system of indirect rule, the Dutch were able to exercise complete authority over the territories within their purview, allowing them to control both the population and the system of agricultural production.

During this period of the colonial era, there was a remarkable mixing of Indonesian and Dutch elements. This was largely due to the fact that the Dutch were far less concerned to impose their own culture and religion on the indigenous population than, for example, the Portuguese in their eastern colonies. This Dutch tolerance of local customs and beliefs is reflected in the town planning of 19th-century urban centres in Java, which clearly show a mixing of local and Western influences. Instead of building administrative centres based on Western principles, the Dutch were content to adhere to existing patterns in a conscious exploitation of traditional spatial models of power and authority. The town layout of the regency capitals, for example, are dominated by the *alun-alun*, or central square. Surrounded by the administrative buildings of the *bupati* and Dutch resident, and the mosque, this constituted the administrative and religious centre of the town. The *kabupaten*, or regent's seat, was situated on either the north or the south side of the square, its symmetrical axis coinciding with the

ARCHITECTURE OF THE 17TH TO 19TH CENTURIES

What began as small, fortified trading centres near existing native settlements grew into thriving urban centres with a town hall, church, hospital, jail and execution square augmenting the basic complement of warehouses, workshops and barracks. Subsequent additions included a paupers' hostel and orphanage which were typical features of Dutch towns back in Holland during this period.

❶ *Market in Buitenzorg (present-day Bogor).*
❷ *The Spin House, Batavia, where prostitutes were sent to spin yarn.*
❸ *The Children's Hospital, Batavia.*
❹ *Brick-making kiln.*
❺ *The Latin and Greek School, Batavia, 1662.*

(Below from left to right)
The Wilhelmina Pavilion in Batavia (present-day Jakarta).

1166 Java Street in Bandung, West Java.

Head office of the N.I.S Bodjong in Semarang, Central Java.

The Beer Hall in Surabaya, East Java.

north-south axis of the *alun alun*. The *lodji*, or resident's office (*lodji* is derived from *loge*, the Dutch word for residence), was normally located on the eastern side of the square, opposite the mosque. Other buildings commonly surrounding the *alun-alun* included the town prison. The formal arrangement of urban space and buildings was strengthened by the symmetrical placement of impressive banyan trees and small guard houses in relation to the north-south axis of the *kabupaten* and *alun-alun*.

The 19th-century administrative capitals which acquired their form under the Dutch colonial government are an urban expression of a balance of power between foreign and indigenous rule and of cultural tolerance on the part of the Dutch. The typical blend of Dutch and Indonesian elements which characterises 19th-century towns, particularly in Java, makes the 'Indies' town a remarkable phenomenon in colonial urban history.

Later Developments

The Indies town continued to exist after the abolition of the Cultuurstelsel, or Cultivation System, which operated between 1830 and 1870. This system of forced agricultural production under colonial government supervision was introduced to fill an empty treasury and resulted in the severe exploitation of the population of Java. The Cultivation System was eventually found to be untenable and was replaced by the Dutch parliament in 1870 by a new set of policies which opened up the colony to private enterprise.

New crops for the world export market, such as tobacco and coffee, boosted the emergence and development of plantation towns such as Banyumas, Bondowoso, Jember, Lumajang and Pasaruan, which rapidly grew into busy centres of agricultural production. Often plantations were situated miles away from the nearest town, so that the local Dutch club (*kamar bola* or *soos*) became an important feature of colonial life in these remote areas.

By the end of the 19th century, an elaborate system of administration and agricultural production had evolved, supported by hill stations which were established in cooler mountainous regions to serve as recreation centres for the European population who had their workplace in the blistering heat of the tropical lowlands.

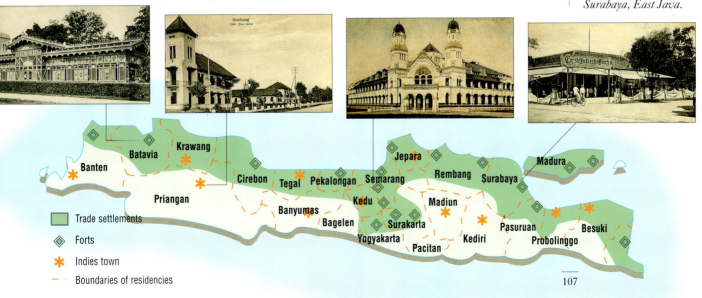

107

Batavia: the Realisation of an Ideal City

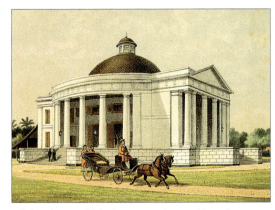

A unique feature of present-day Jakarta is the old quarter of Kota which displayed certain characteristics of an early 'planned' city in the Dutch Indies. The evolution of most towns is typically a fairly random process, representing a series of haphazard accretions, clustered round a modest nucleus. The building-up of Batavia, however, was achieved by strict adherence to a carefully planned layout. Within a period of forty years a complete, walled city was established on the northern coast of Java. By the 19th century, visitors of Batavia came to know it as the 'Queen of the East'.

»» *The Williams Church of the royal square, Batavia. Drawing taken from W.A. Van Rees's* Nederlandsch-Indie, *1881.*

An Ideal City

Following the siege of the Javanese city of Jayakarta (previously known as Sunda Kelapa) and its demolition by the Dutch in 1619, it was decided to build the headquarters of the Dutch East India Company (Vereenigde Oost-Indische Compagnie, or VOC) on the site. Simon Stevin, a prominent 17th-century mathematician, scientist and advisor to the Dutch Prince Maurits, was commissioned to design a comprehensive plan for the future settlement based on his concept of the 'ideal city'. His response was a rectangular, walled town, bisected by the river Ciliwung which was to be channelled into a straight canal. This layout can still be clearly recognised today on either side of the Kali Besar. The fortress represented the centre of power and main focal point of the city to which the street plan and housing blocks were related. The townhall, markets and other public buildings and civic institutions were distributed, for the most part, in accordance with Stevin's ideal model. Around 1730, Batavia grew into a wealthy metropolis with some 20,000 townspeople of various nationalities within the wall and another 100,000 outside.

The Surrounding Countryside

With Batavia properly established as a fortified centre of trade and commerce, the Dutch turned their attention to the surrounding countryside which they explored and subsequently developed for the cultivation of sugar and later coffee. Wealthy merchants began to buy land outside the city walls and build themselves country residences, ranging from simple dwellings built of local materials to grandiose mansions in the European manner. Canals, like the Molenvliet, were constructed to irrigate the

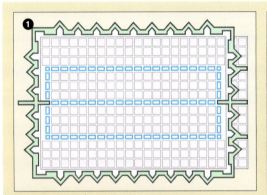

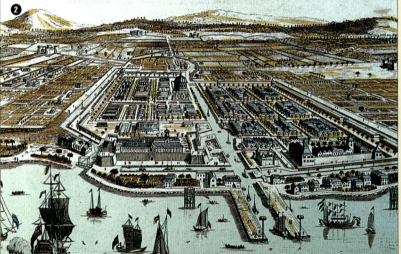

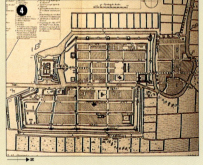

BATAVIA: THE FIRST 100 YEARS
The development of Batavia, from its early beginnings as a fortified settlement with a rudimentary street plan, to the realisation of Stevin's master plan can be traced through a series of contemporary maps and views of the city.
❶ The ideal city of Simon Stevin, with its grid-like layout of streets and canals reflects a burgeoning spirit of scientific rationalism which manifested itself in Europe during the early 17th century. ❷ The grid plan of Simon Stevin's ideal city is clearly discernible in this 17th-century impression of Batavia. ❸ The siege of Batavia in 1629 when Javanese troops surrounded the city. The fortress is still under construction and the Ciliwung River has yet to be turned into a canal.
❹ Early 18th century plan of Batavia from Henri Chatelain's *Atlas Historique*, which was published in Amsterdam between 1705 and 1720.

ARCHITECTURE OF THE 17TH TO 19TH CENTURIES

(Left) The old City Hall (Stadhuis) of Batavia, now Taman Fatahillah, was completed in 1710 and inaugurated by Governor-General Abraham van Riebeeck on 10 July of the same year. This building was built over the site of the demolished second City Hall of Batavia. The plan was drawn by W.J. van der Velde and the structure was built by chief carpenter J. Kemmer.

land, facilitate the transport of agricultural produce and to drive the watermills that operated the sugar presses. A protective circuit of five fortresses was also built to defend outlying areas from Javanese attack. Several outstanding country estates were also built during this period. Some extant examples include the famous Reiner de Klerk House on the east side of Jalan Gajah Mada. It was built around 1760 and represents a unique example of an almost wholly European-style building in tropical Southeast Asia (see p. 112). In contrast, the Japan house, near Palemerah, represents a contemporary but contrary design concept which takes the Javanese *pendapa* as a starting point.

The Early 19th Century

At the beginning of the 19th century, when the VOC was liquidated and the Dutch government took over its assets, it was decided to quit the by then dilapidated and unhealthy Kota and build a new town centre further inland, near the estate of Weltevreden, now the district of Lapangan Banteng and Medan Merdeka. New government offices, military quarters and the residences of more affluent Batavians were built there, a number of which have survived as striking examples of a specifically Indonesian Neo-classical style from the 19th century. Batavia had thus become a city with two centres: Kota remained the hub of business, where the offices and warehouses of shipping and trading companies were located, while Weltevreden provided a new home for the government, military, the well-to-do and a growing number of shops. These two centres were connected by the Molenvliet Canal and a road which ran alongside it, now Jalan Gajah Mada.

Urban Expansion

It was not until the end of the 19th century that any significant changes in Batavia took place. The abolition of the Cultuurstelsel, or forced cultivation system, in 1870, made way for the rapid development of private enterprise in the Dutch Indies. Numerous trading companies and financial institutions established themselves in Java. For the most part they settled in Batavia and opened their offices in Kota, typically along, or near, Kali Besar. These private companies owned or managed plantations, oil fields and mines. International trade with Europe and other parts of the world boomed, and the corresponding increase in the volume of shipping led to the construction of a new harbour at Tanjung Priok between 1877 and 1883.

A direct consequence of these expanding commercial activities was the immigration of large numbers of Dutch employees and their families. At the same time, many rural Javanese left their *kampung* homes and moved to the city to find work. This resulted in a great demand for housing and land prices soared. New houses were often built closely packed together with *kampung* settlements filling the spaces in between. This feverish burst of development and building, with little regard for the tropical conditions, resulted in too many people, living too close together, in houses with poor sanitation and no public amenities. These circumstances provided an ideal breeding ground for disease and in 1913 the plague broke out in Java.

Periodical adjustments were required in order to keep up with the continuing population growth. A map of present-day Jakarta vividly illustrates the enormous expansion of the city in less than 50 years.

(Below) The Molenvliet Canal flowing through the European residential district of Ryswick, late 1850s.

(Bottom) A street lined by rows of Dutch townhouses in Batavia. Painting by Dessin de M. de Molins.

Country Houses in the 18th Century

As Batavia grew in size during the course of the 18th century, wealthy merchants were the first to flee from the increasingly congested and unsanitary town centre and build themselves grand residences in the surrounding countryside. These so-called *thuyen* or *landhuizen* were initially conceived as replicas of country seats back in Holland, but subsequently came to include many Javanese features, partly in response to the tropical climate and partly owing to the adoption of a more 'local' lifestyle on the part of their owners. This distinctive type of architecture, became known later as the 'Indies Style'.

The entrance to the great palace of Weltevreden, built around 1750, which was home to a succession of Governors-General of the Netherlands East Indies.

»»*Four types of doors from the Reiner de Klerk house.*

A Dutch Indies style country house in the former Arab quarter which is located in the northeastern section outside the old city walls of Semarang.

Country Estates of Batavia

The 17th century saw the increasing importance of Holland as a major maritime nation with a growing commercial empire overseas, particularly in the East. This generated capital for the merchant classes of Amsterdam who began to invest their profits in a second residence outside the city's boundaries. These ranged from modest rural retreats to luxurious country seats along the rivers Amstel and Vecht. In Batavia, a similar development occurred roughly half a century later, when European merchants began to settle beyond the town walls. This only happened after the Ommelanden — the hinterland that lay immediately beyond the fortified city boundaries — had been pacified and kept free from attacks by Javanese insurgents who were trying to evict the Dutch intruders. This was achieved by establishing a circular line of fortified field posts at places like Antjol, Jacatra, Noordwijk, Rijswijk, Anke and Vijfhoek, some ten kilometres outside the town. These forts later became famous as the place names of urban districts which developed on those sites.

Wealthy East India Company officials were the first to build themselves country residences in the newly pacified zone. Their estates were ideally situated between the rivers and roads that led into Batavia, thereby affording them easy access to their business interests in town. The first houses were modest wooden structures, but as time went by these gave way to extravagant palaces set amidst luxurious pleasure gardens complete with their own music pavilion and belfry.

Many country houses were built in other Dutch settlements during the 18th century, such as Galle in Sri Lanka, Cape Town in South Africa, and Curaçao, Netherlands Antilles, but none to surpass the stately homes of Batavia. Indeed, much of Batavia's reputation as 'Queen of the East' rested on the grandeur of these 18th-century mansions.

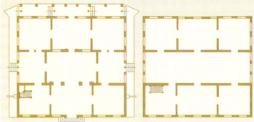

DUTCH STYLE HOUSES (1730-1770)

Compactly designed and solidly built, these two-storeyed country houses are almost exact replicas of their counterparts in Holland. Typical characteristics include a hipped roof, closed façade and high windows arranged in a symmetrical order. The only concession to the tropical climate seems to have been the adoption of a large roof overhang, which can be seen in the Reiner de Klerk house, now the National Archives building. Unlike their Dutch counterparts, the Batavian estates included extensive ancillary quarters to accommodate a large retinue of slaves who served to keep up the grand lifestyle of their owners. The Reiner de Klerk house, named after its builder who later became Governor General, also had godowns for the storage of goods acquired through private trading ventures.

ARCHITECTURE OF THE 17TH TO 19TH CENTURIES

(Below) One finds echoes of the landhuis Cililitan Besar in much later buildings such as this Residency in Palembang, South Sumatra.

(Left) The gracious lifestyle of the great country houses of Batavia in the late 19th century.

TRANSITIONAL DUTCH INDIES COUNTRY HOUSES (1750-1800)

The structure and form of this type of country house reveals a process of acculturation and gradual adaptation to the tropical climate on the part of the Dutch. Cililitan Besar is still a two-storey structure, but now the façades are protected from solar radiation by a large overhanging roof which projects on all sides and is supported by Tuscan columns. The roof profile strongly resembles the local *joglo*-style roof traditionally reserved for the houses of Javanese noblemen (see pp. 34-35) while the walls of the upper storey consist of plaited bamboo panels. The upper floor is reached by an external staircase and the central portion was left open to encourage maximum ventilation; tall windows with louvered shutters ensured the same for the closed-off portions.

INDIES STYLE COUNTRY HOUSES (1790-1820)

The end of the 18th century saw the emergence of a country house style which was more closely identified with indigenous forms of architecture than had hitherto been the case. While earlier hybrid styles evince doubt and hesitation, the new style followed a clear concept, being almost entirely based on the houses of Javanese nobles. This consisted of a single storey with front and rear verandahs — *pringgitan* and *gadri* respectively — covered by a high, pitched roof which extended over the verandahs rather like a protective broad-brimmed hat. Often the verandahs were connected to side galleries for full climatic protection on all sides.

The *landhuis* was ideally situated in a superb location with magnificent views of the surrounding countryside which could be enjoyed from the verandah. Tjitrap is a wonderful example of design integrated with the landscape. With the exception of the typical 18th-century Dutch windows this classic example of the Indonesian style country house bears no resemblance to its Dutch progenitors: two centuries after they had first set foot in the Archipelago, the Dutch had finally accepted the Indonesian way of life and made it their own.

Indonesian-style country houses were built in great numbers but almost all of them have been demolished at some point in time, including the Japan House, which was taken down in 1996. The only building left standing is Camis which is situated on the road to Bogor. Considering the almost complete destruction of the Batavian *landhuizen*, we are fortunate that one prototype of the three major styles survives.

(Top) View of the Tjitrap house in 1840.
(Above) The front façade of the Tjitrap house.

The landhuis Japan represents the perfect expression of a harmonious intermingling of Dutch and Javanese architectural traditions.

Dutch Townhouses

In general, Dutch townhouses of the 17th and 18th centuries were a more or less faithful copy of their counterparts in the Netherlands. They tended to be long and narrow, with steeply pitched roofs and stepped Dutch gables at the end of terraces. The few that remain are a poignant reminder of a long past nostalgia for a distant homeland on the part of Dutch East India Company officials and their families.

A row of terrace townhouses in Batavia (above). The roof profiles reveal an eclectic mix of Dutch and Chinese influences.

Early Examples

The earliest Dutch residences tended to be tightly packed together on narrow sites laid out within the defensive ramparts of trading settlements. Even so these early townhouses were usually a lot larger that their European relatives and could measure up to 110 metres in depth with a 20-metre street frontage. At least two storeys in height, they were built in straight rows along the side of canals. This type of townhouse, which had performed quite well in Europe, proved to be hopelessly unsuited to the tropical climate: poor ventilation and the warm humid air made these townhouses unbearably stuffy places to live in. The only concessions to local conditions were large overhanging eaves. In this respect they followed the precedent of Chinese shophouses which already belonged to a long and established tradition of urban design in a tropical environment.

Toko Merah, on Kali Besar in the historic Kota district of Jakarta, is a typical example of this type of double-plan, 18th-century townhouse. Air wells provide light and ventilation to the middle section of the building which extends back from the street some 50 metres. Another group of modest townhouses which have survived the sweeping changes to the city can be found on Jalan Teh. Here, the party walls which divide individual dwellings from one another extend beyond the surface of the roof and act as a protective device against the spread of fire. The historic town of Semarang in Central Java features an authentic and rare example of a stately 18th-century historic townhouse in a detached setting. The symmetrical front façade is richly decorated and is equipped with typical 18th-century Dutch sash windows.

TOKO MERAH, KALI BESAR.

Toko Merah, or 'Red Shop', was built in the 18th century when Kali Besar was a high-class residential district. It actually consists of two dwellings divided by a party wall. The house on the right was once the home of Governor-General Gustaaf Willem Baron van Imhoff (1705-1750).

❶ vestibules
❷ front rooms
❸ halls (with ornamental ceiling)
❹ inner courtyards
❺ mezzanine floor with cellars underneath
❻ accommodation for servants and slaves

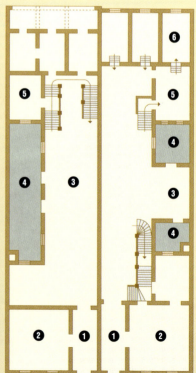

ARCHITECTURE OF THE 17TH TO 19TH CENTURIES

WAYANG MUSEUM
The Wayang Museum on Jalan Pintu Besar Utara was only built as recently as 1912, although its façade is modelled on the Dutch townhouse of the 17th and 18th centuries. Typical features include high sash windows with split shutters and a front door surmounted by a Classical pediment. The Wayang Museum was previously called the Museum of Old Batavia and was opened in 1939 by the last Dutch Governor-General T. van Starkenborch Stachouwer. It was built originally to house the VOC collection of pictures of Old Batavia.

SPANNING TWO CULTURES
The colonial townhouse reached its maturity in the 19th century with the emergence of the Indies Style which reformulated local architectural traditions within a European context. Earlier townhouses belonging to the merchant classes were solidly built, relatively enclosed structures, reflecting an inward-looking European way of life quite alien to the tropics. The Indies Style townhouse, however, was open to the tropical environment, with high roofs and ceilings, and front and rear verandahs that opened on to gardens.

Spatially and structurally the Indies house incorporates many Indonesian and Chinese influences, the arrangement of the open verandahs and adjoining rooms at the front and back of the house, being one example of this. Quite often a Javanese style *limasan* roof was employed. The detailing, however, is unmistakeably European: the doors, windows, Tuscan columns and a flight of three to four steps leading up to a verandah running the full width of the house, are all typical 19th-century elements drawn from a European architectural vocabulary.

The Tygersgracht, Batavia, in the early 18th century. A contemporary observer writes: "Among the Grachts — streets with water channels, the Tygersgracht is the most stately and most pleasant, both for the goodliness of its buildings, and the ornamentation of its streets, which afford a very agreeable shadow to those who pass along the street".

Shophouses and Temples: the Chinese Connection

There is evidence of contact between Indonesia and China as far back as the 5th century AD, and Chinese merchants had settled in Indonesian trading centres long before the first European adventurers arrived on the scene. They brought with them the architecture of their homeland which they adapted to their new surroundings. While temples have continued to be built in accordance with ancient precepts set down as early as the Han dynasty (206 BC-AD 220), the terraced shophouse reflects a mixture of Chinese, European and local architectural traditions.

Forecourt of a traditional Chinese mansion in Java (upper). A few surviving examples of these grand courtyard houses can still be found in some areas of Jakarta, Lasem and Semarang.

The Chinese in Indonesia
The Indonesian shophouse is closely linked to the history of Chinese settlement in the Archipelago: it seems likely that there was already a substantial Chinese presence in northeast Sumatra (Kota Cina) by about the 11th century while Marco Polo mentions fortified Chinese settlements in Sumatra at the end of the 13th century. One cannot know the provenance of these early Chinese settlers, but many later immigrants came from southern China, especially Guangdong Province, and it is the architecture of this region that provided the major formative influence for the Chinese shophouse in Indonesia.

Terraces of shophouses separated by a narrow street, or rows of houses built along a road, are a common feature in Guangdong Province. Architectural elements designed to combat the humid, sub-tropical Guangdong climate, with its typhoons, torrential rains and intense sunlight, meant that the traditional architecture of southern China was well suited to local climatic conditions in Indonesia. Environmentally adapted features include high ceilings, ventilation grilles, airwells and extended eaves to reduce glare and solar radiation.

The Traditional Chinese House
The archetypal Chinese house has a rectangular plan with rooms arranged around a square courtyard. Purlins, rafters and floor joists are embedded in load-bearing gable walls, which typically rise above the roof ridge. Symmetry is an important design principle with the main family altar being located on the longitudinal axis at the far side of the front room as one enters the building. The terraced shophouse can perhaps be best understood as a traditional courtyard house divided in two by a party wall running along its central axis.

Construction Methods
All structural loads are transmitted through the thick, load bearing masonry walls down to stone foundations running along the margins of the site. These load-bearing walls are typically placed between three to five metres apart, which correspond to the length of the wooden beams and purlins available on the market. The curved apexes of these masonry walls are traditional aesthetic embellishments imported from China.

The weight of the roof, with its projecting eaves, is transferred to the wall by sets of wooden brackets. These brackets not only perform a structural function, but also serve as aesthetic elements. The master-builders responsible for introducing shophouse architecture to Indonesia, were highly trained craftsmen, who had developed their skills through years of apprenticeship. This can be seen in the detailing of the wooden balcony balustrading at the front of many shophouses, or in the inner courtyard, as well as the carved interior partitions.

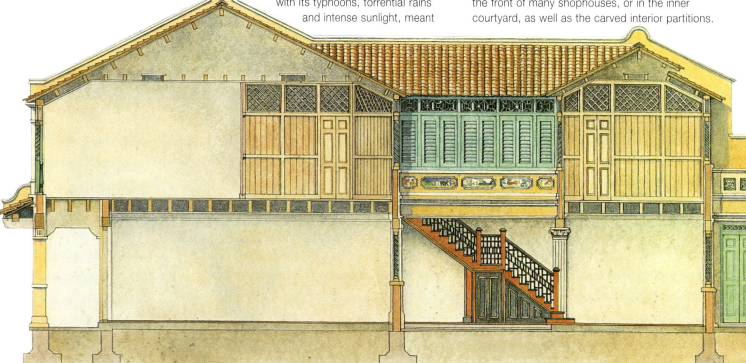

ARCHITECTURE OF THE 17TH TO 19TH CENTURIES

KLENTENG

Chinese temple architecture is extremely conservative: the basic structural elements and their proportional relationships were already firmly established in the Han Dynasty. As in the case of the traditional Chinese house, symmetrically aligned courtyards and walled compounds are key elements, while geomancy (*feng-shui*) dictates the alignment of buildings with natural features of the landscape. Unlike the shophouse, the roof structure is supported by a system of cantilevered units resting on pillars. Roof ridges are typically swept up at the ends in the 'swallow tail' manner and surmounted with a pair of cavorting dragons, symbolising the male and female principles of *yin* and *yang* whose eternal conflict represents the quest for perfect truth. Colours also play an important symbolic role: red which is identified with fire and blood, symbolises prosperity, good fortune, virtue and the male *yang* principle, and is typically used for walls, pillars and interior decorations.

The Klenteng Batu, Semarang (top). The same temple (extreme left). Interior of Chinese temple, Padang (left).

A HIERARCHY OF SPACES

The long and narrow shophouse plan can be conceived as a linear series of interconnected spaces, some of which are open, others closed. The overall impression is one of narrowness, but this arrangement is actually the most efficient way of utilising the limited space available to fulfil a wide range of functions. Furthermore, any feeling of confinement is offset by the illusion of spaciousness created by the inner courtyard or airwell: when one enters the central courtyard from the darker recesses of the building, one's first impression is of openness and brightness.

Taking a section through a typical Chinese shophouse reveals a systematic set of spatial relations between the street, the front arcade, and the courtyard inside the house. Effected by a series of passageways and thresholds, the move from the street to the innermost part of the building represents a shift in spatial values from public to private. The traditional door-cum-window unit at the front of the building is well-suited to a variety of functions. The easily removed double-leafed doors and panels allow for a variety of functions including opening a shop, enclosing a living room, allowing the removal of a coffin or providing a large space for wedding celebrations. The shophouse thus forms an integral component in the social and physical universe of the Chinese settlement.

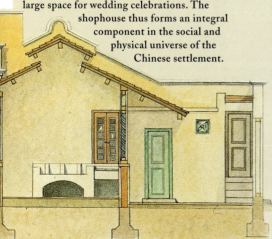

❶ *A street in the Chinese quarters, Batavia.*
❷ *Batavian shophouse.*
❸ *Interior of Chinese shophouse.*
❹ *Cooking facilities in a 19th-century Batavian shophouse.*

115

The Introduction of New Building Types

The abolition of the Cultivation System in 1870 ushered in a new era in the history of the Netherlands Indies as the colony opened up to private enterprise. Large scale agricultural production for the world market required new facilities for processing, storage, distribution and commerce. As a consequence, a new range of building types appeared to meet these emerging needs.

The Baroque bell towers and portico of the south entrance to the Gereja Blenduk, Semarang.

A Colonial Bureaucracy

Up until the last decades of the 19th century, the Netherlands Indies was organised along the lines of a traditional, hierarchical Indonesian society governed by a colonial administration, the Binnenlands Bestuur, or Civil Service. Almost every major building was owned, used and designed by the government, as were the roads, railways, ports and other public utilities. The range of government buildings, included administrative offices, military barracks, warehouses, opium factories, pawnshops and *pasanggrahan*, or rest houses. The latter were situated in remote locations and used by travelling civil servants on tours of duty. Designed by the Civil Public Works Department, or Departement voor Burgerlijke Openbare Werken, most prominent government buildings, almost without exception, were built in the prevailing Neo-classical style which was perceived as the most appropriate expression of empire.

Private Enterprise and Modernisation

The Agrarian Law of 1870, which replaced the oppressive, government-run Plantation System with free enterprise and private ownership, encouraged a massive influx of immigrants from Europe who were eager to take advantage of the new economic opportunities in the profitable colony. Banks and trading companies (*handelskantoren*) sprang up in the cities and new port facilities were established to accommodate the increase in trade.

New building regulations were also introduced which transformed the appearance of city centres. In downtown Batavia, for example, it was required that new buildings be provided with a covered walkway, or colonnade, to provide protection from the fierce tropical sunshine and monsoon rains.

Railways and Railway Stations

The first railway line in Java was opened in 1867 and soon expanded into an island-wide network connecting inland towns, and their surrounding sugar factories and tobacco, coffee and rubber plantations, with the coast and its busy ports. As was the case in the Netherlands, stations were classified according to their importance.

Standard designs were used for each category of railway stations in the Dutch East Indies, ranging from mere halts and small country stations to spacious, fully equipped facilities in the major urban centres such as in Batavia (Jakarta), Bandung, Semarang, Surabaya and Yogyakarta. The latter, with their monumental design, represented new landmarks in the architecture of the Dutch East Indies.

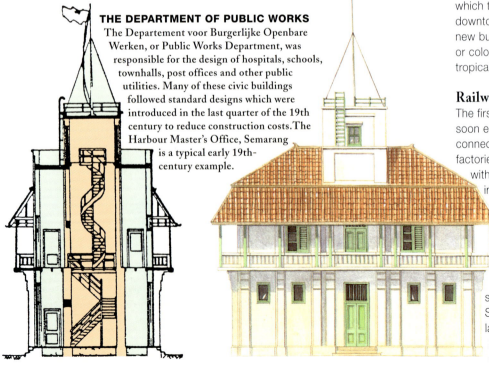

THE DEPARTMENT OF PUBLIC WORKS

The Departement voor Burgerlijke Openbare Werken, or Public Works Department, was responsible for the design of hospitals, schools, townhalls, post offices and other public utilities. Many of these civic buildings followed standard designs which were introduced in the last quarter of the 19th century to reduce construction costs. The Harbour Master's Office, Semarang is a typical early 19th-century example.

ARCHITECTURE OF THE 17TH TO 19TH CENTURIES

THE ARCHITECTURE OF COMMERCE

Architecturally, the changes brought about by the introduction of private enterprise to the Dutch Indies were most apparent in the larger cities. European trading houses and banks had established their offices in downtown Batavia, Semarang and Surabaya well before the end of the 19th century, with branch offices in Medan and Makassar (Ujung Panjang) shortly after 1900. Neo-classicism fell from favour as the preferred architectural style of the Indies to be replaced by somewhat contrasting enthusiasms for the Neo-gothic and Dutch Rationalism. The chain of Javaasche Bank offices in Bandung, Surabaya, Medan and Batavia (below) which were designed around 1910 by the Amsterdam partnership of Cuypers and Hulswit, reflect these new architectural sensibilities.

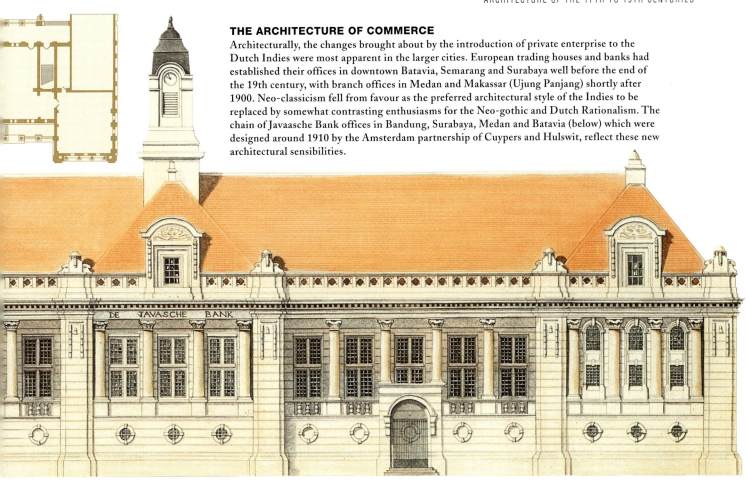

NEW BUILDING TYPES

Railway stations were another major new component in the late 19th- and early 20th-century cities of Java and Sumatra. As was the case in the Netherlands, stations were classified according to their importance.

1. The Railway Station Building in Surabaya.
2. Javanese Bank Building in Batavia.
3. Hong Kong Bank, Batavia.
4. Godowns, offices and railway station, Tanjong Priok.
5. Offices of van Arcken & Co.
6. A new factory building in the Batavian suburb of Noordwijk.
7. Telephone exchange at Weltevreden, a suburb of Batavia.

117

❶ *Museum in Taman Mini, Jakarta.*
❷ *The MPR/DPR building (Parliament Building), Jakarta..*
❸ *The main administration building, Universiti Indonesia, designed by G. Tjahjono and B. Sukada.*
❹ *The Wisma 46 Bank Nasional Indonesia, Jakarta.*
❺ *The Gateway Office Building, Jakarta. Architects are Ir. Suntana and Sdr. Zamrudh.*
❻ *The Senen Triangle buildings, Central Jakarta.*
❼ *Ancol Recreation Park, Jakarta.*
❽ *Grand Melia Hotel, Jakarta.*

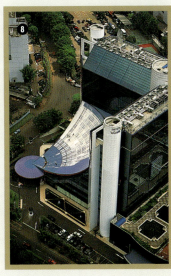

MODERN ARCHITECTURE AND IDENTITY

The final decades of the 19th century were years of profound change in the Netherlands East Indies. They saw the emergence of a new political awareness accompanied by increasing demands for autonomy from Holland and self-government. This burgeoning nationalism manifested itself architecturally in the quest for a new style of architecture — one that reflected the cultural identity of the region. The architects who responded to this call can be divided into two schools. The first, which included architects such as A.F. Aalbers, based their work on strictly functionalist principles in line with the Modernist Movement in Europe. The second, however, sought to temper the Modernist ethos by including indigenous architectural elements, thereby creating a distinctively Indonesian style of modern architecture: Maclaine Pont and Karsten were the leading exponents here.

In the 1950s, as Indonesia emerged as a newly-liberated nation, the quest for national unity became paramount. This sentiment was expressed architecturally in an all-embracing acceptance of Modernism, which was very much in line with the prevailing Internationalism of the times. This trend continued well into the 1960s despite years of political turbulence, but even so there were some Indonesian architects who continued to explore the traditional architecture of the region as a source of ideas for national architecture.

The 1970s saw an increasing involvement of the private sector in building projects and during this period, economic rationalism inevitably prevailed over aesthetic sensibilities, resulting in the appearance of a great many box-like buildings. In the public sector, however, architects were actively encouraged to turn to the region's architectural heritage for inspiration and many local government buildings began to sprout 'traditional' roof profiles. At the same time, a new generation of Indonesian architects, many of whom had studied overseas, also began to introduce fresh perspectives on the nature of the built environment and the purposes that architecture should serve.

In the last two decades of this century we have seen the rapid growth of these new ideas and approaches, together with increased globalisation and economic progress, and these new conditions have made themselves felt in an architectural context which seems to be of a much greater variety than before. The designs of buildings and environments range from those which are based on practical and rational considerations to those which embrace the local and traditional values of Indonesia's architectural heritage.

The Emergence of a New Indies Style

The early years of this century saw an increasing dissatisfaction with the prevailing Neo-classical style of colonial architecture in the Dutch Indies. Faced with the task of finding effective solutions to the problems of designing for a tropical environment, Dutch architects turned to indigenous architectural forms for their inspiration. These they translated into a Modernist idiom, thereby giving rise to a neo-vernacular school of architecture which, they then combined with Art Deco elements, to create what is known today as the New Indies Style.

(Above) The Schonburg Building, Weltevreden, represents the transitional Tropical Style.

The flat roofs and clean lines of the Semarang railway station reflect the rationalist aesthetics and philosophy of the Modernist movement.

Designing for the Tropics

During the 19th century, Neo-classicism was universally accepted as the most appropriate architectural style through which to express the greatness of empire. By the turn of the century, however, this form of architecture had become so degraded that newly arrived architects from Holland agitated for a fresh approach to architectural design in the Indies. Their aim was to create a style of architecture which was both appropriate for the tropical climate and could also be identified specifically with the Dutch Indies. This new school of architecture, while it initially continued to adhere to an essentially Classical form, incorporated elements especially designed to combat the fierce sunlight and heavy rains of the tropics. The most important innovation was the introduction of double-façades which was the first time that this idea had appeared in modern architecture. These new form of environmentally sensitive architecture subsequently became known as the Tropical Style.

Modernism and the Neo-vernacular

The rise of what is commonly referred to as the 'New Indies Style' can be linked, in part, to the Modern movement. At the end of World War I, the Dutch colonial administration of the Netherlands Indies actively sought the assistance of professional architects in setting up a new infrastructure for urban centres in the region. This led to an influx of young Dutch architects who arrived in Java to work for the municipal governments of the major cities, or else to set up their own private practices in the commercial sector. They brought with them European architectural influences such as Art Deco and de Stijl which prepared the way for the introduction of a Modernist agenda subsequent to World War II. Although Modernism advocated a rationalist and functional approach to architectural design, the earliest attempts to employ these principles in the Indies were not altogether successful: the rigorous application of architectural features such as flat roofs and sheer façades, which had previously only been

EAST MEETS WEST

Popularly known as the Gedung Saté, on account of the flanged pylon which crowns the apex of the roof like a giant *sate* skewer, the Office of the Governor of West Java, Bandung, was designed by the Dutch architect, J. Gerber and completed in 1920. The multi-tiered roof over the centre of the building echoes traditional mosque architecture — for example, the Masjid Agung at Yogyakarta (left) — while the façades combine Art Deco orders with Classical Hindu-Buddhist motifs.

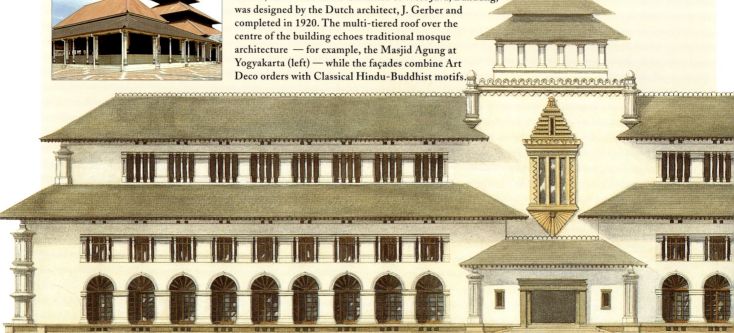

F.J.L GHIJSELS

Fran Johan Louwrens Ghijsels was born in Tulung Agung in Java in 1882. In 1903 he began to study architecture at the polytechnic in Delft, where some of his fellow students included several future East Indies architects, Thomas Karsten and Henri Maclaine Pont among them.

Ghijsels' first appointment after graduation was as a government architectural supervisor in Amsterdam, but in 1910 he was accepted for the post of engineer by the Municipal Works Department in Batavia. This signalled the beginning of a 20-year career in the Netherlands East Indies, initially in the service of the colonial government, but which later became a private practice.

The Kota Railway Station in Batavia (bottom right) is one of Ghijsels' best known works. The elegant building is remarkable for its restrained use of Art Deco ornamentation and its spacious interiors; a gallery around the first storey provides access to administrative offices. Another notable building by Ghijsels is the Nijm office in Yogyakarta (top right).

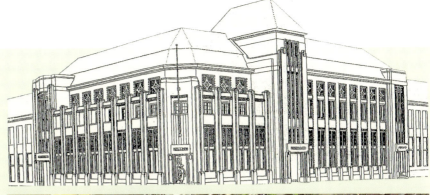

seen in Europe, resulted in buildings which were totally unsuited to the tropical climate with its torrential monsoon rains, high humidity and intense solar radiation. In the end, the young revolutionaries had to accept that many of the design principles endorsed by the Modern masters were quite inappropriate in the tropics. This led them to explore indigenous architectural forms as a source of possible solutions for dealing with the local climate.

The 1920s and 1930s saw the progressive development of this school of thought which consciously sought to combine traditional elements of Indonesian architecture with new technologies and Modernist architectural principles from Europe. Indigenous roofs were singled out for particular attention and there were many interesting syntheses of local and European forms and construction techniques. This exchange of ideas worked in both directions: the interest of Modernists in the dynamic interplay of geometrical elements was soon incorporated into the New Indies Style and led to bold experiments that combined these structural forms with traditional vernacular ornamentation.

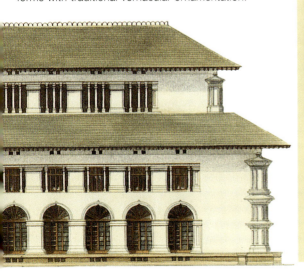

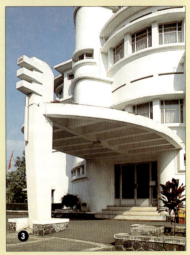

OTHER EXOTIC INFLUENCES

Modernism was not the only European movement to influence the architecture of the Dutch Indies in the early years of this century. One also finds versions of Art Nouveau, Art Deco and Expressionist styles of architecture. At the same time, the New Indies Style itself was evolving rapidly and subsequently gave way to what became known as the Dutch Indies Freestyle. The last of these European schools to reach the Indies was the Nieuwe Zakelijkheid Style.

❶ *PT Java Maluku Building, Surabaya, which was designed by H.P. Berlage in 1900 — Art Nouveau.*
❷ *Detail from the same building.*
❸ *Villa Isola in Bandung — Expressionist.*
❹ *A building in Pasuruan — New Indies Style.*

121

Attempted Synthesis: Dutch Architects in the Indies

Twentieth-century Dutch architects in the Netherlands Indies can be divided into two broad groups, namely those who followed the European tradition in which they had been trained and those that sought to achieve a synthesis of eastern and western architectural styles. The latter were responsible for producing some of the most innovative and interesting tropical architecture of the 20th century.

(Above) The Governor's office, Surabaya.

↗ *The symmetrical arrangement of doors and windows for the front elevation of Karsten's Netherlands Steam Navigation Company Offices, Semarang, looks back to the archetypal Dutch* landhuizen *of the 17th century as exemplified by the former Reiner de Klerk residence (now the National Archives Building).*

(Below) Thomas Karsten's Joana Stoomtram Maatschappij, Semarang.

W. Lemei

The colonial governor's office at Surabaya, East Java, is a good example of a building which for the most part conforms to the European pattern. Designed by W. Lemei in 1931 it was built as part of the colonial government's decentralisation plan. The use of flat roofs, towers and cubist forms, suggest affinities with the Hilversum City Hall (1930), designed by the Dutch architect Willem Dudok. Other obvious European influences include the use of Art Deco motifs in the ornamentation of windows and ventilation openings. But despite the stylistic similarity between the governor's office and Hilversum City Hall, there are departures between the two buildings in terms of their response to climatic considerations. In the case of the Surabaya building, this was designed around a rectangular ground plan with a cloistered inner courtyard. The latter feature, while providing access to various parts of the building, also enabled good natural cross-ventilation and reduced the effects of solar radiation on the internal walls.

Thomas Karsten

Herman Thomas Karsten (1884-1945) was one of the foremost Dutch architects who practised in Batavia in the 1920s and 1930s. The son of a philosophy professor and a graduate of the Delft High School of Technology (Technische Hogeschool de Delft), Karsten worked as a town planner and later became the professor of town planning at the Bandung Institute of Technology.

The former office for the Netherlands Steam Navigation Company – Stoomvart Maatschappij Nederland (SMN) – in the old city centre of Semarang, is one of Karsten's best known works. This two-storeyed building, which later became the offices of the national shipping line, Jakarta Lloyd, was built in 1930. Its rectangular plan maximises site coverage. The symmetrical front façade is dominated by six vertical columns, surmounted by a rather curious hipped roof which is curved in its lower part.

Karsten's concern for the tropical climate can be seen in a number of special features, such as the high windows and ventilation grills, which reach from floor to ceiling. The large, and steeply sloping, expanse of roof provides good insulation from solar radiation and efficient run-off for monsoon rains. Corridors, at the front and sides, on the ground floor and first storey, also assist thermal insulation.

The former offices of the Dutch steamtram company, Joana Stoomtram Maatschappij, are another fine example of Karsten's work in Semarang. Built in the same year as the SMN offices, the architectural style is very different and shows evidence of a more overt Indonesian influence. Unlike the typical city centre locations which jammed buildings together along the streets, the Joana Stoomtram Maatschappij office is located in what was once an outlying district of the city. This allows Karsten to place his building in the middle of his site with plenty of space on all sides. The ground plan of this single-storeyed building is identical to that of a traditional Javanese *joglo* house: tall columns support a hipped, two-tiered roof, which facilitates cross ventilation of the roof cavity.

MODERN ARCHITECTURE AND IDENTITY

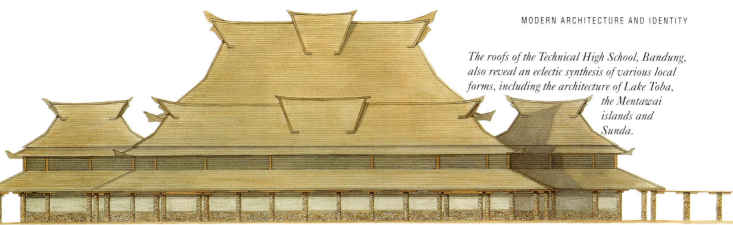

The roofs of the Technical High School, Bandung, also reveal an eclectic synthesis of various local forms, including the architecture of Lake Toba, the Mentawai islands and Sunda.

Henri Maclaine Pont

Henri Maclaine Pont was born in 1885 in what is now Jatinegara and like his contemporary, Karsten, he was a graduate of the Technische Hogeschool de Delft. Maclaine Pont was greatly interested in the indigenous architecture of the region and published several works on the Hindu-Buddhist temples of Java. The influence of local architectural forms is more apparent in his work than in Karsten's as can be seen in his masterpiece, the Technical High School at Bandung.

The original Technische Hogeschool complex consisted of three main groups of buildings, which are linked by colonnaded walkways springing from a central peristyle entrance. These principal buildings are set out on a north-south axis which aligns with the volcano Tangkuban Perahu to the north. The arrangement is clearly inspired by ancient cosmological precepts.

Maclaine Pont employed highly original construction techniques for the most important buildings in the complex, such as the auditorium. The main structural elements, such as the columns, are made up from layers of teak bound together by iron hoops.

Interior of Maclaine Pont's church at Pohsarang. It represents another attempt by Pont to incorporate Hindu-Buddhist elements into a Western building.

NEW TECHNOLOGIES

The Modernist movement was accompanied by technological innovations and the use of new building materials which gave architects the freedom to experiment with more plastic architectural forms. During the 1920s and 1930s Karsten was responsible for a remarkable series of municipal markets including Pasar Gede, in Surakarta (1929) (left and below), and Pasar Johar, in Semarang (1938) (top left). The split level roof, which exploits the advantages of natural lighting and ventilation, reflects Karsten's interest in the relationship between architecture and the tropical environment.

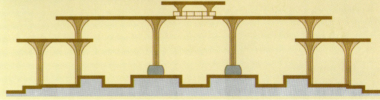

External galleries create a double façade which shields the interior of the building from the direct sunlight while cooling towers at either end ensure good ventilation.

THE SEMARANG-CHERIBON STEAM TRAM COMPANY

The Semarang-Cheribon Steam Tram Company headquarters in Tegal, Java, which was designed by Henri Maclaine Pont, is an astounding example of innovative tropical architecture. With an elongated elevation aligned on an east-west axis, the building is provided with perfect natural ventilation, alternately taking full advantage of a cool sea breeze in the morning and a land breeze in the evening. The same orientation also minimises the effect of solar radiation in that the morning and afternoon sun only strikes the narrow end façades of the building.

Maclaine Pont also provided the long north and south elevations with galleries and a double façade, with 'breathing' ceilings and ventilation shafts at both ends. The Semarang-Cheribon Steam Tram Company's building represents a new departure in terms of its design principles which incorporate a passive, yet extremely effective, response to the problems of designing for a tropical climate.

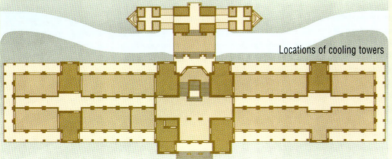

Locations of cooling towers

Garden Cities and Suburban Bungalows

The beginning of the 20th century saw a rapid growth in the size of the colonial town and its European population. The newcomers from Europe brought with them European sensibilities and conventions which ultimately were responsible for transforming the Indies way of life for both colonist and native alike. This shift in social values is reflected in the domestic architecture of the period and corresponding changes in the plan and administration of major urban centres, particularly in Java.

An example of the eclectic style from Solo.

By the 1930s, Art Deco styling had become an ubiquitous feature of the Dutch colonial villa. These examples come from Gresik (below) and Semarang (bottom).

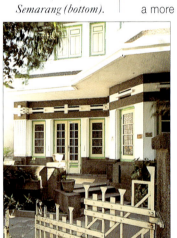

The Rise of the Tropical Garden City
The rapid growth of the colonial town in the early years of the 20th century led to a tremendous shortage of available building sites and a corresponding rise in the price of land. As a result, the colonial house and garden became much smaller in size, reflecting the more modest income and aspirations of the burgeoning middle classes.

Town planning boards were established and building ordinances introduced to cope with the demand for new housing, and this led to a more orderly distribution of houses and facilities in suburban areas. At the same time, the increasing number of motor cars and improved public transport systems allowed for more dispersed neighbourhoods so that the newly laid out European residential areas began to take on the atmosphere of a Dutch garden city. The Indies town, especially the major urban centres of Batavia, Semarang and Surabaya acquired a more 'colonial' appearance as the architecture of these cities was explicitly modelled on European prototypes. Bandung, in particular, was revered as 'the Paris of the East'.

Early 20th-Century Colonial Villa
The early years of the 20th century witnessed an era of architectural eclecticism with villas constructed in the romantic and picturesque style. This did not last long, as around the beginning of World War I, a new type of colonial villa came into being. The new form was both more modern in appearance and designed to meet the needs of living in a tropical climate. Abandoning contemporary European influences, the archetypal ground plan of these new dwellings was closer in spirit to the Indies tradition. As in the case of the 19th-century colonial bungalow, an entrance hall was very often omitted, being replaced by a small verandah at the front of the house. The grand reception rooms of yesteryear were reduced to a large circulation area which functioned as a drawing room, while the dining area was located at the back. Sometimes there was a staircase leading to bedrooms upstairs, while the kitchen, bathrooms and toilets were usually external to the main part of the house. In contrast with former times, the servants no longer resided in the compound but lived outside the European residential areas in *kampung* settlements.

The 1920s and 1930s
The 1920s and 1930s saw the advent of a new archetype for the Dutch colonial house which subsequently became so well established that examples can be found in just about every region of the Archipelago. The basic model consisted of a modest, single storey, detached house, with a tiled roof, plastered walls and teak (*jati*) windows, placed on a stone plinth or basement. More commodious examples ran to two storeys with garages and outbuildings. These type of houses were designed as homes for conventional, middle-class European families and marked a transition from the 19th-century way of life in the Indies to a more European urban culture which established itself in Indonesia at the turn of the century. The antecedents of this social revolution lay in the abolition of government controlled agricultural

MODERN ARCHITECTURE AND IDENTITY

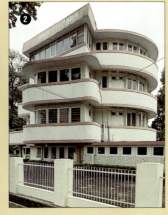

A.F. AALBERS AND THE MODERNIST MOVEMENT

The 1920s and 1930s saw the advent of Modernism in the Dutch Indies. Typical features included flat roofs and cubic forms, though Art Deco ornamentation was also often incorporated into the design. A.F. Aalbers was one of the foremost representatives of the Modern movement in Indonesia before the Second World War: his work has been favourably compared with that of the Dutch architect Jan Duiker and the Swiss Grand Master of Modernism, Le Corbusier. Aalbers arrived in Indonesia from Rotterdam in 1928 and started working for the architect-contractor J. Bennink; in 1930, he established his own *atelier* in Bandung. Aalbers' work is characterised by its clean-cut, functionalist elevations, which often feature curved lines, and the absence of external ornamentation and other purely decorative devices.

❶ One of three Modernist villas in Jalan ir. H. Juanda, Bandung, designed by Aalbers in 1936; contemporaries christened them "The Three Locomotives".
❷ Another Aalbers residence in Jalan ir. Juanda, built in 1938.
❸ Aalbers' Modernist masterpiece, the Savoy Homan Hotel (1939), was constructed around a steel skeleton and like many of his houses featured curved lines and textured external surfaces. The building reflected plans to create a more high-rise, city-like street façade for Bandung.
❹ Modernist villas, Salemba.

production in 1870. The relaxation of government control over the economy opened the doors to private enterprise in the Indies and encouraged a massive influx of European entrepreneurs from Holland and elsewhere. What had previously been a society of civil servants was rapidly transformed into a society of '*partekleer sadja*' (small-scale European businessmen). The latter brought with them their womenfolk who encouraged the revival of European social values and standards of behaviour. This change to a more explicit European way of life can be clearly identified in the changing design of European townhouses. The openness of the typical Indies house was replaced by the closed structure of the European model: front and rear verandahs became incorporated into the main part of the building, while bay windows and arts and crafts detailing evoke the cosiness of urban life back in Holland.

Leafy Suburbs

Living in a European residential area guaranteed an optimal level of municipal services such as sanitation, schools, hospitals, shopping centres and well constructed roads. The environmental quality of these districts conformed to the late Victorian ideal of a 'garden city', with an open-plan layout, tree-lined avenues and lots of green spaces; large private gardens contributed greatly to the quantity of the residential environment. Examples included Menteng in Jakarta, Candi Baru in Semarang, Darmo in Surabaya, Polonia in Medan and most famously the north side of Bandung. The municipal councils took responsibility for the maintenance of the environment and services while the building ordinance of Batavia in 1919 stipulated that "owners of buildings and compounds are obliged to keep buildings in a proper condition and at least once a year — in the month of June — to paint their properties white in colour".

*A weekend cottage (*pondok*) in the hills: like the British in India and neighbouring Malaya, the Dutch established a number of hill resorts in order to take advantage of the cooler climate at higher elevations.*

The 1930s witnessed large-scale suburban developments on the outskirts of major urban centres. Van Heutz Boulevard, Menteng, Batavia.

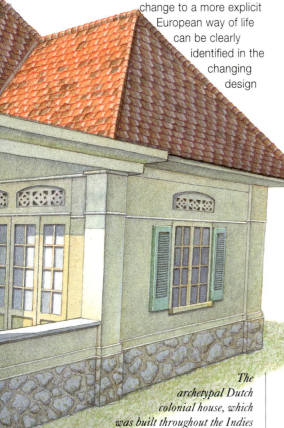

The archetypal Dutch colonial house, which was built throughout the Indies in the period before World War II.

Modernism and the International Style

Modern architecture in Indonesia has its origins in the final decades of the colonial era, when Dutch architects introduced a rationalist imperative to the architecture of the Dutch Indies. Since Independence, Indonesian architects have continued to look to Europe and America for inspiration, at first taking up where their Dutch Modernist predecessors left off and then later adopting the International Style of Walter Gropius, Mies van der Rohe and Philip Johnson.

(Above) A panoramic view of the Monas in Central Jakarta.

(Opposite, left) The lobby and conference room of the Hotel Indonesia. (Below) The hotel is designed by Sorensen, a Danish architect.

(Bottom) The STEKPI campus is designed by architects from PT Atelier-6.

Modernism in the Sixties

The programme of nationalisation, which was introduced in 1957, led to the repatriation of Dutch lecturers at the Bandung Institute of Technology (ITB) and their replacement with Indonesian teachers. Many of this first generation of Indonesian lecturers had studied in the USA, Germany, England and the Netherlands and they continued to endorse the Modernist agenda advanced by their Dutch predecessors.

The early 1960s saw the return of a new generation of Indonesian students who had studied abroad in Europe and America. This group included Sujudi, Suwondo and their peers, many of whom were enrolled as junior staff members at the ITB where they promoted the modern and progressive ideas of their idols, the German Bauhaus masters, Walter Gropius and Mies van der Rohe, the French Swiss, Le Corbusier, and the American Frank Lloyd Wright. For better or worse, a significant Modernist movement in Indonesia began to take shape during the 1960s: Chicago-style skyscrapers, the biomorphic forms of Oscar Niemeyer's Brasilia and the rational functionalism of the 'International Style' were the principal enthusiasms which informed the teaching and practice of architecture in Indonesia at the time.

Nationalism and Contextualism

In the wake of President Soeharto's 'New Order' in 1966, many more Indonesian students went abroad to study architecture and on their return they too set about creating new skylines for the cities of their native land. The buildings they designed were still largely derivative of Western models and bore little relation to any Indonesian context. However, courses in anthropology and geography were introduced to the architectural syllabus in Indonesian universities in the late 1960s and this in turn encouraged a reappraisal of the country's rich architectural heritage. This was partly fuelled by the quest for a national identity — every form of artistic expression had to advance an Indonesian perspective or stem from Indonesian origins. The traditional architecture of the Archipelago was seen as an exemplary symbol of Indonesian nationhood.

The Indonesian pavilion for the Osaka Expo (1967-1968) was designed by Robi Sularto (Atelier-6) who drew his inspiration from Borobudur and the terraced irrigated rice fields of Java. The structure itself was decidedly modern, being situated obliquely on the square plot and using space frame construction techniques to span the central mass. Nevertheless, the message was clear: modern architects should look to Borobudur and similar antiquities as symbols of national identity.

There were other creative young architects in the late 1960s who also tried to combine a Modernist agenda with a new formal and spatial syntax which could also be related to specifically Indonesian contexts. The audacious freelance architect, Mangunwijaya, and Adhi Moersid (Aterlier-6) were both Aga Khan winners, carrying the torch of progress by producing startling new designs out of commonplace building types. These experiments ran into various theoretical design problems but in spite of the obstacles, this era saw the rise of 'contextualism' in Indonesian architecture.

MODERN ARCHITECTURE AND IDENTITY

❶ *The People's Assembly building (MPR/DPR) is designed by Sujudi in 1963. It reflects features of Late Modernist architecture.*
❷ *The Japan Embassy, Jakarta (1964), represented the first example of a Late Modern and International Style building.*
❸ *The Bappindo Bank along Jalan Gondanglia Lama.*
❹ *The Istora Senayan in Jakarta was designed by Russian architects in 1958.*

(Below) The Gedung Dharmala, designed by Paul Rudolph, shows how local themes can be incorporated into a modern design using slender posts and shading.

New Directions, New Styles

During the 1970s, Indonesia experienced a sustained period of economic development following a boom in world oil prices. The government played a major role in this programme and many new government buildings were commissioned. Although the latter were constrained by tight annual budgets which restricted their design to largely functional and economic considerations, many regional and local governments insisted on the incorporation of traditional roof types in the design of public buildings.

During this period, a number of large-scale construction projects were also executed. One notable example, was a 90 x 120 metre structure to house Jumbo jets at the Soekarno-Hatta Airport. Ary Mochtar Pedju (PT Encona), who designed it, was an engineering-oriented architect who taught advanced structural design and construction management. His approach to architecture was led by technological criteria, the form being largely determined by construction techniques and the nature of building materials employed.

In the private sector, Indonesia's newly acquired affluence was reflected in bourgeois indulgences in the domestic sphere which spawned a rash of pseudo-Classical villas, with Greek or Roman columns, and futuristic 'capsule' houses.

The Architecture of Early Independence

Indonesian architecture during the early years of Independence was still largely informed by Dutch Modernism, and in particular the Delft and De Stijl schools of architectural design. This was largely due to the fact that most Indonesian architects at this time had either studied under the Dutch or else had worked for Dutch construction companies before World War II. There were also a number of prominent Dutch architects still attached to the Public Works Department in the period immediately following Independence and several others who continued in private practice until they were obliged to leave as a consequence of the nationalisation programme launched by the government at the end of the 1950s.

Two buildings using the box-frame-cum-rational grid system. (Top) Bank Nasional Indonesia and (middle) the Election Building. (Bottom) Yankee-style housing in Kebayoran Baru in the early 1950s.

(Below, from left, clockwise) Hotel Borobudur, Jakarta. Sekolah Pertanian Menengah Atas, Bogor. Kalibata cemetery.

The Legacy of the Dutch

The architecture of the early Independence period has its origins in the attempted restoration of a Dutch Indies government following the capitulation of Japan in 1945. After four years of conflict, the prospect of a peaceful settlement between Holland and Indonesia at last emerged and the Dutch returned to a programme of civic building works undisturbed. At that time, and in the ten years or so that followed Independence, most new buildings were either designed by Dutch architects or Indonesian architects who had studied under the Dutch. Some were followers of the Delft school, which combined box-building with a rational grid-system that allowed the manufacture of pre-fabricated elements to be used for external walls; others adhered to the Functionalist style, which included the architecture of De Stijl. The pre-war interest in creating a modern architecture which nevertheless embraced Indonesian characteristics, was also revived, resulting in a number of contemporary buildings with a 'traditional' style roof placed on top. The latter style became the dominant trend in government architecture.

Housing Schemes

The district of Kebayoran Baru, south of Jakarta, was the first new housing project initiated by the Dutch after retaking Indonesia from the Japanese. Conceived as a satellite of the city, Kebayoran Baru was intended to provide housing facilities for government employees, though the private sector was also allowed to participate in the scheme in order to create variety. The project was notable for the involvement of the Indonesian architect Susilo, a former assistant of the Dutch urban designer, Thomas Karsten. Especially interesting was the provision of mass-housing for low rank government employees and flats for middle ranking officials. The higher echelons of government servants were also provided with accommodation, consisting of either terrace or detached houses which were distinguished by their sloping walls and skewed columns. This distinctive style of architecture, which was actually a technical solution arising out of specific construction techniques, came to be known as the Yankee Style. Later, in the 1950s, another new style of architecture emerged, known as the Villa Style; it was popular among private house builders.

FREIDRICH SILABAN AND TROPICAL ARCHITECTURE

Freidrich Silaban was one of the first Indonesian 'avant-garde' architects. He received his earliest instruction in building techniques at the Royal Wilhelmina School (KWS) in Batavia, from which he graduated in 1931. He started working for the government and in his enthusiasm to advance his prospects, he often attended evening courses in design. In 1950, he went to Holland after which he re-entered government service on his return to Indonesia and eventually rose to the position of Head of the Public Works Department in Bogor before his retirement in 1965. He also ran a private practice from his home in Bogor.

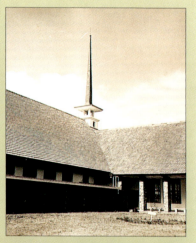

MODERN ARCHITECTURE AND IDENTITY

The First Indonesian Architects

The early Independence period is notable for the emergence of the first fully-fledged Indonesian architects. They can be divided into two groups according to the manner in which they received their architectural training and experience. The first group gained their expertise in the 1930s, typically as staff in a Dutch-owned construction firm. They could be described as architects by training. They included such prominent names as Susilo, Suhamir and Silaban (see box). Silaban himself was inspired by a Dutch architect Ir. Antonisse, one of the initiators of the 'Indo-Europeesche Stijl'. The second group of architects, on the other hand, attended the newly established school of architecture at the Bandung Institute of Technology and were thus architects by virtue of their education. The first generation of this latter group — those who graduated in 1958 and the years that followed — included Suhartono (the son of Susilo), Hasan Purbo and Achman Noe'man. Suhartono went on to become the founder and first chairman of the Institute of Indonesian Architects (IAI) in 1959 and later became head of the Architecture Department at the Parahyangan University, Bandung, where he still holds a teaching post to this day.

The majority of Indonesian architects only started producing their own work at the end of the 1950s, when they replaced Dutch architects who left for their own country following the introduction of a programme of nationalisation by the Indonesian government. The early works of the first group inevitably reflect their architectural roots and show a strong influence of Dutch Classical and Rationalist traditions. Those who trained at the Bandung Institute of Technology, on the other hand, had been exposed to a wider range of influences expounded by their Dutch lecturers and the architectural literature of the Modern Movement. Although their outlook was decidedly contemporary, they nevertheless made some attempt to adapt their modernist agenda to suit local conditions.

A Final Break With the Past

The period of early Independence was a short-lived one. It ended in 1957 when the Indonesian government began to take over Dutch assets and investments in the country under a programme of collective nationalisation. The Dutch responded by withdrawing all their experts from Indonesia, professional architects and educators among them. Then, in 1959, President Soekarno announced his Presidential Decree preparing the way for a new era in the political economy of the nation known as the 'Guided Democracy' period. At this point the historical continuity between modern Indonesian architecture and the architectural traditions of the Dutch Indies was finally severed altogether.

Buildings designed by Freidrich Silaban: (above) the Masjid Istiqlal, Jakarta, which was built in 1960, the Hotel Indonesia (left) and Bank Jabar (bottom left).

(Below) The Nurses' Dormitory in Bandung displays some Yankee-style features.

The Architecture of Modern Indonesian Cities

The urban fabric of most present day Indonesian towns and cities represents an overlay of successive, and often widely differing, ideas about city formation, reflecting the geographical and cultural diversity of the Archipelago, and the individual historical circumstances which led to their formation and development. This means that although it is possible to discuss Indonesian urbanism in terms of local or regional contexts as, for example, in the case of the Javanese town, it is difficult to identify an archetypal Indonesian city or town.

(Top) Buildings under the Kampung Improvement Programme of Jakarta which won the 1980 Aga Khan award for Architecture. (Above) New urban houses in the outskirts of the Jakarta city.

The Colonial Municipality

For the first two hundred years of colonial rule, Dutch influence on Indonesian urban life was essentially limited to Batavia (Jakarta). Although Batavia, which was modelled after Dutch cities back in the Netherlands, introduced the concept of an autonomous city administration to the region, it was not until the early 20th century (1905-06) that certain towns in Java and elsewhere in the Archipelago were granted the status of municipalities (*gemente*), in accordance with the implementation of the Ethical Policy in 1901. The primary concern, here, was to decentralise the authority of the central government, but the actual result was to increase colonial control at the local level. Subsequently, a kind of dualism developed in that while these towns were generally considered to be European enclaves, they nevertheless included a significant native population, living in their own settlements or *kampung*. The latter were regarded as falling outside the administrative jurisdiction of the municipality and until recently, were not considered in town development programmes, being left instead as pockets of urban stagnation where living conditions deteriorated as population densities increased.

EARLY 20TH-CENTURY CITIES
Conferences held in the 1950s and 1960s, led to the subdivision of Indonesian cities into segregated areas, each defined according to their purpose: residential, commercial, industrial, circulation and recreation. The years since then, however, have seen a shift in emphasis from land usage to more abstract, non-physical definitions of space usage. Dichotomies such as modern vs. traditional, formal vs. informal, planned vs. unplanned, were hotly debated against a social background of political turmoil, migration and demographic growth. (Top to bottom) Semarang, Central Java; Bandung, West Java; and Surabaya, East Java.

The Colonial City in the 20th Century

During the latter years of the colonial era, municipal towns underwent important transformations. Town Development Plans established new residential districts, mostly for Dutch residents, which were planned along the lines of a

MODERN ARCHITECTURE AND IDENTITY

'Garden City'. A range of public buildings, such as townhalls, post offices and banks, were built to create new civic centres, which together with the residential areas they served, were situated in a park-like setting. Smaller houses for low-income groups — mostly local Indonesians — were also built and inserted into the new European residential districts according to a pattern of urban development advocated by Thomas Karsten, a prominent Dutch architect and town planner.

In 1926, fearing the unhealthy *kampung* areas might breed disease — the Java plague of 1913 had provided a shocking precedent — some municipalities launched programmes to improve sanitation and amenities in these blighted areas (Semarang Conference on Public Housing, 1925). These schemes and housing projects, intended for the Dutch and local populace alike, were part of a multi-pronged policy aimed to develop the colonial town and enhance the quality of all its residents in every walk of life.

Early Independence and Town Planning

Dutch colonial rule in Indonesia ended with the Japanese invasion in 1942. During the three and a half years of occupation, both the economic situation and the physical conditions of Indonesian cities deteriorated. Following the Japanese surrender in 1945, Indonesia declared its independence, but urban development continued to stagnate whilst the Dutch tried to re-establish themselves as colonial masters. However, in 1947, the Dutch succeeded in implementing a set of planning regulations for urban development — the SSO/SVV (Stadsvormings-ordonantie/Stadsvormings-verordening) — which had been drawn up before the war.

In 1950, the Dutch finally left and their residences and properties were taken over by the Indonesian government. The Dutch departure saw a massive influx of rural people into urban areas in response to widely held perceptions of the city as a place of economic opportunities. The *kampung* areas swelled and overflowed, filling all available vacant areas.

Recent Urban Development

Since 1970, the national development policy has been focused primarily on economic growth and achievement. This situation has pushed housing programmes to the fore and encouraged the emergence of a large number of housing projects in the private sector. Government housing schemes have also been implemented to cope with the growth of urban populations, whilst *kampung* improvement programmes have been reintroduced to improve conditions in existing areas. Despite the success of the latter policies they have been discontinued because they were considered to be too biased towards improving the physical infrastructure solely.

During the 1980s, urban development started to spread outwards away from city centres, creating new towns in the process. Within the existing urban fabric, smaller sites have been acquired for high-rise projects, while larger parcels of land have been subdivided for low-key projects such as the building of new shophouses. Meanwhile, the construction of skyscrapers and other large scale projects result in the removal of kampongs from the inner city areas and the destruction of many historical buildings.

Towering skyscrapers dominate the skyline of the vibrant and dynamic city of Jakarta in the 1990s. (Above left) The Menara Emporium, Kuningan, Jakarta. (Above) The Menara Batavia, Central Jakarta.

(Below) The Jakarta skyline during the mid-evening, drawing contrast between the short kampung *houses in the foreground and the tall skyscrapers at the back.*

Regionalism and Identity in Contemporary Architecture

The Indonesian population comprises more than 200 ethnic groups, each with its own specific cultural traditions and identity. They are spread unevenly across the Archipelago which comprises roughly 13,000 islands grouped together into 29 provinces. Often one particular ethnic group is singled out as representative of an entire province — for example, West Java is typically identified as the homeland of the Sundanese, despite the fact that the Sundanese are actually only the second largest ethnic group in the region. Naturally, architecture plays an important part in the expression of this regional identity.

(Above) A design-sketch of the Museum Toraja.

(Right) The Timorese house, designed by Yori Antar and Marco Kusumawijaya, came out of a project to create modern and healthy house types for the Timorese people.

(Below) Designs of biu-biu houses in Jimbaran, Bali, by Jay Subiyakto.

Regional Signifiers

The vernacular architecture of Indonesia is distinguished by the prominence of different roof forms which are usually sufficient to identify a particular building with a specific locality. Often the function of a particular building, or the social status of its occupants, is signalled by the type of roof form adopted, while in other instances, a single structure may exhibit a variety of roof forms reflecting a range of different activities taking place within.

Regionalism and the Neo-vernacular Style of Architecture

Dutch architects in the early decades of this century were the first to recognise the potential of Indonesian regional architecture as a means of developing a truly local style of contemporary architecture for the Indies. This led them to adopt a neo-vernacular form of architecture which appropriated and re-interpreted existing building traditions. However, in general, the only successful synthesis of local and modern traditions lay in various combinations of vernacular roof forms, and construction principles, with modern Western building techniques, as exemplified by Henri Maclaine Pont's Technische Hogeschool, Bandung, and an assortment of European residences built in the 1920s and 1930s.

The first generation of Indonesian architects in the early Independence era continued the search for appropriate blend of European and Indonesian architectural forms, the most urgent requirement at that time being the need to create a strong sense of national identity. In time, the use of traditional roof forms became increasingly rarefied, eventually becoming little more than a simple geometrical outline. This development can be seen as an attempt to create new architecture for the modern Republic of Indonesia whilst still preserving a sense of tradition and continuity with region's historic past.

The Revival of Regionalism in the 1970s

There was a resurgence of regionalism in Indonesian architecture during the 1970s as revenues from the sale of crude oil were directed towards development and improving the nation's infrastructure. This revival of interest in local architectural forms can be seen as a reaction against the anonymous and alien aesthetic of the 'International Style' which had come to dominate the Indonesian architectural scene of the previous decade. Moreover, the 1970s also saw the emergence of the idea of Indonesia as the 'summit of local cultures', a development which was reflected in the construction of the Taman Mini Indonesia Indah theme park, promoting Indonesia's cultural diversity and riches.

TRADITIONAL ELEMENTS IN CONTEMPORARY BUILDINGS

Following the early experiments by Maclaine Pont and Karsten in the pre-war era, Dutch and Indonesian architects alike continued to try and incorporate traditional features in their work. In the early years this synthesis of local and modern elements was fairly conservative, but as time went by, architects began to play with more abstract ideas and forms with varying degrees of success. The post-modern era has witnessed much cruder attempts to incorporate local references: often the 'solution' has been simply to place a traditional roof form on top of an otherwise entirely modern structure.

❶ *The Bandung Institute of Technology is designed by the eccentric Maclaine Pont.*
❷ *The Carita Beach Resort, Sunda Straits, employs traditional multi-tiered roofs to good effect.*
❸ *The Hotel Amankila in Karangasem, Bali incorporates references to traditional 'floating pavilions' in its design.*
❹ *A 1930s private house in Bandung.*
❺ *The Karo Batak pavilion at Taman Mini, Jakarta.*

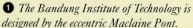

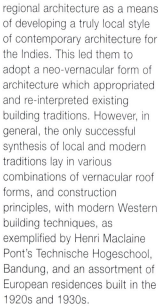

MODERN ARCHITECTURE AND IDENTITY

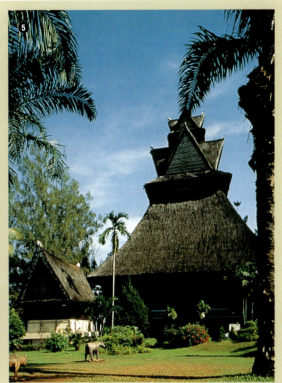

The demand for regional architecture, at this time, was so strong that many local governments decided that all public buildings within their area of jurisdiction would incorporate local architectural elements in their design. In most instances, however, this consisted of no more than simply taking a tradi-tional roof type and enlarging it to suit whatever new purpose it was intended to serve. Similar policies were adopted in the private sector and in every town and major urban centre, commercial buildings of every description — hotels, offices, banks and shopping centres — sprouted vernacular roof forms with very little regard for aesthetic sensibilities.

The new international Soekarno-Hatta airport at Cengkareng, west of Jakarta, which was built in the late 1970s, employed a similar strategy, being conceived as a conventional modern building which was then topped by enlarged versions of indigenous roof forms. In this instance, the architect responsible was a Frenchman, P. Andreau, who had previously designed the Aeroport du Paris — presumably the intention here was to provide a suitably regional flavour for the main gateway to the country.

A National Architectural Identity

In September 1984, a seminar held by the Indonesian Institute of Architects explored the issue of a common national architectural identity. Two main arguments dominated the forum. The first favoured the development of a national architectural identity through references to traditional forms, and sought to implement this strategy in government building projects. The second view argued for the creation of an entirely new cultural image — an image which would also include Western architectural values and precepts. In the latter instance, a specifically Indonesian identity would gradually emerge over time as what were initially foreign elements became adapted to local conditions and needs.

Postscript

Regional architecture was again optimistically embraced by Indonesian architects in the 1980s with the emergence of Post-modernism on the international scene. The eclectic manner of pluralistic references advocated by the Post-modernist school gave rise to the anticipation that modern regional architecture would be revived and would once again inform contemporary architecture. Sadly it was a Classical revival which took hold and occupies a dominant position in Indonesian architecture today, though this position is now being challenged by Deconstruction and the New Modernist school.

(Top left) Front elevation of the Mina Bay Resort Hotel, Batam.
(Top) Novotel Toraja, Tana Toraja, south Sulawesi.
(Above) A design model of the Amanjiwo hotel, Yogyakarta, Central Java.

Towards the Maturity of Indonesian Architecture

The architectural scene in modern Indonesia is extremely complex with a multiplicity of different forms and solutions appearing in a wide range of contexts. In this respect, it is difficult to identify a mainstream of architectural development. In many urban centres, however, the 'International Style' continues to prevail resulting in the suppression of local elements which are all too often entirely absent from the most prestigious sectors of modern Indonesian cities. Critics have referred to this as a 'crisis of cultural identity'.

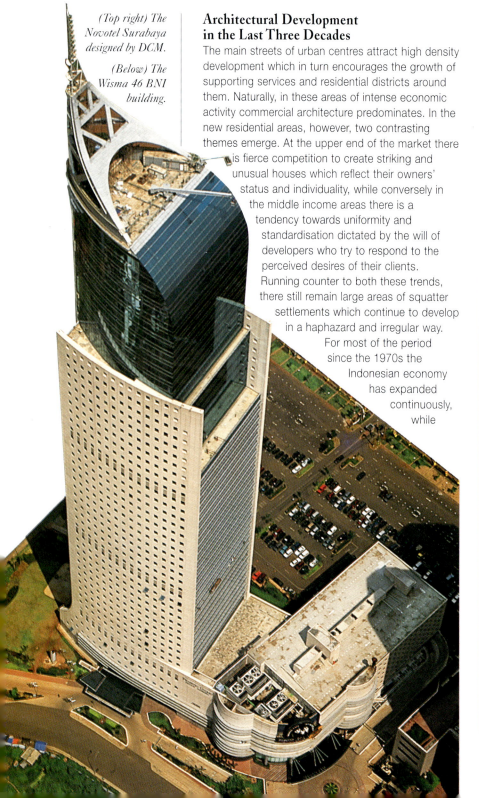

(Top right) The Novotel Surabaya designed by DCM.

(Below) The Wisma 46 BNI building.

Architectural Development in the Last Three Decades

The main streets of urban centres attract high density development which in turn encourages the growth of supporting services and residential districts around them. Naturally, in these areas of intense economic activity commercial architecture predominates. In the new residential areas, however, two contrasting themes emerge. At the upper end of the market there is fierce competition to create striking and unusual houses which reflect their owners' status and individuality, while conversely in the middle income areas there is a tendency towards uniformity and standardisation dictated by the will of developers who try to respond to the perceived desires of their clients. Running counter to both these trends, there still remain large areas of squatter settlements which continue to develop in a haphazard and irregular way.

For most of the period since the 1970s the Indonesian economy has expanded continuously, while between the late 1980s and the mid-1990s, there was also a massive increase in foreign investment. This injection of overseas capital into joint-venture property and construction projects with local developers, brought many foreign architects to Indonesia and they have played a significant role in shaping the architecture of new Indonesian towns and cities. However, unlike the Dutch architects of the 1930s, many of these expatriate architects were unfamiliar with designing for the tropics, while their local partners, who often had received a similar Modernist architectural training, were either equally ignorant or else lacked the authority to propose alternative solutions to those of their foreign counterparts. As a result, the downtown areas of many Indonesian cities gradually came to resemble those of big cities in the West and often at a high environmental cost: massive high-rise buildings consume huge amounts of energy in terms of air-conditioning and other services.

MODERN ARCHITECTURE AND IDENTITY

The DCM trio, B. Hendropurnomo, S. Sutanto and D. Hendrasto, won the IAI award for Tugu Park Hotel in 1997 and was responsible for designing a wide range of buildings including Novotel Surabaya, Novotel Semarang (below and right).

IAI Awards

Attempting to avoid any further worsening of this situation, the Indonesian Institute of Architects has instituted an awards scheme which is held every three years, the IAI Awards. Both architects and owners are eligible for either an award or a citation in a number of different categories, the choice being decided upon by a panel of experts. Past winners have included: Sonny Sutanto, Budiman Hendropurnomo, Sardjono Sani, Mr. Juned of Team 4, Gunawan Tjahjono and Budi Sukada, and Mangunwijaya. Not every modern building of note has received an award. Some of these buildings are Danamon Square by Henry Cobb, Dharmala Tower by Paul Rudolph, Niaga Tower by KPF and Grand Hyatt by HOK.

Aspiring Young Architects

Arsitek Muda Indonesia (AMI) group was founded by a group of young architects, some of them are IAI recipients, who have actively sought to promote their work through public exhibitions. The most significant contribution of this group to the Indonesian architectural scene is their regular critical discussion programme. This programme is often held in conjunction with an 'open house' at any completed new buildings by its members. The works of AMI's members often follow new global trend. A few of them have even successfully incorporated into their work cultural aspects of design; a good example is the award-winning East Timor house project by Yori Antar and Marco Kusumawijaya.

FUTURE OF INDONESIAN ARCHITECTURE

existence of AMI has greatly enriched the Indonesian architectural trum. The emergence of a critical consciousness in the minds of a new eration of Indonesian architects can be seen as a maturing process, with y innovative and experimental designs now appearing on the drawing rds. Inevitably, foreign elements have been incorporated, but these been adapted to suit local needs and sensibilities, creating a nctive form of architecture which is at once Indonesian and modern.

❶ *The Sewa Dago office in Bandung, designed by award-winning A.D. Tardiyana, S. Silalahi and B. Wahyudin.*
❷ *The twin towers of Danamon square by Henry Cobb.*
❸ *Agha Khan award-winning house by S. Sani.*
❹ *Novotel apartments in Surabaya were designed by DCM (Duta Cermat Mandiri).*
❺ *Bank Niaga building designed by US-based Kohn Pederson and Fox.*

Glossary

A

alang-alang : *imperata cyclindrica*, a tall grass. It is usually found covering areas where forest has been repeatedly burned.

alun-alun : public square to the north of a Javanese palace.

antefix : carved triangular element which is used for decorations for the tops of walls and **cornices**.

B

bahal : Nepalese term for a two-storied temple of the Vajrayana sect, which was extremely influential in Indonesian Buddhism.

basement : see **stereobate**; the lowest storey of a building, usually below or slightly below the ground level.

Bauhaus : school of design founded by German architect, Walter Gropius, which existed in Germany from 1919 to 1933. It sought to combine the finer elements of art and technically expert craftsmanship.

box frame : box-like form of concrete construction, where the loads are taken on cross walls. Suitable only for buildings consisting of repetititve small cells or units.

C

candi : architectural remains from the Classic Period.

cantilever: horizontal projection such as step, balcony, beam or canopy supported by a downward force behind a fulcrum.

cella : inner room containing the statue of a divinity.

clerestorey : arrangements of windows on the walls of a room which is carried higher than the surrounding roofs to light the interior.

colonnade : row of columns supporting a row of horizontal **mouldings**.

corbel : projecting block, usually made of stone, supporting a beam or other horizontal members.

cornice : decorated projection at the top of the wall to protect the wall face or to be used as a kind of ornamentation.

D

Delft School : term applied to conservative Dutch architects associated with the Technische Hogeschool in Delft, The Netherlands, in the 1920s and 1930s. Characteristics of the Delft School style of architecture are sloping roofs and simple and sobre design details.

De Stijl : art movement founded by a painter-architect Theo van Doesburg in Leiden in 1917. Based on abstraction of form and colour. These forms were well-suited to the International Modern Movement and had considerable influence on the **Bauhaus** in the 1920s.

dolmen : descriptive term for **megalithic** chamber tomb. In Southeast Asia, it is usually used to refer to a large flat rock supported on one or more small rocks so that the whole structure looks like a stool.

E

entablature : upper part of an order, consisting of architrave, **frieze**, and **cornice**.

eave : lower portion of a sloping roof near the walls, especially a part projecting beyond the walls and forming an overhanging drip for water.

F

frieze : middle of three main divisions of an **entablature**. Also refers to any long and narrow horizontal panel used for ornamentation purposes.

I/J

ijuk : native palm tree (*Arenga pinnata*).

joglo : type of roof with two roof ridges.

joints : union between two pieces of wood. There are two classes of joints. Parallel joints are created by joining two paralled pieces of wood side by side, usually with the grain of wood along the long dimension. An example of this joinery method is the lapped joint. Right-angled joints are created by joining two pieces of wood end to end or crosswise, usually at right-angle to each other and across the grain of the wood.

architrave
frieze
cornice
pillar

lapped joints

mortise-and tenon joint

136

Examples of this method of joinery are mortise-and-tenon joints and lapped joints.

K

kampung : term for a village or rural settlement.

kala : motif found over temple doorways and niches for statuary in Java, Sumatra and Bali.

king post : post standing on a tier or collar-beam and rising to the apex of the roof where it supports a ridge-piece.

kota : modern Indonesian term for city. Hindi in derivation, it originally describes a walled settlement or fort and subsequently came to designate an urban centre.

kraton : Indonesian term for palace, the residence of the ruler.

L

limasan : type of roof with five roof ridges.

lingga : phallic symbol representing **Siva**, often found in Hindu temples together with its female counterpart, the **yoni**.

lumbung : rice barn.

M

makara : mythical beast with an elephant's trunk, a lion's mane, a parrot's beak and a fish's tail. A sculptured form placed at the wings of stairways in Sumatran and Javanese temples, and at lower corners of niches for statues.

mandala : mystic symbols in the form of concentric circles; used as aids to meditation; territory under a cakravartin.

marae : designates a public place reserved for the social and religious activities of the community.

megalithic : pertaining to monuments constructed primarily of large stones; associated with Preclassic societies.

menhir : type of **megalithic** construction; a tall monolith.

meru : mountain abode of the gods at the centre of the universe.

moulding : general term applied to all the varieties of outline or colour given to the angles of various subordinate parts and features of buildings.

P

party wall : wall built between two pieces of land belonging to two different proprietors. The purpose is to provide a wall of sufficient thickness and strength to afford a degree of privacy.

pendapa : from South Indian mandapa, a 'pillared hallway'; in Indonesian, a term for an unwalled pavilion.

peristyle : range of columns surrounding a building or open court.

pilaster : imitation pillar carved on the walls of Javanese temples.

porch : roofed structure, usually open at the sides; it projects from the front of a building and is used to protect the entrance from the elements.

punden berundak : Indonesian counterpart to the Polynesian **marae**; a series of stepped terraces associated with religious worship.

purlin : horizontal timber laid parallel with the **wall plate** and the ridge-beam some way up the slope of the roof, resting on principal **rafters** and supported by common **rafters**.

R

rafter : roof timber sloping up from the **wall plate** to the ridge.

ridge pole : board or plank at the apex of a roof against the sides of which the upper ends of the **rafters** abut.

S

salient : part of a fort which projects out to enemy territory.

Siva : Hindu deity, one of the major trinity, the most widely revered god in ancient Java. He is usually represented by a **lingga**, although occasionally statues are used, such as at Candi Lara Jonggrang.

stereobate : solid mass of masonry serving as a base usually for a wall or a row of columns.

stud : upright timbers.

T

tie beam : horizontal tranverse beam in a roof, connecting the feet of **rafters**, usually at the height of the **wall plate**, to counteract the thrust.

W

wall plate : timber laid longitudinally on top of a wall to receive the ends of the **rafters**.

wali songo : 'nine saints' who had supposedly introduced Islam to the island of Java.

Y

yoni : female counterpart of **lingga**, female principle. Used to represent Parvati, the consort of **Siva**.

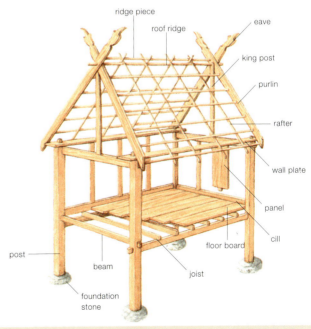

REPRESENTATION OF BALINESE DEITIES IN PAINTING ON P. 52			
Dewi Sri	goddess of rice and fertility	Dewi Uma	Siwa's consort
Dewa Budha	Buddha	Resi Waraspati	one of the five godly seers; corresponds to Thursday
Dewa Tintya	the symbol of the One God		
Dewa Brahma	one of the Trimurti; the god of creation	Resi Raditya	one of the godly seers; corresponds to Sunday
Dewa Wisnu	one of the Trimurti; the god of preservation	Resi Budha	one of the godly seers; corresponds to Wednesday
Dewa Guru (Siwa)/ Iswara/ Mahadewa	one of the Trimurti; the god of destruction	Resi Anggara	one of the godly seers; corresponds to Tuesday
Siwa Raditya	the Sun God	Resi Somo	one of the godly seers; corresponds to Monday
Dewi Uma	goddess of the realm of illusion		

Bibliography

GENERAL WORKS

Bellwood, P. 1985. *Prehistory of the Indo-Malaysian Archipelago.* Sydney: Academic Press.

Feldman, J.A. 1985. *The Eloquent Dead: Ancestral Sculpture of Indonesia and Southeast Asia.* Los Angeles: UCLA Museum of Cultural History.

Fox, J. (ed). 1993. *Inside Austronesian Houses: Perspectives on Domestic Designs for Living.* Canberra: The Australian National University.

Jones, D. & Mitchell, G. (eds.). 1977. *Vernacular Architecture of the Islamic World and Indian Asia.* London: Art and Archaeology Research Papers.

TRADITIONAL ARCHITECTURE

Blust, R. 1987. 'Lexical Reconstruction and Semantic Reconstruction: the case of Austronesian 'House' Words', *Diachronica* IV (1-2), pp. 79-106.

Clamagirand, B. 1975. 'La Maison Ema Timor Portugais', *Asie du Sud-Est et Monde Insulindien* 6 (2-3). pp. 35-60.

Cunningham, C. 1964. 'Order in the Atoni House', *Bijdragen tot de Taal- Land- en Volkenkunde* 120, pp. 34-68.

Dawson, B. & Gillow, J. 1994. *The Traditional Architecture of Indonesia.* London: Thames and Hudson.

Dumarçay, J. 1987. *The House in South-East Asia.* Singapore: Oxford University Press.

Forth, G. 1981. *Rindi: An Ethnographic Study of a Traditional Domain in Eastern Sumba.* The Hague: Martinus Nijhoff.

Hamzuri. n.d. *Rumah Tradisionil Jawa.* Jakarta: Departemen Pendidikan dan Kebudayaan.

Howe, L. 1983. 'An Introduction to the Cultural Study of Traditional Balinese Architecture', *Archipel* 25. pp. 137-58.

Izikowitz, K & Sørensen, P. (eds.). 1982. *The House in East and Southeast Asia: Anthropological and Architectural Aspects.* London: Curzon.

Keeler, W. 1983. *Symbolic Dimensions of the Javanese House.* Working Paper No. 29. Clayton: Centre of Southeast Asian Studies, Monash University.

Kis-Jovak, J. 1980. *Autochthone Architektur auf Siberut.* Zurich: Eidgenossische Technische Hochschule.

Kis-Novak, J.W., Nooy-Palm, H., Schefold, R. & Schulz-Dornburg, U. 1988. *Banua Toraja: changing patterns in architecture and symbolism among the Sa'dan Toraja, Sulawesi, Indonesia.* Amsterdam: Royal Tropical Institute.

Ng, C. 1993. 'Raising the House Post and Feeding the Husband-Givers: The Spatial Categories of Social Reproduction Among the Minangkabau', in J. Fox (ed.) *Inside Austronesian Houses: Perspectives on Domestic Designs for Living.* Canberra: The Australian National University.

Sargeant, G & Saleh, R. 1973. *Traditional Buildings of Indonesia, Vol. 1: Batak Toba; Vol. 2 Batak Karo; Vol. 3 Batak Simalungan/Mandailing.* Bandung: REHOCE (Regional Housing Centre).

Sibeth, A. 1991. *The Batak Peoples of the Island of Sumatra.* London: Thames and Hudson.

Soebadio, H. 1975. 'The Documentary Study of Traditional Balinese Architecture: Some Preliminary Notes', *Indonesian Quarterly* 3, pp. 86-95.

Soelarto, R. 1973. 'Villages Balinais: Tradition, Restoration, Renovation', *L'Architecture Aujourd'hui* 167, pp. 44-49.

Tan, R. 1967. 'The Domestic Architecture of South Bali', *Bijdragen tot de Taal-, Land- en Volkenkunde* 123 (4), pp. 442-75.

Tjahjono, G. 1989. *Cosmos, Centre, and Duality in Javanese Architectural*

Traditions: the Symbolic Dimensions of House Shapes in Kota Gede and Surroundings. Ph. D Dissertation, University of California.

Viaro, A. 1980. *Urbanisme et Architecture traditionnels du Sud de L'Ile de Nias*. Paris: UNESCO.

Waterson, R. 1990. *The Living House: An Anthropology of Architecture in Southeast Asia*. Kuala Lumpur: Oxford University Press.

INDONESIA'S CLASSICAL HERITAGE

Atmadi, P. 1988. *Some Architectural Design Principles of Temples in Java: a Study Through the Buildings Projection on the Reliefs of Borobudur Temple*. Yogyakarta: Gadjah Mada University Press.

Bullough, N. 1995. *Historic East Java: Remains in Stone*. Singapore: East Javanese Tourism Promotion Foundation.

Chihara, D. 1996. *Hindu Buddhist Architecture in Southeast Asia*. (trans. Rolf W. Giebel). Leiden: E.J. Brill.

Dumarçay, J. 1978. *Borobudur*. Singapore: Oxford University Press.

—. 1986. *The Temples of Java*. Singapore: Oxford University Press.

—. 1986. *Candi Sewu dan Arsitektur Bangunan Agama Buda di Jawa Tengah*. Jakarta: Departemen Pendidikan dan Kebudayaan.

—. 1991. *The Palaces of South-East Asia: Architecture and Customs*. Singapore: Oxford University Press.

—. 1993. *Histoire de l'Architecture de Java*. Paris: Publications de l'Ecole Française d'Extrême-Oriente.

Ismiyono, M., Sumedi, B., Siswoyo, B. & Winarto. 1983. *Laporan Studi Teknis Muara Teknis Bidang Tekno Arkeologi*. Jakarta: Direktorat Perlindungan dan Pembinaan Peninggalan Sejarah dan Purbakala.

Kempers, B.A.J. 1959. *Ancient Indonesian Art*. Amsterdam: van der Peet.

—. 1977. *Monumental Bali: Introduction to Balinese Archaeology Guide to the Monuments*. Den Haag: Voor Goor Zonen.

—. 1978. *Herstel in Eigen Waarde: Monumentenzorg in Indonesië*. Amsterdam: de Walburg Pers Zutphen.

Manguin, P.Y. 1987. 'Etudes sumatranaises I. Palembang et Sriwijaya: anciennes hypotheses, recherches nouvelles (Palembang Ouest)', *Bulletin de l'Ecole Française d'Extrême-Orient* 76, pp. 337- 402.

Miksic, J.N. 1990. *Borobudur: Golden Tales of the Buddhas*. Hong Kong: Periplus Editions Ltd.

—. 1990. *Old Javanese Gold*. Singapore: Ideation.

Pigeaud, Th. G. Th. 1960-1963. *Java in the 14th Century: a study in cultural history — the Nagarakertagama by Rakawi Prapanca of Majapahit 1365 A.D*. 5 vols. The Hague: Martinus Nijhoff.

Schnitger, F.M. 1937. *The Archaeology of Hindoo Sumatra*. Leiden: E.J. Brill.

Suleiman, S. 1981. *Monumen monumen Indonesia Purba*. Jakarta: Pusat Penelitian Arkeologi Nasional.

Sumadio, B. (ed). 1984. *Sejarah Nasional Indonesia II: Jaman Kuna*. Jakarta: Balai Pustaka.

CITIES, MOSQUES AND PALACES

Beek, A. van. 1990. *Life in the Javanese Kraton*. Oxford University Press.

Frishman, Martin & Khan Hasan-Uddin. 1995. *The Mosque: History, Architectural Development & Regional Diversity*. London: Thames and Hudson.

Guillot, C., Ambary, H.M. & Dumarçay, J. 1990. *The Sultanate of Banten*. Jakarta: Gramedia Book Publishing Division.

Maass. A. 1939. *Die Kunst bei den Malaien Zentral-Sumatras*. Berlin: D. Reimer.

Macdonald, C. (ed.). 1987. *De la hutte au palais: sociétes 'à maison' en Asie du Sud-Est insulaire*. Paris: CNRS.

Smithies, M. 1986. *Yogyakarta: Cultural Heart of Indonesia*. Singapore: Oxford University Press.

ARCHITECTURE OF THE 17TH TO 19TH CENTURIES

Akihary, H. 1996. *Ir. F.J.L. Ghijsels: Architect in Indonesia [1910-1929]*. Utrecht: Seram Press.

Djauhari, S. 1978. *Kompendium Sejarah Arsitektur*. Bandung: L.P.M.B.

Faber, G.H. 1931. *Oud Soerabaia*. Surabaya: H. Van Ingen.

—. 1936. *Nieuw Soerabaia*. Surabaya: H. Van Ingen.

Heuken, A. 1989. *Historical Sights of Jakarta*. Singapore: Times Books International (3rd edition).

Jessup, H. 1982. 'Four Dutch Buildings in Indonesia', *Orientations* vol. 13 (9-12).

—. 1984. 'The Dutch Colonial Villa Indonesia', *MIMAR* 13.

Lombard, D. 1982. 'Villes Coloniales', *Urbi* VI Liege-belgigue.

MODERN ARCHITECTURE AND IDENTITY

Dana, D. W. 1990. *Ciri Perancangan Kota Bandung*. Jakarta: PT Gramedia Pustaka Utama.

Nas, P.J.M. 1986. *The Indonesian City*. Dordrecht: Foris Publications.

Nix, T. 1940. *Stedebouw in Indonesie en de Stedebouw-kundige Vormgeving*. Bandung: A.C. Nix.

Index

A

Aalbers, A.F., 119, 125
    residence, *125*
acculturisation, 111
Aceh, 86, 96
adat, 25
Aeroport du Paris, 133
Aga Khan award for Architecture, 130
Agastya, 62, 69
Ageng, Sultan, 98, 99
Agung, Sultan, 98, 107
agrarian polity, 85
ahu, 11
Air Tiris, 97
air wudlu, 96
Airlangga; king, 72, 73
Aksobhya, 66
alang alang, 17, 41
alun-alun, *88*, *90*, 90, 102, 106
Amal Bakti, 97
Amangkurat, 102, 103
Amarasi house, 44
Ambarrukmo, 99
Ambarwinangun, 99
Ambon, 96, 97
amin, 32, 33
Amitabha, 66
Amoghasiddhi, 66
Anak Wungwu, king, 78
anastylosis, 81
ancient ruins, 7
Ancol Recreation Park, *117-118*
Andreau, P., 133
Angkor, 81
Antar, Yori, 133
antefixes, 58, 60
Antonisse, Ir., 129
apsaras, heavenly creatures, *60*, *66*
Arca Domas, 73, *80*
Archaeological Association of Yogyakarta, 80
archaeological remains, 73
Archaeological Service Museum in Trowulan, 72
Archaeological Service, 80
Arsitek Muda Indonesia (AMI), 135
Art Deco, 48, 120, 121, 124
    motifs, 122
    ornamentation, 121, 125
Art Nouveau, 121
Asta Kosala Kosali, 36
Atlast Historique, 108
Atoni Meto, 44
    Atoni house, *18*, *44*
Austronesian, 14
    ancestry, 9
    animism, 36
    archetype, 34
    architecture, 11
    expansion, *9*
    house, 8, 10
    legacy, 12
    morphology, 83
    pile structures, 40
    tradition, 38, 83
    word list, 11
    -Indonesian connections, 10-11
Avalokitesvara, 66

B

Badui, 72
    house, *8*
Badut, 81
Bahal I, *77*
Bajangratu, 71
balai kambang, 99
bale, 30, 41, 70
bale bele, 41
bale kambang, 97 also see floating pavilion
Bale lantang, *38*
Bali Aga
    houses, *38*
    villages, 38
Bali museum, Denpasar, *90*
Balinese
    architecture, 71
    houses, 36-37, *36-37*, 38-39
    palace, *90*
    pantheon, 52
    rice barn, 17
bamboo rafts, 85
Banda Aceh, 84
Bandung Institute of Technology, 122, 126, 129, *132-133*
Bandung, 116, 124, 130
    private house, *133*
Bank Jabar, *129*
Bank Nasional Indonesia, *128*
Bank Niaga, *135*
Banten, 89, 96, 102
    city plan, *103*
    minaret, *86*
    mosque, *103*
Bappindo Bank, 127
Batak, 55
    architecture, 16, 24-25
    homeland, 24
Batavia, 105, *108*, 108-109, 109, 110, 116, 124
    map of, *104-105*
    Batavian shophouse, 115
Batu Aceh, 101
batu umang, 78, *78-79*
Beer Hall, *107*
Banjarmasin, 97
Bennink, J., 125
Berlage, H.P., 121
Besakih, *50*
biu-biu houses, 132
Bock, Carl, 83
bodhisattva, 66

Bojong residency, *106*
Borobudur, 6, *12*, *50*, 59, 61, *64*, *65*, 66, *80*, 80, 81, 85
    hidden foot of, 59
Bosch, F.D.K., 76, 95
Bottle Cave, 79
box frame(s), 16, 17
Brahma and Visnu temples, 81
Brahma, deity, 62, 63
brahmamula, 95
brick
    architecture, 70-71, *71*
    structures, 76-77
    temples, 55, 76-77, *77*
    -making kiln, *107*
Buddha Vairocana, 66
Buddhist
    architecture, 66-67
    temples, 67
Buitenzorg, market in, *107*
Bukit Menore, 64

C

Calon Arang, 78
canals, 108
candi, 54, 58, 83
    C. Abang, 54
    C. Angsoka, 76
    c. apit, 58, 59, 63
    C. Arjuna, 55, 55
    C. Badut, 7
    C. Bajangratu, 58, 70
    c. bentar, 87, 89
    C. Berahu, *70*, 70
    C. Biaro Bahal III, *77*
    C. Bima, *55*
    C. Borobudur, *8*, 64-65, 65
    C. Brahma, 63
    C. Ceto, 75
    C. Darmo, 71
    C. Gebang, 63, 81
    C. Ijo, 63
    C. Jabung, 71
    C. Jago, *58*, 69, *98*
    C. Jao, 59
    C. Jawi, *52*, 67, *69*, 81
    C. Kalasan, *50*, *52*, 66, *67*, 81
    C. Kedaton, 70
    C. Kidal, 58, 68, 69
    C. Lara Jonggrang, 6, *52*, *57*, 60, *58*, 61, *62*, 63, *79*, *80*, 81, *81*
    C. Lor, *70*
    C. Lumbung, 57
    C. Mahligai, *76*, *77*
    C. Mendut, *59*, *67*, 81, *81*
    C. Morangan, 63
    C. Mulungan, *52*
    C. Ngawen, *60*, *81*
    C. Panataran, *50*
    C. Pari, 70
    c. perwara, 63
    C. Plaosan, *52*, 66, 67, *66-67*
    C. Sajiwan, *67*
    C. Sari, 66, *66*
    C. Selogriyo, *62*
    C. Semar, 55, 62
    C. Sewu, 66, *80*
    C. Singasari, 69
    C. Siva, *62*, 63
    C. Sukuh,73
    C. Sumberawan, *52*
    C. Surawana, 69
    C. Tikus, *71*
    C. Tugurejo, *52*
    C. Visnu, 63
    C. Wringin Lawang, 70
    C. Yudha, *72*
    candi mouldings and perspective effects, *69*
Cardeel, J.L., 103
Carita Beach Resort, *132-133*
Casparis, J.G. de, 62, 65
caves
    artificial see *batu umang*
    sacred, 54
    hermit, 87
cemeteries see tombs
    also see royal cemetery at Imogiri
Central Java, 78-79
ceramic plates/objects, 87, 95, 96
ceremonial stone terraces, 11
Chatelain, Henri, 108
chief's house, *31*
Children's Hospital, Batavia, *107*
Chinese, 114
    house, 114
    shophouse, 115
Cililitan Besar, 111, *111*
Ciliwung River, 108
Cirebon, 79, 98
    Chronicle, 98
    mihrab, 95
    Cirebonese batik, *86*
cities, 82-103 also see modern cities
City Hall, *109*
Civil Public Works Department, 116
Classic era, 6, 51, 54, 76, 83, 88
    also see Early Classic
    also see Late Classic
    also see Middle Classic
Classic Indonesian architecture, 51, 52
Classical heritage, 6, 50-81
Classical style, 86
    also see Dutch Classical
    also see European classicism
Cobb, Henry, 135
colonial
    architecture, 120
    bureaucracy, 116
    municipality, 130

town, 124
columns see pillars and columns
Commission in Netherlands India for Archaeological Research on Java and Madura, 80
communal gallery, 33
conservation, 80-81
construction
    methods, 14, 56, *56*, 114
    rites, 20-21
    techniques, 16-17, 26, 47
contextualism, 126
cook houses, 47
country houses, 110-111
crossed-log foundation, 13, 16, 24
Cultivation System, 107, 116
cultural identity, 134
Cunningham, Clark, 44
Cuypers and Hulswit, 117

D

Dagada houses, 45
dalem, 35
Danamon Square, 135, *135*
Dani
    Compound, 46-47, *47*
    Men's house, 46
    settlement, *47*
    patterns, 46
Dayak
    carpenters, *16*
    longhouse, 32
    settlement, *12*
DCM trio (B. Hendropurnomo, S. Sutanto and D. Hendrasto),135
de Klerk, Reiner, 105
    house, 109, 110, *110*, 122
de Molins, Dessin de M., 109
de Stijl, 120, 128
deconstruction, 133
deities, 66
Delft High School of Technology, 122, 123, 128
Demak, 83, 94, 103
    mosque, 94-95
Department of Public Works, 116
Dewi Sri, 70
dharma, 36
Dharmala Tower, 135
Dieng Plateau, *54*, 54, 55, 59, 62, 66, 78
Directorate for the Conservation and Protection of the National Heritage, 80
Dong Son drum, *14*
Dra. Bintarti, 73
Duiker, Jan, 125
Durga, 62, 69
Duta Cermat Mandiri see DCM
Dutch Classical, 129
Dutch East India Company (Vereenigde Oost-Indische Compagnie or VOC), 108, 112
Dutch East Indies, 116
Dutch Indies Freestyle, 121
Dutch Rationalism, 117
Dutch residences, 112
Dutch townhouses, 112-113

E

early 20th-century cities, 85, 130
early 20th-century colonial villa, 124
early architecture (17th to 19th century), 114-117
Early Classic, 51, 78
early Dutch settlements, 105
early Independence, 128-129
early Islamic
    architecture, 86-87
    cities, *85*
    mosques, 88, 89
    palace, 86
Election Building, *128*
Ethical Policy, 130
European
    architecture, 7
    classicism, 105
    -Indian features, *97*
exotic influences, 121
Expressionist, 121

F

factory building, *117*
family compounds, 38
feng shui see geomancy
floating pavilion, 87 also see *bale kambang*
Fort Rotterdam, *106*
Fort Speelwijk, *103*

G

gandarwas, heavenly creatures, *66*
Gandhara, 54
Ganesha, *60*, 62, 63, 69
gardens, 98-99
    of Java, 98-99
    outside Java, 99
garden cities, 124-125
garuda statues, *73*
Garudeya, 68
Gateway Office Building, *118-119*
gateways, 71, *87*
    to *Pendopo Jinem*, *86*
    to the *sitinggil*, *86*
Gautama Buddha, 64
Gedong
    Songo, *54*, 54, 62, *62*

Songo VI, *55*, 55
Songo 9, *50*
Gedung
    Batu, 103
    Dharmala, 127
    Saté, *6*
geomancy, 115
geometric motifs, 60
Gereja Blenduk, *116*
German Bauhaus masters, 126
geriten (head house), 49
Ghijsels, F.J.L., 121
Goa Gajah (Elephant Cave), 78, 79
godowns, *117*
gorahua newali, 30
Governor's office, Surabaya, *122*
granaries, 45
Grand Hyatt, 135
Grand Melia Hotel, *117-118*
Grand Mosque at Banten, 102
Grand Mosque, Banda Aceh, *82*
graves, 73, *83*
    Christian, 48
Great Mosque gateway, *87*
Great Mosque of Demak, 97
Great Mosque of the Kasepuhan Palace, 95
Groneman, 80
Gropius, Walter, 126
Guided Democracy period, 129
Gunung Agung, 36
Gunung Gangsir, 70
Gunung Jati, 101
Gunung Kawi, *78*
    building of, *79*
    candi at, *78*
Gunung Padang, 11, 72, 73
gunungan, 98

H

Haji, Sultan, 103
Hall of Justice, 99
Hamengkubuwono I, 93, 98
Han dynasty, 114
Harbour Master's Office, *116*
Hasta Kosali, 90
Heine-Geldern, R. von, 73
Hendropurnomo, Budiman, 135
hermit caves, 87
Hilversum City Hall, 122
Hindu
    architecture, 56, 62-63
    architectural motifs, 63
    deities, 52, 78
    sites, 62
    temple complexes, 54
    trinity gods, 81
    -Buddhist architectural elements, 88
    -Buddhist era, 83
Homann Heirs Nuremberg, 104
honai, 47
Hong Kong Bank, Batavia, *117*
horned houses, 15 also see Minangkabau houses
Hotel Amankila, *133*
Hotel Borobudur, *128*
Hotel Indonesia, *126*, 129
houses for the dead, 48-49
housing schemes, 128
housing, yankee-style, *128*

I

Iban longhouse, *32*
Ibrahim, Malik, tomb of, 100, *100*
idjambe, 48
Ijzerman, J.W., 80
inaugural rites, for house, 21, 29
Indian temple, *54*
Indies Style, 113
    country houses, 111, *111*
Indo-Europeesche Stijl, 129
Indonesian architects, 129
Indonesian Directorate for the Preservation and Protection of the National Heritage, 95
Indonesian Institute of Architects, 133, 135
Institute of Indonesian Architects (IAI), 129
    IAI awards, 135
International Style, 126-127, 134
    building, 127
    skyscrapers, *7*
Iskandar Muda, Sultan, 97
Iskandar Tani of Aceh, 98
Islam, 83, 94
    spread of, *96*
Islamic
    architecture, 7
    Hijrah era, 101
    influence, 83
    kingdoms, 88
    period, 88
    structures, 88
    tombs, 100
Istora Senayan, 127

J

Jakarta Lloyd, 122
Jalah Gajah Mada, 109
Japan Embassy, 127
Japan House, 109, *111*
Java Street, *107*
Java, 95, 100 also see Central Java
Javaasche Bank offices, *117*
Javanese Bank Building in Batavia, *117*
Javanese
    architecture, 70
    cemetery, 101
    house, 34-35, *34*, *35*
    inscriptions, 72

Saka, 101
  stonework, 60-61
  temples, 58-59, 68, *68*, 89
Jayakarta, 103, 108
Jepara, 103
Jina (Conqueror) Buddhas, 81
Joana Stoomtram Maatschappij Semarang, *122*
joglo, 34, 105
  house, 122
  -style house, *34*
  -style roof, *15*
Johnson, Philip, 126
joints
  gendered joinery, *20*
  mitre, *56*
  mortise and tenon joints, *56*
  reinforced joints, 56

K

Ka'abah, 94
kabupaten, 106, 107
Kadiri, 73
kala head, *51, 60, 61, 78*
Kali Besar, 108, 109, 112
Kalibata cemetery, *128*
Kalimantan, 78-79
  longhouses of, 32-33
  Ma'anyan of, 48
kalpataru, 60
kamar bola, 107
Kampung Improvement Programme buildings, *130*
kampung, 34
  -style house, *34*
Kanoman palace, 87, 98
Karangasem, 99
Karo Batak, 16, 25
  granary, 13
  House, *6*, 17
  houses, 14
  Skull Houses, *49*
Karsten, Herman Thomas, 119, 121, 122, 128, 131, 132
Kasepuhan
  gateway, *86*
  palace, 72, *86, 87*, 98
  palace of Cirebon, *7*
Kebayoran Baru, 128
keben, *52, 52*
Kedu Plain, 64
Kelabit people, 49
Kemmer, J., 109
kendi, 60
Kenyah
  mausoleums, *49*
  settlements, 32
  society, 32
keramat, 101
Khmer of Angkor, 85
kiblat marker, 94, *95*
kinnara, 60
Klenteng Batu, *115*
Kosala, *72*, 73
Kota, 108, 109, 112
Kota Cina, 77, 85
Kota Railway Station, *121*
Kraton Kasepuhan, 89
kraton, 83, 90
Krisna, 63
kubur or makam, 100
Kudus, 87, 95, 103
  drumtower, 7
  houses, 102
  menara at, *86*
  Tower, 86
kuren, 38
Kusumawijaya, Marco, 133

L

landhuizen, 110, 111
Lara Jonggrang see c. Lara Jonggrang
Late Classic, 51, 86
  stone temples, *68*
Latin and Greek school, *107*
Le Corbusier, 125, 126
liang, 48, 49
limasan
  roof, 113
  -style house, 34, *34*
lindo puang, *18*
lingga 52, *54*, 55, *61*, 63, 68, 69
  -*yoni* rituals, 20
Lingsar garden, *90*
lion motif, *60, 81*
Lombard, Denys, 98
Lombok, 40, 99
longhouse, 28, 29, *29*, 38, 42
  of Kalimantan, 32-33
  society, 28
  also see village longhouse
lopo, 44
lumbung, 17, 41

M

ma'bubung, 21
Macan Putih, *80*
Mahabalipuram, *54*, 56
Mahakala, 63
Mahakarmavibhangga, 59
Majapahit, 71, 72, *73*, 83, 85
  brick temples of, *70*
  court, 79
  early period, 68
  Era, 69, 70, 83
  kingdom, 101
  relief, 72
  sunburst motif, 101
Makara, *61, 95*, 97
Makassar, 106
  of South Sulawesi, 48
Maluku, 96
mandala, 66, 90
mandapa, 70
Mangunwijaya, 126, 135
marae, 11, *72*
marapu, 42
Marco Polo, 100
Masjid Agung, 82, 88 also see Grand Mosque
Masjid Istiqlal, *129*
Masjid Jamik, *96, 102*
Masjid Kudus, *89*
Masjid Prasasti, *97*
Masjid Raya, *97*
Matin, Andra, 135
mausoleums, 48, *102*
  Kenyah, 49
Mayura, 99
  water palace, 40
Medan, 117
megaliths, 30-31, 49
  megalithic culture, 74
  megalithic tomb of Umbu Sawolo, *49*
melapas, 36
Melayu, *77*
Menak Jingga, 70
Menara Batavia, 131
Menara Emporium, 131
Mendut, 81
menhirs, 30, 49, *72*, 73
Mentawai
  longhouses, *28*, 28-29
  uma, *18*
Merak, 81
meru
  roof, *89*
  towers, *88*
Middle Classic, 51, 77
Mina Bay Resort Hotel, *133*
Minangkabau, 18, 55
  graves, 48
  Great House, 26-27
    also see *rumah gadang*
  house, *15, 27*
  ice-barn, *82*
  style mosques, *96*
modern architecture, 118-135
modern cities, 130-131
Modern movement, 129
Modernist, 7, 48
  modernisation, 116
  modernism, 120-121, 121, 126-127, 128
  movement, 119, 120, 123, 125
  school, 133
  training, 134
  villas, *125*
Moersid, Adhi, 126
mokhsa, 36, 68
Molenvliet canal, 108, 109
Monas, *126*
mosque, 41, 82-103, *94, 97*
  early, 88, 89
  regional, 96-97
motifs, 77, 87 also see lion motif
mountains
  Mt. Argapura, 73
  Mt. Gamalama, 96
  Mt. Karuhan, 73
  Mt. Kombeng, 78
  Mt. Lawu, 62, 73
  Mt. Merapi, 93
  Mt. Meru, 56, *52, 53*, 58, 71, 78, 87
  Mt. Muria, 73, 103
  Mt. Penanggungan, *72*, 73, 79, 81
  Mt. Perahu, 62
  Mt. Rinjani, 40
  Mt. Sumeru, 73
  Mt. Ungaran, 62
  Mt. Welirang, 73
MPR/DPR building, *117-118*
Mpu Prapanca, 70
Muara Jambi, *77*
  temple at, *76*
Muara Takus, 76, 77
Municipal Works Department, 121
mural at Umah Rukum Damai, *32*
Musi river, 85
Muslim Pancasila Foundation, 97

N

Nagarakrtagama poem, 69, 70,72, 79
Nandin, 62
Nandiswara, 63
Napoleonic Wars, 106
Narmada, 40, 99
  garden, 98
national architectural identity, 133
National Archives building, 105, *122*
nationalism, 126
Nawanatya, 84, 85
negara, 84
Neo-classicism, 117, 120
  Neo-classical style, 109, 116, 120
Neo-gothic, 117
neo-vernacular, 120-121, 132
neolithic era, 73
Netherlands Indies, 116
New Indies Style, 7, 120-121, 121
New Order, 126
Ngaju of Kalimantan, 48
Ngaju ossuary, 49
Ngawen II, 81
ni ainaf, 44
N.I.S Bodjong, *107*
Niaga Tower, 135
Nias, 30-31, 49, 73
  houses, *30, 31*
  villages, 30
Niasan architecture, 12
Niemeyer, Oscar, 126
Nieuwe Zakelijkheid Style, 121
Nijm office, *121*
Noe'man, Achman, 129
notched-log entry ladders, 33
Novotel Semarang, *135*
Novotel Surabaya, *134, 135*
Nuaulu of Seram, 20
Nurses' Dormitory, *129*
Nusa Tenggara, *42*

O

omens and auguries, 28-29
omo sebua see chief's house
organic building materials, *17*
origin temple, 38
origin-houses see *tongkonan*
Orissa, *54*
Osaka Expo, 126

P-Q

Padang Lawas, 77
paduraksa, 95
  gate, 71, *87*, 101
palaces, *7, 14*, 82-103, *83, 86, 87, 110*
Palembang, 96, 97
  residency, *111*
Panataran, 81
pangkalan, 27
papanggu, 11
parholian, 48
Parvati, 61
pasanggrahan, 116
Pasar Gede, 123
Pasar Johar, 123
Pasaruan, *121*
Pasernah, 73
pavilions, 37, 98
  also see *bale*
  also see *bale kambang*
  also see floating pavilions
Pawon, 80
Pedju, Ary Mochtar, 127
pendapa, 35, *90*, 105, 109
pendopo, 89
peringgitan, 35
Perquinn, 81
perspective effects, 58-59
Pesisir, 102-103
piagem, 57
pilasters, *60, 61*
pile
  dwelling, 32
  foundations, 12-13, 34
  structures, 16, 30
pilgrimage places, 101
pillars and columns, 54, 55
Plantation System, 116
plantation towns, 107
Plaosan Kidul, 67
Plaosan, 79
plinth (*mbelembele*), *31*
Pont, Henri Maclaine, 119, 121, 123, 132
  church at Pohsarang, *123*
Pontianak, 97
ports, *84*
Postmodernism, 7
posts, 29, 43
  and beam structure, *16*
Prambanan, *62*, 80, 81
  temple ruins, *54*
Progo River, 64
Protestant Church, 105
PT Java Maluku Building, *121*
Puang Matua, 22
Pulo temple ruins, *77*
punden berundak, 11, 72, *73*, 73
Pura Besakih, 75
pura dalem, *75*
Purbo, Hasan, 129
Purworejo Regency, 78
pusaka, 81
Qur'an, 94, 100

R

Railway Station Building in Surabaya, *117*
railways, *117*
Rakai Garung, 67
Ramayana, 63
Rationalist traditions, 129
  also see Dutch Rationalism
Ratnasambahava, 66
Ratu Boko, 54, 79
Ratu Lara Kidul, 93
reconstruction, 80-81
regionalism, 132-133
rice barn, *22*, 40
rimata, 28
Rindi, 21
roof
  extended roof ridges, 14-15
  roofing, *20*
  roof formation, 34
  roof forms, 132, *133*
  stressed roofbeam technique, 55
  traditional roofs, 15
  also see *joglo*-style
Roti, 21
Rotinese house, *18*, 48
royal cemetery at Imogiri, *101*
Royal Wilhelmina School, *128*
Rudolph, Paul, 135
ruma gorga, *24*
ruma siampore, 24
rumah anjung-anjung, 25
rumah gadang, *26-27, 48* also see Minangkabau Great House
Ryswick, 109

S

Sa'dan Toraja, 16, *17*, 20
sacred caves, 54
Sang Hyang Komara, 39
Sang Hyang Komari, 39
Sani, Sardjono, 135
Santiko, Dr. Hariani, 73
Sari, 81
Sasak
  house, 40-41, *41*
  settlements, 41
Savoy Homan Hotel, *125*
Schonburg Building, *120*
School of Modern Architecture, 7
Segaran, 71, 98
Seguntang Hill, 76
Sekolah Pertanian Menengah Atas, *128*
Selo Soemardjan, 93
Selomangleng, 79
  cave, *78*
Semarang, 103, 105, 112, 116, 124, 130
  railway station, *120*
Semarang-Cheribon Steam tram
  company, *123*
Sendang Duwur, 81, *101*
Senen Triangle buildings, *117 118*
senthong, 35
Seplawan limestone hills, 79
serambi, 95, 97
Sewa Dago office, *135*
Sewu, 79, 81
shahbandar, 102
shophouses, 114-115
  also see Chinese shophouse
sibayak see *rumah anjung-anjung*
Siberut *sapou*, *28*
Silaban, Freidrich, 128, 129
sili, 46, 47
Simalungun house, *24*
Sindok, king, 72
Sindok, 73
Singasari, 68, 73
Singhasari period, 72
sinong, 33
sitinggil, 87
Siva, 54, 58, 61, 62, 63
  Plateau, 79
  Temple, 81
sleeping pavilions, 37
Soeharto, President, 97, 126, 129
Soekarno-Hatta airport, 133
soko guru, *18*, 89, 94, 95, 96, 105
soko tunggal, 89, *89*
Spin House, Batavia, *107*
Sriwijaya, 77, 98
Steam Navigation Company Offices, *122*
STEKPI, *126*
Stevin, Simon, 108
stilt foundations see pile foundations
stone
  age tool kit, 10
  architecture, 54-55, 68-69
  building methods, 56-57
  construction techniques, 57
  courses, *56*
  markers, 67
  plaques at Mantingan, *89, 94*
  temples of East Java, *68*
  wedges, *56*
  also see ceremonial stone terraces
  also see Javanese stonework
stupa, 52
Suai house, *45*
suburban bungalows, 124-125
Sufism, 88
Suhamir, 129
Suhartono, 129
Sujudi, 127
Sukada, Budi, 135
Sukendar, Dr. Haris, 73
Sularto, Robi, 126
Sumba, 20, 21, 42, 49, 94
  clan house, 15, *42, 43*, 49
  Sumbanese clan house, *42*
  also see *uma mbatangu*
  Sumbanese village, *43*
Sumurupas, 70
Sunan Bonang, 89
Sunan Kalijaga, 95
Sunda Kelapa, 102
Sunda Pajajaran, 102
Sungai Langsat, 77
Sunyaragi, 79, 98, 99
Surabaya, 116, 124, 130
Surakarta
  kraton, 90, *90-91*
  palace of, 90
  vicinity, *90-91*
surau, *96*
Surosowan, 102
Susilo, 128, 129
Sutanto, Sonny, 135
Syek Jafar Sadek, 96
synthesis, 122-123, 132

T

Taj Mahal, 100
Talang Tuwo, 98
Taman Fatahillah see City Hall
Taman Ghairah of Aceh, 99
Taman Mini, *117-118*
  also see Karo Batak
Taman Sari, 79, 98
tambak, 48
Tana Toraja, 22
Tanahabang, 76
Tanjung Anom, 77
Tanjung Priok, 109
tano niha, 30
Tapak Raja Suleiman, 24
Tara of incense, 66
Tara of music, 66
Tasik Ardi, 99
Tawang railway station, 105
Team 4, 135
Technical High School at Bandung, 123, *123*
Tegurwangi, 69
Telaga Warna, 78
telephone exchange, *117*
temple, 114-115
  complexes, 79
  construction, 56
  layout, 56
  precints, 62-63
  sites, 74-75
  also see Javanese temples
  also see Prambanan temple ruins
  also see Pulo temple ruins
  also see Indian temple
temple-founding ritual, 57
terraced sites, *73*, 74-75
terracing, 73
The Three Locomotives, *125*
timber
  framework, 16
  houses, 85
Timorese houses, 44-45, *133*
Tjahjono, Gunawan, 118, 135
Tjitrap house, *111*
to minaa, 21
Toba Batak, 48
  dwelling, 24
  graves, 48
  house, 13, 14, *24* also see Toraja house
  rice barn, 15 also see *sopo ruma gorga*, *24*
toko 15
Toko Merah, 112, *112*
tombs, 48, *100*, 101, 100-101
  also see Ibrahim, Malik
  also see Kalibata Cemetery
Toraja, 48, 49, 55
  origin-house, *14, 21*
  rice barn, *14*
  tombs, 48
  tongkonan, 8, *18, 21, 22, 23*, 22-23
  villages, *23*
town formation, 106-107
townhouses, *112*
  colonial, 113
  Dutch, 112-113
trading
  centres, 85
  port, 85
  settlements, 106-107
traditional architecture, 8-49
Tralaya, 101
tropical garden city
  see garden cities
Tropical Style, 120
Trowulan, 70, *72*,73, 72-73, 83, 85, *98*, 101
Tuban, 89
tugu, 48
tulak somba, 14, *23*
tumpal, 60
tumpang sari, 34, 35
Tygersgracht, *113*

U

Ubud, 90
Ujung Pandang, 105, 106
Ujung Panjang, 117
uma dadoq see longhouses
uma kamudungu, 43
uma maringu, 43
Uma Mbatangu see Sumba clan house
uma see longhouses
Umbul Winangun, 99
UNESCO, 81
Universiti Indonesia, *117-118*
urban tradition, 84-85

V

Vajrayana Buddhism, 77
van Arcken & Co., *117*
van der Rohe, Miles, 126
van der Velde, W.J., 109
van Imhoff, Gustaaf Willem Baron, 112
Van Rees, W.A., 108
van Riebeeck, Abraham, 109
van Starkenborch Stachouwer, 113
verandah, *34*
vernacular architecture, 6, 8, 12, 14, 16, 22, 34, 38, 83, 84, 132
Villa Isola, *121*
Villa Style, 128
village longhouses, *3*
  also see *bale lantang*
Visnu, 58, 62, 63, 68

W-Z

W. Lemei, 122
wali songo, 95, 101
Wallace, Alfred Russel, 99
wayang kulit, 98
Wayang Museum, *113*
wayang, 35
Weltevreden, 109
Wetu Telu mosques, 41
Wheatley, Paul, 84
Wilem Dudok, 122
Wilhelmina Pavilion, *107*
Williams Church, *108*
Wisma 46 Bank Nasional, *117 118*
Wisma 46 BNI building, *134*
wong bali aga, 38
wooden architecture, 54
Wright, Frank Lloyd, 12 6
Wringin Lawang, 71
Ying-yai Sheng-lan, 85
Yogyakarta, 83, 116
  kraton, *93*, 93
yoni, *61*, 63
Zheng He, 103
ziarah, 101

Photo Credits

Unless otherwise specified, pictures have been taken from Editions Didier Millet's private collection.

The Publisher acknowledges the kind permission of the following for the reproductions of photographs.

Chapter Openers:
Traditional Architecture, all illustrations by Julian Davison; Borobudur relief by Tara Sosrowardoyo; and Badui construction detail by Tantyo Bangun.
Indonesia's Oldest Buildings, Candi Panataran and Borobudur by Leo Haks; Panataran's kala by Tara Sosrowardoyo; Dieng kala head by Tantyo Bangun; and Plaosan kala by John Miksic.
Cities, Mosques and Palaces, Aceh mosque by Kal Muller, palace of Kutei and living near tombs by Kasinathan Manoharan, Goa palace by John Falconer.
Architecture of the 17th to 19th Centuries, Batavia by Antiques of the Orient.
Modern Architecture and Identity, museum by Guido Rossi, Gateway Office building by Yori Antar, and MPR/DPR building, UI Administration building, Wisma 46 BNI, Ancol Park, Senen Triangle and Grand Melia Hotel by Tara Sosrowardoyo.

Accor Asia Pacific, p. 133, Novotel Toraja.
Amanresorts, p. 133, Amanjiwo hotel.
Ping Amranand, p. 55, Candi Bima.
Yori Antar, p.116, Baroque bell towers; p.121, Isola villa; p. 123, Pasar Gede; p. 124, eclectic villa; p. 126, museum; p. 127, Gedung Dharmala; p.128, villa house and Yankee style house; p. 133, ITB and Timor house project; p. 134, Danamon Towers and Sewa Dago building; and p. 135, Bank Niaga building.
Antiques of the Orient, p. 10, sailing vessel; p. 12, Dayak settlement; p. 16, Dayak carpenters; p. 20, erecting a house; and p. 113, Tygers Gracht.
Tantyo Bangun, p. 18, Mentawai uma; p. 29, man sitting in front room, pig skulls, and fetish basket; and p. 38, bale lantang and longhall; p. 52, Candi Lara Jonggrang; p. 78, Gunung Kawi and cloister; p. 102, Banten mosque; p. 121, PT Java Maluku building and building detail; p. 126, Hotel Indonesia and MPR/DPR; and p. 127, Istora Senayan and Japan Embassy.
Bauast Nedam International B.V., P. 122, Joana Stoomtram Maatschappij.
Nigel Bullough, p. 71, Candi Bajangratu.
Yu-Chee Chong Fine Art, London, p. 88, Surabaya mosque.
Alain Compost, p. 21, Rindi house; p. 27, modern Minangkabau house; p. 43, entrance platform; p. 74, menhirs; p. 97, Masjid Raya; and p. 100, tomb from Airmata.
Gilles Crampes, p. 19, Sumbanese columns; p. 22, rice barn under construction; p. 43, buffalo horns and house interior; and p. 49, megalithic tomb and carved stella.
Duta Cermat Mandiri, p. 135, Menara Asia, Novotel Semarang (2 pictures) and Novotel apartments.
John Falconer, p. 80, Matjan Poetih, ruins at Arca Domas and Borobudur gateway; p. 83, Goa palace; p. 106, Bujong residence; p. 107, the spin house, children's hospital, brick-laying, and the Latin and Greek school; p. 108, Williams Church; p. 109, Batavia in 1629; p. 113, entertaining guests and at the rice table; p. 120, Governor-General of Rijswijk's palace; and p. 131, Batavia in 17th century.
James Fox, p. 44, Atoni house and Amarasi house.
Jill Gocher, p. 115, interior of Chinese temple.
Leo Haks, p. 93, Yogyakarta kraton and Sultan of Yogyakarta; p. 117, Hong Kong Bank and new factory building; and p. 130, Surabaya, Bandung and Semarang.
Ahnamul Hanim, p. 58, Bajangratu and p. 123, central office.
Rio Helmi, p. 7, Jakarta skyline; p. 12, Borobudur relief; p. 15, relief; p. 23, Toraja houses on hills; p. 24, Ruma gorga relief; p. 32, mural; p. 33, notched-logged, amin apartment and communal gallery; p. 43, spatial organization in Sumba; p. 46, Dani compound; p. 47, a group of women; p. 78, Goa Gajah; p. 99, entrance to Taman Sari; and p. 106, Fort Rotterdam.
Hotel Indonesia, p. 127, Hotel Indonesia (2 sketches).
Paul Koh, p. 43, male and female ancestors.
Leong Kai Tong, p. 115, inside Chinese shophouse.
Linbinjarah, p. 76, Muara Jambi and p. 77, Candi Biaro Bahal III.
John Miksic, p. 7, Kasepuhan palace; p. 34, joglo house; p. 36, family shrine; p. 54, Mahabalipuram; p. 55, Candi Arjuna spout, Bhitargaon, and Gedong Songo IX; p. 58, Sambisari antefix; p. 59, karmavibhangga relief; p. 62, Candi Selogriyo, Candi Lara Jonggrang, and Dieng Plateau; p. 63, lions in niches, parrot motif, bearded rsis, Ganesha, and Mahakala and Nandiswara; p. 70, Candi Lor and Candi Gunung Gangsir; p. 71, Candi Tikus, and Candi Jabung; p. 72, Majapahit relief; p. 74, Candi Yudha; p. 75, Candi Sukuh (2 pictures), carved relief, Candi Cetoh, and Argapura; p. 77, dancing figures, Pulo ruins, Candi Mahligai, and mandala brick; p. 78, Selomangleng kala; p. 81, caryatid lion at Ngawen; p. 84, Aceh; p. 85, iron artefact and houses on rafts; p. 86, Banten minaret, gateway to Sitinggil, and Cirebonese batik; p. 89, soko tunggal and Kudus stone carving; p. 90, cannons, and pendopo at Lingsar; p. 94, Demak door and Mantingan mosque; p. 96, Masjid Jamik, decorated mosque, surau, carved wooden panel and mosque at Palembang; p. 97, Masjid Prasasti and Penyengat mosque; p. 98, Gunungan Aceh and Narmada gardens; p. 101, Tralaya grave, Imogiri gateway; p. 102, entrance to Jamik mosque, Gresik cemetery, and Kudus wood carving; p. 109, Molenvliet Canal; p. 112-113, townhouse; and p. 123, Pohsarang church interior.
Kal Muller, p. 20, Sumba house roofing; p. 23, house decoration; p. 40, man climbing into rice barn; and p. 49, man with Kenyah sandong.
Hugh O'Neil, p. 102, Sendang Duwur.
Cor Passchier, p. 125, another Aalbers residence, modernist villa and weekend cottage.
Photobank, p. 7, Candi Badut (LT); p. 14, Toraja house (KM); p. 22, extended roof (JD); p. 43, women preparing cotton (KM); p. 47, Dani settlement (KM) and outer palisade wall (LT); p. 58, Candi Lara Jonggrang and Candi Kidal (LT); p. 59, Dieng Plateau (MF) and Candi Jago (LT); p. 66, niches on Sari (LT); p. 67, Candi Kalasan (LT); p. 68, Candi Jawi and Candi Kidal kala (LT); p. 70, Candi Brahu; p. 74, Ratu Boko; and p. 99, Klungkung.
PT Atelier-6, p. 126, STEKPI campus; and p. 133, Carita Beach Resort.
Guido Rossi, p. 131, city of Jakarta.
Reiner Schefold, p. 28, Siberut sapou; and p. 29, interior of gable end and painted wood carving.
Amir Sidharta, p. 120, Masjid Agung; and p. 133, Hotel Amankila.
Sandi Siregar, p. 128, Nurses' Dormitory; and p. 133, Bandung private residence.
Tara Sosrowardoyo, p. 6, Gedung Sate; p. 19, pendapa columns and soko guru Demak mosque; p. 34, limasan roof form, front verandah, and kampung-style house; p. 35, tumpang sari; p. 52, Candi Lara Jonggrang; p. 67, Candi Mendut; p. 86, Kudus menara and Pendopo Jinem; p. 87, Kanoman palace and Kudus menara plates; p. 91, Surakarta kraton, main pendopo and Sitinggil; p. 93, north gate and Sultan's living quarters; p. 94, roof finial; p. 95, 3 ceramic plates; p. 99, Taman Sari pool and backyard; p. 101, paduraksa gateway and pendopo; p. 109, Taman Fatahillah; p. 110, Dutch Indies style house; p. 115, Chinese temple in Semarang; p. 121, house in Pasuruan and Kota Station; p. 124, art deco houses in Gresik and Semarang; and p. 129, Mosque Istiqlal.
Budi Sukada, p. 128, Election building and Bank Nasional Indonesia; p. 129, Bank Jabar and Hotel Indonesia; and p. 133, Taman Mini.
Roxana Waterson, p. 13, Karo Batak house; p. 14, palace of Simalungun; p. 18, hearth in Rotinese house; p. 19, north gable; p. 21, Toraja house ritual and navel post; p. 41, platform beneath rice barn; and p. 48, Christian graves.
Mike Yamashita, p. 40, thatching a Sasak house.

Illustrators:
Anuar Bin Abdul Rahim, p. 36, anthropocentric measurements; p. 52, kebens and stupas; p. 54, Indian temple with decorated columns; p. 57, Candi Apit; p. 59, candi mouldings; p. 63, cross section of Candi Merak; p. 64, splitting boulders; p. 64-65, the construction of Borobudur; p. 65, carving reliefs; p. 67, Candi Sajiwan elevation; p. 68-69, rendering of Candi Jawi; p. 69, candi mouldings; p. 72-73, street in Trowulan; p. 78-79, Gunung Kawi; p. 80-81, Candi Ngawen; p. 88, Banten minaret; p. 89, Kudus menara; p. 95, Cirebon mihrab; p. 99, Taman Sari; p. 100, ten tombstones; and p. 116, Harbour master's office section through.
François Brosse, p. 54, relief of wooden structure; p. 55, Candi Semar and Candi Bima; and p. 59, Borobudur's hidden foot.
Julian Davison, p. 6, Karo Batak house; p. 10, stone tools; p. 11, Toba Batak house; p. 14, Minangkabau house; p. 14-15, Toraja house; p. 15, Sumba clan house and rice barn; p. 17, Karo Batak house section through and Toraja rice barn section through; p. 22-23, Toraja tongkonan; p. 24, Simalungun house; p. 34, different types of roofs; p. 35, Javanese house compound; p. 41, Sade house, cross section and Wetu Telu mosque; p. 46, Dani house; p. 47, cook house; p. 49, Kenyah charnel house and Karo Batak skull house; p. 66-67, Candi Plaosan; p. 71, Candi Jabung; p. 111, wayang museum; p. 112, Reiner de Klerk House; p. 113, Indies Style house and Cilitan Besar house; p. 114-115, Chinese shophouse; p.116, Harbour Master's office; p. 116-117, Javaasche bank; p. 120-121, Gedung Sate; p. 122, Karsten's Netherlands Steam Navigation; and p. 123, ITB elevation.
Atang Fachruroji, p. 56-57, temple construction; and p. 78-79, carving of Gunung Kawi.
Bruce Granquist, p.87, paduraksa gateway, candi bentar and gateway to Grand Mosque; p. 89, Mantingan coral stone plaque; p. 91-92, Surakarta kraton and its environs; p. 93, Yogyakarta kraton; and p. 115, Chinese klenteng.
Bruce Granquist and Studio Satumata, p. 11, megalithic tomb; p. 13, Sulawesi pile formations; p. 14, Dong Son detail; p. 15, Sulawesi house horns; p. 16-17, Balinese rice barn; p. 17, plaited bamboo panels, roof shingles and atap gable; p. 20, Javanese house joinery; p. 25, Karo Batak house; p. 31, Southern Nias house; p. 33, Kenyah longhouse; p. 35, Javanese tumpang sari; p. 36-37, Balinese house compound; p. 39, Bali Aga house; p. 42, Sumba house; p. 45, Suai house, section-through, Dagada Lautem house, interior and granary; p. 60-61, all illustrations; p. 72, kemuncaks; and p. 124-125, colonial style house.
Mark Hopkins, p. 40, Sasak lumbung.
Kasinathan Manoharan, p. 28-29, Mentawai longhouse; p. 30, Northern Nias house; p. 71, Candi Bajangratu; p. 74, Kosala; and p. 85, Malay village.
Ujang Suherman, p. 56, temple-founding rituals; p. 74, Ratu Boko and p. 75, Candi Sukuh.
The following illustrators have also contributed to the making of this book:
Osman Asari
Chia Boon Khiang
Teo Eng Hean

EDM would like to thank the following persons for their kind assistance in the preparation of this volume: **Tim Bradley, Janet Hoskins, Helen Jessup, Tim Jessup, Lai Chee Kien, Amir Sidharta, Sandi Siregar and Roxana Waterson.**

The publishers have made every effort to ensure that all photographs and illustrations contained in this volume have been correctly credited, and apologise if any omissions or errors have occurred. These will be amended in the next printing.